Certificate of Proficiency in Insolvency

Question Bank

For the June 2014 examination

Certificate of Proficiency in Insolvency Question Bank

ISBN 9781 4453 5838 3

Seventh edition 2013

British Library Cataloguing-in-Publication Data
A catalogue record for this book
is available from the British Library

We are grateful to the Insolvency Practitioners Association for permission to reproduce past examination questions.

Published by

BPP Learning Media Ltd
BPP House, Aldine Place
London W12 8AA

www.bpp.com/learningmedia

Printed in the United Kingdom by

CPI Antony Rowe
Bumper's Farm
Chippenham
Wiltshire
SN14 6LH

Your learning materials, published by BPP Learning Media Ltd, are printed on paper sourced from sustainable, managed forests.

A note about copyright

Dear Customer

What does the little © mean and why does it matter?

Your market-leading BPP books, course materials and e-learning materials do not write and update themselves. People write them: on their own behalf or as employees of an organisation that invests in this activity. Copyright law protects their livelihoods. It does so by creating rights over the use of the content.

Breach of copyright is a form of theft – as well as being a criminal offence in some jurisdictions, it is potentially a serious breach of professional ethics.

With current technology, things might seem a bit hazy but, basically, without the express permission of BPP Learning Media:

- Photocopying our materials is a breach of copyright
- Scanning, ripcasting or conversion of our digital materials into different file formats, uploading them to Facebook or emailing them to your friends is a breach of copyright

You can, of course, sell your books, in the form in which you have bought them – once you have finished with them. (Is this fair to your fellow students? We update for a reason.) But the e-products are sold on a single user licence basis: we do not supply 'unlock' codes to people who have bought them second-hand.

And what about outside the UK? BPP Learning Media strives to make our materials available at prices students can afford by local printing arrangements, pricing policies and partnerships which are clearly listed on our website. A tiny minority ignore this and indulge in criminal activity by illegally photocopying our material or supporting organisations that do. If they act illegally and unethically in one area, can you really trust them?

Contents

BPP
LEARNING MEDIA

Introduction

This is the seventh edition of BPP Learning Media's Question Bank for the Certificate of Proficiency in Insolvency.

It complements the BPP Learning Media CPI Study Manual and is published specifically for the June 2014 CPI exam.

Features include:

- All the CPI exams from 2000 to 2013 with answers prepared by BPP Learning Media
- Fully up to date at 30 June 2013
- A user-friendly style for easy navigation
- Designed to be easy to use and easy on the eye

The questions have been updated where appropriate to reflect changes in the legislation up to 30 June 2013.

Moving on to JIEB

BPP Learning Media will publish its range of JIEB study manuals in November 2013, for the November 2014 exam session. The ideal companion for JIEB studies, these study manuals will maximise your chances of success.

For further information, or to order, call 0845 0751 100 (within the UK) or +44 (0)20 8740 2211 (from overseas) or order online at www.bpp.com/learningmedia

Structure of the paper

There is one three hour paper divided into three parts (parts A, B and C). The entire paper covers:

- Personal insolvency (bankruptcy and individual voluntary arrangements)
- Company voluntary arrangements
- Administrative receiverships (including LPA and fixed charge receiverships)
- Administration
- Liquidations
- Matters relating to insolvency generally

Part A of the paper is divided into two sections. The first part consists of multiple choice questions worth one mark each. The second part consists of questions where a short written answer is required. These questions carry the marks as indicated. In total Part A is worth 40% of the marks on the paper.

Part B and C of the paper comprise questions to which either standard essay-style or numerical answers have to be given and cover the entire syllabus. Four questions in total have to be answered from these sections. The only choice you have in the examination therefore (given that all the questions in Part A and B are compulsory) is which two questions to choose out of Part C.

The questions asked vary in each section between very practical questions ('list the steps....', 'outline the strategy for....'); general questions ('comment on the validity.....', 'state the merits of the claims....', 'List the advantages and disadvantages...'); as well as numerical questions requiring the production of a statement of affairs or a schedule of creditor's claims.

Clearly it is not possible to pass the exam on the basis of knowledge of Personal or Corporate Insolvency alone. Over 30% of the paper is on Personal Insolvency issues.

Questions are based on the law and best practice as at 5 January in the year the exam is set.

Tackling multiple choice questions

Multiple choice questions comprise 10% of the total marks available for this paper.

Most of the multiple choice questions (MCQs) in your exam contain four possible answers although some may contain five. You have to choose the option that best answers the question. The three or four incorrect options are called distracters. There is a skill in answering MCQs quickly and correctly. By practising MCQs you can develop this skill, giving you a better chance of passing the exam.

You may wish to follow the approach outlined below, or you may prefer to adapt it.

Step 1 Skim read all the MCQs and identify what appear to be the easier questions.

Step 2 Attempt each question – starting with the easier questions identified in Step 1. Read the question thoroughly. You may prefer to work out the answer before looking at the options or you may prefer to look at the options at the beginning. Adopt the method that works best for you.

Step 3 Read all the options and see if one matches your own answer. Be careful with numerical questions, as the distracters are designed to match answers that incorporate common errors. Check that your calculation is correct. Have you followed the requirement exactly? Have you included every stage of the calculation?

Step 4 You may find that none of the options matches your answer.

Re-read the question to ensure that you understand it and are answering the requirement.

Eliminate any obviously wrong answers.

Consider which of the remaining answers is the most likely to be correct and select the option.

Step 5 If you are still unsure, make a note and continue to the next question. You have an average 1.8 minutes per multiple choice question (including reading time). Some questions will take you longer to answer than others. Try to reduce the average time per question, to allow yourself to revisit problem questions at the end of the exam.

Step 6 Revisit unanswered questions. When you come back to a question after a break you often find you are able to answer it correctly straight away. If you are still unsure have a guess. You are not penalised for incorrect answers, so never leave a question unanswered!

Tackling essay style questions

When working through the question bank, the following points are worth remembering:

Do not simply read the questions and then look up the answer. You need to practise the skill of interpreting questions, in other words, learning what the examiner is looking for. The best way of practising this is to either:

Attempt the question in exam (ie timed) conditions. Remember you should allow 28 minutes for a Part B or C 15 mark question: or

Read the question carefully, plan your answer on a single side of A4 paper (give yourself approximately 10 minutes) and then review the answer.

The former is better for practising time management, the latter for covering a lot of ground where time is short.

The model answers should be viewed as an 'aide memoire'. Markers in the exam do have discretion to award bonus marks – so that additional points made by you in your attempts at the question may have scored marks on the day despite the fact that they do not appear in the solution.

Exam technique

Always read the requirements of a question first

Pay very close attention to the demands of the question. Exactly what is it asking you to do? You may be asked to prepare a particular type of account or to show workings or to give reasons for proposed actions and marks will be thrown away if these instructions are not adhered to. Begin by reading the requirements at the end of the question before you read the facts. Underline the instructions and address yourself to them when answering. In addition you should note the marks allocated to each part to ensure that you do not spend too much time on any one part. As a guide one mark equates to 1.6 minutes after allowing for reading time. Therefore you should spend approximately 25 minutes on a 15 mark question.

Use the format

If you are asked to write a letter or a memo set out your answer in that format. You will get 'free' marks for this!

Use the 'ISAC' method

For many of the essay style exam questions, particularly those involving a scenario, the best way to approach your answer is to use the 'ISAC' method, ie

- **Identify** the issue
- **State** the law
- **Apply** the law to the facts of the question and
- **Conclude**

Let's take each one in order.

Identify the issue

Though you would rarely get a mark for identifying the issue in a question, it is a good discipline to focus your mind with this stage first. Sometimes, there are a number of issues raised by a particular question and this first stage also ensures that you do not miss any of them in the hurry of trying to get the answer down on paper.

State the law

Where you are required to state or explain the law in a particular area, state relevant provisions of the Act and Rules as concisely as possible. You do not need to remember the wording of a section by heart, but you do need to be able to paraphrase such provisions accurately (ie without changing their underlying meaning).

When you quote cases, quote the name of the case (if you remember it) and the proposition of law for which it is authority. You do not need to memorise the dates of cases. Neither are you required to reproduce details of the facts of the case, unless these are directly relevant to the facts of the question (in other words the question reminds you of what happened in the case).

When you quote statutory provisions it is perfectly acceptable to abbreviate the name of a statute (eg IA 86). If you remember a section number or rule number put it down (it adds to the general authority of your answer) but do not devote time simply to memorising section numbers: it is the substance of answers which score the marks.

Always quote the rules which you are applying if this is relevant to the demands of the question. Quotation should be concise. Concentrate on drawing out the core elements of the rule rather than regurgitating it.

Apply the rules to the facts of the questions

Many questions will be primarily concerned with application rather than knowledge so take time to apply the law or rules to the facts of the question.

Conclude

Always reach a conclusion.

Numerical or computational questions

In numerical or computational questions:

- Always head up your work and underline the heading
- Provide notes, workings and assumptions if the question requires it or if it helps you to explain to the examiner what you have done. Make sure that you cross reference all your notes or workings to the account you are preparing. This helps the marker identify how you have reached a particular number.
- Don't worry if you can't do all the entries; no one scores 100% in questions of this type. Concentrate on getting down the correct pro-forma (eg for a statement of affairs) and on putting in all the simpler entries which you can do. Try not to overrun on time.

Exam analysis

Liquidations

Year	Question	Description
2012	B 22	CVL putting company into CVL – procedure.
2012	C 25	CVL Statement of affairs and deficiency account.
2011	C 24	CVL closure, R&P account.
2010	C 34	Compulsory liquidation, distraint and execution.
2009	C 23	S216 considerations.
	C 25	SIP 2 investigations, steps to be taken by the liquidator prior to declaring a dividend, admission/rejection of creditor claims.
2008	C 31	Remedies available to the liquidator to recover funds for creditors. Duties of the liquidator to submit reports on the conduct of directors as outlined in SIP 4.
2007	C 31	Factors considered by the Disqualification Unit, what information to append to a disqualification report, definition of a shadow director.
2005	C 32	CVL, Dealing with creditor claims, ROT, interest, set-off, employees, calculation of bank's preferential wages claim.
2005	C 33	Preparation of a deficiency account, investigations by liquidator.
2003	C 34	CVL, Preparation of bank reconciliation, VAT calculation, Receipt and payments account.
2001	B 32	Liquidation committee: certificate of constitution, sale of assets to committee members, reports to committee, liquidator's remuneration, sanction of committee.

Administrations

Year	Question	Description
2012	C 23	Creditors' committee in administration.
2011	B 21	Options in respect of unsecured creditors and calculation of dividend.
	C 25	Progress reports and challenge to administrators remuneration.
2010	C 23	Procedure to appoint administrator, SIP 16, creditor's meeting.
2009	B 21	Matters to include in administrator's statement of proposals
	C23	SIP 16 – conduct of parties in a preparation of a pre-pack sale, matters to be disclosed re a pre-pack sale
2008	B 29	Standard tests of insolvency, who may appoint an administrator, effect of administration, strategy for achieving a going concern sale.
2007	C 33	Matters to consider re administration, terminating administration.
2006	B 29	Power of administrator to dispose of charged assets, distributions to creditors.
2006	C 33	Selling the business.
2005	B 29	Content of administrator's proposals, ending administration.

2004	C 34	Comparison of insolvency procedures available to a company, purpose of an administration order, steps to enter administration.
2000	C36	Voting requirements, disposing of fixed charge assets, powers of administrator.

Bankruptcy

Year	Question	Description
2012	B 21	Calculate Secretary of state fees, dividend and estimated outcome statement.
2012	C 24	Bankruptcy estate and antecedent transactions.
2011	B 22	Matrimonial home and assets.
	C 23	Options for debtor.
2010	B 22	Antecedent transactions.
2009	B 22	Statutory and practical matters that trustee should attend to within first few days following his appointment.
	C 24	Statutory obligations of the bankrupt to co-operate with trustee. Court procedures to be invoked to secure bankrupt's compliance. Recovery of pension contributions.
2008	B 30	Dealing with former matrimonial home and establishing a claim to current property.
2007	B 29	Effect of bankruptcy, options for an insolvent individual, advantages and disadvantages of bankruptcy.
2007	C 32	Void dispositions of property, duties to trustee, functions of trustee, which assets vest in trustee.
2006	B 30	Establishing extent and value of bankrupt's interest in matrimonial home, options to deal with equity.
2005	B 30	Protecting, establishing and realising debtor's interest in a matrimonial home.
2004	B 33	Obtaining information re bankrupt's estate, calculation of bankrupt's interest in matrimonial home.
2003	B 33	Estimated outcome statement, order for possession of matrimonial home, release of trustee.
2003	C 36	Proofs of debt, proxies, voting.
2002	B 33	Income payments order, obtaining information from bankrupt, agreement of creditor claims, closure checklist.
2001	C 34	Available assets, matrimonial home, challenge of transactions by trustee.
2000	B 32	Grounds to avoid a bankruptcy order, grounds for annulment, seizure of bankruptcy assets, court control of trustee, challenging acts of trustee.

Individual Voluntary Arrangements

Year	Question	Description
2010	C 24	Ethics.
2008	C 32	Preparation of income and expenditure account. Discussion of options available to a debtor to settle credit card debts.
2006	C 32	Contents of proposal.
2005	C 31	Advantages and disadvantages of a voluntary arrangement v bankruptcy.
2004	C 35	Role and duties of nominee and supervisor, interim order, statement of affairs.
2001	B 31	Failure of voluntary arrangement, assets available in a subsequent bankruptcy.

Company Voluntary Arrangements

Year	Question	Description
2010	C 25	Voting in CVA.
2004	C 36	Advantages of CVA, conditions for moratorium, effect of moratorium, duty of nominee to monitor company's performance.
2002	C 35	Ethical considerations, statement of trading contributions, requisite majorities, estimated outcome statement.
2001	C 35	Content of proposals, report of creditors meeting, annual reports.

Receiverships

Year	Question	Description
2002	C 34	Administrative receivership: Dealing with practical issues re landlord, employees, utilities, ROT, petitioning creditor.

Estimated outcome statements

Year	Question	Description
2012	B 21	Bankruptcy.
2011	B 21	Administration.
2006	C 31	CVL v CVA.
2003	B 33	Bankruptcy.
2003	C 35	CVL v CVA.
2002	C 35	CVA.
2002	C 36	Bankruptcy v IVA.
2000	B 33	Administrative receivership.
2000	C 35	Bankruptcy v IVA.

Statement of Affairs

Year	Question	Description
2012	C 25	CVL Statement of affairs and deficiency account.
2010	B 21	CVL Statement of Affairs and deficiency account.
2009	B 21	Administration Statement of Affairs.
2008	C 33	Preparation of Statement of Affairs. Requirements of SIP 13 re disclosure of a sale of assets to a director.
2007	B 30	CVL Statement of Affairs and deficiency account.
2006	C 33	Administration Statement of Affairs.
2004	B 32	CVL Statement of Affairs.
2003	B 32	CVL Statement of Affairs.
2002	B 32	CVL Statement of Affairs and deficiency account.
2001	C 33	CVL Statement of Affairs.

Part A:
Exam Questions

Note that where applicable this exam paper has been updated to reflect changes in the legislation.

1 The IP: Key professional issues

1 What SIP deals with the presentation of financial information in insolvency proceedings? (6/12)

(a) SIP 1
(b) SIP 7
(c) SIP 10
(d) SIP 13

---

2 In appropriate circumstances you send a document by electronic delivery but a hard copy is requested. How long do you have to comply with this request? (6/11)

(a) 5 business days
(b) 5 days
(c) 7 days
(d) 7 business days

---

3 In accordance with the Rules within what period should a Trustee's remuneration be determined by either the creditors' committee or a meeting of creditors? If not so determined, how will it be fixed? (6/11) **(2 marks)**

---

4 A partner of your firm was appointed as administrator of Nuts & Bolts Limited on 1 February 2011.

(a) Set out the requirements to report to creditors and the contents of the Administrator's progress report to creditors in accordance with the Rules. **(10 marks)**

(b) Set out the matters applicable and procedure for creditors to challenge an Administrator's remuneration or other expenses as being excessive under the Rules. (6/11) **(5 marks)**

(Total 15 marks)

---

5 Which statement of Insolvency Practice deals with the use of proxy forms? (6/09)

(a) SIP 8
(b) SIP 10
(c) SIP 12
(d) SIP 14

---

6 Under r4.218 list four types of expenses or costs which are payable out of the assets of a company in priority to the remuneration of the liquidator. **(4 marks)**

(6/09)

---

7 (a) List four things SIP 9 states creditor committees should have regard to when considering fee applications. **(2 marks)**

(b) According to SIP 9, what information should an office holder provide to creditors' committees where agreement is being sought on fees? **(2 marks)**

(06/08) **(Total 4 marks)**

---

8 Which Statement of Insolvency Practice deals with an officeholder's investigations into the affairs of companies in Administration and Insolvent liquidation? (06/07)

(a) SIP 1
(b) SIP 2
(c) SIP 4
(d) SIP 9

---

9 How often must a Supervisor report to creditors? (06/07)

(a) Not less often than once every 6 months
(b) Not less often than once every 12 months
(c) On first anniversary and then by agreement with creditors
(d) As often as the proposal directs

---

10 For what period should the Insolvency Practitioner's Case Record be retained? (06/07)

(a) 5 years from the date of appointment

(b) 10 years from the date of appointment

(c) 5 years from the date of release or the date on which the specific bond in respect of the case expired, whichever is the later

(d) 10 years from the date of release or the date on which the specific bond in respect of the case expired, whichever is the later

---

11 Which of the following is a statutory basis for fixing the Trustee's remuneration? (06/07)

(a) As a percentage of the value of the assets which are realised and/or distributed

(b) As a percentage of the value of assets remaining after distribution to unsecured creditors

(c) At a fixed rate determined by the petitioning creditor having regard to the complexity of the case

(d) At a fixed rate determined by the appointing creditor/Secretary of State having regard to the complexity of the case

---

12 (a) Under Statement of Insolvency Practice 9, what is the distinction between Category 1 and Category 2 expenses? **(1 mark)**

(b) Under Statement of Insolvency Practice 9, how should the following expenses be treated?

(i) Photocopying of circulars to creditors

(ii) Train fares incurred on estate business

(iii) Internal document storage, calculated by reference to square footage of office occupied by estate files and boxes

(iv) Allocation of rental costs of a firm's photocopier

(v) Mileage allowance paid by a firm to staff travelling on estate business

(vi) An office holder's specific penalty bond **(½ mark per point)**

(06/07)

---

13 An administrator's progress reports to creditors shall cover what periods? (06/06)

(a) Three months commencing on the date the company entered administration and every subsequent period of three months

(b) Three months commencing on the date the company entered administration and every subsequent period of six months

(c) Three months commencing on the date of the approval of the administrator's proposals and every subsequent period of three months

(d) Six months commencing on the date the company entered administration and every subsequent period of six months

(e) Six months commencing on the date of the approval of the administrator's proposals and every subsequent period of three months

---

14 Where an office holder is appointed in one capacity to an estate and is subsequently appointed in another capacity to the same estate, in which of the following circumstances will a second specific penalty bond not be required? (06/06)

(a) When a supervisor of a company voluntary arrangement is appointed liquidator
(b) When a nominee of a company voluntary arrangement is appointed supervisor
(c) When a members voluntary liquidator becomes a creditors voluntary liquidator
(d) When an administrator becomes supervisor of a company voluntary arrangement
(e) Where a supervisor in an individual voluntary arrangement becomes trustee in bankruptcy

---

15 A company enters administration with the following assets and liabilities:

	£
Fixed charge assets	80,000
Floating charge assets	90,000
Amount due to fixed charge creditor	60,000
Amount due to floating charge creditor	100,000
Amount due to preferential creditors	30,000
Amount due to unsecured creditors	150,000

Calculate the sum for which the administrator should bond. Ignore costs. **(4 marks)**

(06/06)

---

16 Excluding any hourly rate charges, what flat rate fee will the Official Receiver now be entitled to for administering a bankruptcy estate where he is trustee? (06/05)

(a) £1,715
(b) 20% of realisations
(c) £1,950
(d) 17% on realisations over £2,000 up to a maximum of £100,000
(e) 15% on the first £50,000 and on a reducing scale thereafter

---

17 A summary of which of the following need not be included in an administrator's final progress report? You should assume that the company entered administration after 15 September 2003. (06/04)

(a) The administrator's proposals
(b) Any major amendments to or deviations from, those proposals
(c) The steps taken during the administration
(d) The outcome
(e) Any unrealised assets of the company

---

18 (a) State whether a liquidator is allowed to recover costs in a liquidation he/she is dealing with. Where you have stated that he/she can recover such costs state, with your reasons, whether or not the basis of the cost recovery must be disclosed and authorised by those who approve the liquidator's remuneration.

(i) Specialist copying carried out on the liquidator's firm's photocopier for a circular to creditors

(ii) Case advertising

(iii) The liquidator's office and equipment rental costs

(iv) Room hire for a creditor's meeting at the liquidator's business premises

(v) Reimbursement of a member of the liquidator's staff in respect of an invoice which the staff member has paid for international air travel incurred in connection with a contract debt owed to the company in liquidation

(vi) Document storage costs in respect of old records of the company in liquidation which are stored in the liquidator's basement. **(½ mark for each correct answer)**

(3 marks)

(b) Where the liquidator wishes to make a recovery of the expenses which require approval from those who authorise his/her remuneration, what will be persuasive evidence of the reasonableness of the charge he/she wishes to make? **(1 mark)**

(06/04) **(Total 4 marks)**

---

19 In accordance with the Insolvency Practitioners Regulations 2005 an office holder must have in place an enabling bond with a surety under which certificates of specific penalty for each appointment are granted. For how much is this enabling bond? (06/04)

(a) £50,000
(b) £100,000
(c) £250,000
(d) £500,000
(e) £1 million

20 Where a document to be served is to be sent by first class post on which day is it deemed to have been served? (06/04)

(a) The day after the date of posting unless the contrary is shown
(b) The business day after the date of posting unless the contrary is shown
(c) The second day after the date of posting unless the contrary is shown
(d) The second business day after the date of posting unless the contrary is shown

---

21 Which of the following are specifically excluded by s246 of the Act – Unenforceability of liens? (06/02)

(a) Cash books and financial records
(b) Contracts
(c) Documents of title
(d) Leasing and finance agreements

---

22 Who approves the remuneration of an administrative receiver? (06/02)

(a) The creditors' committee
(b) The creditors
(c) The court
(d) The appointing debenture holder

---

23 Which insolvency rule says that 'a proxy holder should not vote in favour of any resolution which would directly or indirectly place him, or any associate of his, in a position to receive any remuneration out of the insolvent estate, unless the proxy specifically directs him to vote in that way'? Is it: (06/01)

(a) Rule 8.6
(b) Rule 8.7
(c) Rule 9.5
(d) Rule 9.6
(e) None of these

---

24 What is the minimum bond value that may be attributed to an individual estate under the Insolvency Practitioners Regulations? Is it: (06/01)

(a) £500
(b) £1,000
(c) £5,000
(d) £10,000
(e) £25,000

---

25 In which one of the following insolvency procedures is the value of the specific penalty bond not to be based on the value of the assets disclosed in the statement of affairs? (06/00)

(a) Administrative receivership
(b) Provisional liquidation
(c) Creditors' voluntary liquidation,
(d) Company voluntary arrangement

---

26 In a compulsory liquidation commencing on 2 February 2009 you have realised £113,000. After costs you distribute £65,000 to creditors. You have tried unsuccessfully to obtain a resolution from creditors to approve your remuneration. Therefore, you take your remuneration on the Schedule 6 scale.

Requirement

(a) How much remuneration are you entitled to draw?

(b) Which SIP says that you must try to obtain creditor approval prior to relying on the Schedule 6 Scale?

Please show your workings. **(4 marks)**

(06/00)

---

27 Where a creditor claims that the trustee's remuneration is excessive (Rule 6.142(1) of the Rules), any secured or any unsecured creditor, with the concurrence of what % in value of the creditors including that creditor, may apply to court to challenge the level of remuneration? (06/13)

(a) 5%
(b) 10%
(c) 25%
(d) 50%

---

28 What SIP deals with office holders' remuneration? (06/13)

(a) SIP 7
(b) SIP 8
(c) SIP 9
(d) SIP 10

---

29 Realisations of £10,000 have been made and of this £2,000 is available for distribution. Calculate the Trustee's remuneration using Schedule 6 to the Rules. (06/13)

(2 marks)

2 Key ethical issues

1 (a) The Insolvency Code of Ethics sets out 5 fundamental principles which Insolvency Practitioners and their staff should abide by. What are these principles? Your answer should briefly explain what is meant by each principle. **(10 marks)**

(b) If a supervisor presents a default petition against a debtor in an IVA and a bankruptcy order is made terminating that IVA, in accordance with the Insolvency Code of Ethics what matters should he take into account when considering whether or not he may act as trustee in bankruptcy? **(2 marks)**

(c) An Insolvency Practitioner wishes to act as trustee in bankruptcy of a bankrupt's estate but a partner in his firm is acting as liquidator of a company which has a claim against the bankrupt. This claim is disputed by the bankrupt. What particular issue arises in these circumstances which the Insolvency Practitioner should take into account in considering whether to accept the appointment? Why might acting as trustee give rise to difficulties? **(3 marks)**

(6/10) **(Total 15 marks)**

---

2 Specify the particular threats under the Code of Ethics which may need to be considered in the following circumstances:

(a) An Insolvency Practitioner ('IP') has been instructed to assist in placing a company into Creditors Voluntary Liquidation. The IP's wife owns a business which will have a large claim in the Liquidation although this is disputed by the company's director. **(2 marks)**

(b) An IP is investigating a transaction at undervalue with a view to making a claim against the insolvent company's director. However the director continually threatens to report the IP to his regulator for alleged technical failures in dealing with the insolvency. (06/13) **(2 marks)**

(Total 4 marks)

---

3 SIP 16 and SIP 13

Your principal has been instructed to advise the board of directors of Wrapped Up Limited in relation to placing the company into Administration and completing a 'pre-packaged' sale to the directors' new company.

Requirement

(a) In accordance with SIP 13, what are your principal's duties whilst acting in an advisory capacity prior to his appointment as Administrator? **(5 marks)**

(b) Your principal is appointed and a sale completes as planned. In accordance with SIP 16, what information concerning the sale should be disclosed to creditors? **(7 marks)**

(c) Within what time frame should the above information be given and in what circumstances might the above information not be given? **(3 marks)**

(06/13) **(Total 15 marks)**

---

3 Insolvency computations

1 John Smith, a sole trader, was made bankrupt on 3 January 2011 on the petition of the Commissioners of Revenue & Customs. You were appointed trustee in bankruptcy of the debtor's estate on 16 February 2011.

You have now progressed the bankruptcy to a position where it can be closed following a distribution to the creditors. The debtor did not submit to the proceedings and his wife defended the possession proceedings, albeit no costs were awarded against her.

The matrimonial home was sold for £187,800 and after paying the costs of sale of £5,600 and discharging the outstanding mortgage of £105,000 and a valid charging order of £7,800 against Mr Smith's share of the equity, the net proceeds were divided equally between the Trustee and the debtor's wife who was a joint owner. The trustee's net interest was paid into the Insolvency Service Account ('ISA').

Apart from the deposit on petition the only other realisations made by the trustee were a car for £7,000 and an insurance policy for £8,520. His tools of trade, valued at £1,000, were treated as falling within the provisions of S283(2) of the Insolvency Act 1986.

The non-VATable payments through the bankruptcy estate were the Official Receiver's costs of £1,715; Bond of £180; and Petitioning Creditor's Costs of £1,850. Payments for Statutory Advertising of £150, Agents' Charges of £1,200 and Legal Fees of £8,400 all included VAT.

Your outstanding time costs are £15,840 incurred over 103.25 hours at an average rate of £153.41 per hour. Your Category 2 disbursements are £135 for printing and photocopying and £85 for mileage.

At a meeting of creditors held on 15 May 2011 you sought to fix your remuneration in accordance with Rule 6.138(2)(b) of the Insolvency Rules 1986 on the basis of time costs with authority to draw Category 2 disbursements. The only creditor present or represented at that meeting approved the basis on time costs, but limited to a maximum of £12,000, excluding VAT. Category 2 disbursements were not approved.

You have received and admitted 16 claims totalling £94,020. This included one former employee who had no arrears of pay, but was entitled to two weeks' notice pay, two weeks' accrued holiday pay and three weeks' redundancy pay. His average wage was £7.50 per hour for a 40 hour week.

The debtor was not registered for Value Added Tax purposes.

Ignore ISA Banking Fees and Cheque Issue Fees.

Requirement

(a) Calculate the Ad Valorem Fee charged to the estate by the Secretary of State. Show your full workings. **(5 marks)**

(b) Calculate the dividend to Non Preferential Creditors. Show all workings. **(4 marks)**

(c) Prepare an Estimated Outcome Statement for presentation to the final meeting of creditors. **(6 marks)**

(6/12) **(Total 15 marks)**

2 Ashton Controls (1995) Limited (A Proposed Voluntary Liquidation)

You have accepted instructions to assist the directors of Ashton Controls (1995) Limited to wind up the company under a creditors' voluntary liquidation. The meeting of creditors has been fixed for 30 June 2012.

Part of your engagement is to produce the company's statement of affairs and ancillary documentation for presentation to the S98 meeting of creditors.

The directors have provided you with the following information relating to the company's financial position:

The last audited accounts as at 31 July 2011, (from where the book values for assets derive), showed an excess of liabilities over assets of £167,300. No dividends have been paid to the shareholders in subsequent periods.

The company has a bespoke computer system designed by Control Designs with a book value of £50,000. Your agents have valued this at £17,000.

The goodwill of the business has a book value of £150,000 and the directors consider it to have a realisable value of £100,000.

Trade debtors have a book value of £275,000 and for the purpose of the statement of affairs there needs to be a specific provision for bad debts of £65,000 and a general provision for doubtful debts of 15%.

The fixtures and fittings have a book value of £55,450 and your agents value them at £35,000.

Control Designs holds a fixed charge over the computer equipment dated 24 November 2010. The amount outstanding under the charge is £32,000.

ABL Lenders Limited holds a fixed and floating charge debenture dated 30 September 2011 and the amount due to them is £24,600.

Midwest Bank was granted a fixed and floating charge debenture over the company's assets on 17 June 2005. The Bank entered into a Deed of Priority with ABL lenders to afford the latter priority for their full lending. The sum due to Midwest Bank is £362,000.

Your investigations reveal that all charges have been properly registered at Companies House.

The creditors include HMRC for PAYE/NIC of £228,300 and VAT of £35,200; trade creditors of £263,500; Directors' loans of £95,350; subcontractors of £36,750 and 20 employees owed £19,825 - being all holiday pay.

The paid up share capital is £25,000 being ordinary shares of £1 each.

Requirement

(a) Prepare a summary of the Company's Statement of Affairs for discussion purposes with the Directors. Show your full workings. **(10 marks)**

(b) Prepare an Estimated Deficiency Account. Show your full workings. **(5 marks)**

(6/12) **(Total 15 marks)**

3 A partner in your firm was appointed two months ago as Administrator of Summer Limited by Best Bank plc which holds fixed and floating charges over the company's assets created on 20 September 2007. You have been provided with the following receipts and payments account and other information in relation to the case.

Administrator's Receipts and Payment Account

Statement of Affairs £		**£**	**£**
	Asset Realisation		
160,000	Book debts	30,000	
175,000	Freehold property	175,000	
10,000	Plant and Machinery	13,846	
5,000	Stock	6,924	
Uncertain	Goodwill	17,307	
10,000	Motor Vehicles	6,923	
			250,000
	Cost of realisations		
	Statutory disbursements	1,000	
	Legal fees	13,500	
	Agents' fees	5,000	
	Administrator's remuneration	20,865	
			(40,365)
	Funds held		209,635

- The amount due to Best Bank plc at the commencement of the Administration was £400,000. There have been no payments to the Bank since the Administrator's appointment.
- At the date of appointment the outstanding book debt ledger stood at £200,000. The directors were not aware of any known bad or doubtful debts, however they considered it prudent that a general provision of 20% be applied against the debts when preparing their estimated statement of affairs. Since the appointment you have discovered that there are certain debtors who have rights of set-off in respect of sums owed to them as creditors of the company, totalling £30,000. Furthermore one debtor who owes £10,000 has recently gone into liquidation with no prospect of a dividend to creditors. The Administrator considers that a 20% general provision against the remaining debts continues to be appropriate.
- Agents are to be instructed to assist in the collection of the remaining ledger for a commission of 10% of sums collected.
- Shortly after the administrator's appointment a sale of the company's business and assets on a going concern basis was completed as follows:

	£
Freehold property	175,000
Stock	10,000
Plant and Machinery	20,000
Goodwill	25,000
Motor Vehicles	10,000
	240,000

- The consideration in respect of the purchase of the business and assets was payable as follows:

  On completion, £175,000 was paid for the purchase of the property and £25,000 was paid as an initial payment against the other assets (apportioned pro rata to the purchase consideration). The balance of the consideration was payable in 2 equal payments of £20,000 on the 1st of each of the following 2 months.

- Agents' fees of £5,000 have been incurred, 25% of which relates to dealing with fixed charge assets.
- Legal fees of £3,500 have been incurred directly in dealing with the sale of the property. A further £10,000 has been incurred in dealing with the sale and purchase agreement and appointment formalities.
- Insurance costs have been incurred of £1,500 of which £500 directly related to the insurance of the property.
- Employee claims from employees dismissed in the month prior to administration have been received as follows:

	£
Wages	6,800
Holiday pay	8,200
Compensation in lieu of notice	12,500
Redundancy	16,250
	43,750

Wages claims relate to 4 employees owed £1,700 each.

- The following sums are due to HM Revenue and Customs:

VAT	£12,500
PAYE/NIC	£30,000

- According to the directors' statement of affairs trade creditors are owed £450,000.
- The Administrator's remuneration has been agreed as follows:

  5% of fixed charge realisations

  15% of all other realisations
- The estimated cost of distributing funds to unsecured non-preferential creditors is £3,500.

  The Administrator has been asked to provide an update report to the Bank.

(a) Prepare an estimated outcome statement providing details of the amounts anticipated to be recoverable by the Bank under its charges, based on the information provided. **(10 marks)**

(b) Set out the options available for the Administrators in relation to the distributions to unsecured creditors. **(2 marks)**

(c) Based on the information available calculate the estimated dividend to unsecured creditors. **(3 marks)**

(6/11) **(Total 15 marks)**

---

4 Mr McEnery is dismissed as a senior manager of Roundabout Limited on 28 February 2010 because of the company's insolvency. He is owed salary from 1 February 2010 onwards. Mr McEnery's gross salary is £600 a week. Under his contract of employment he has an annual holiday entitlement of 36 days. The company's holiday year runs from 1 January, and Mr McEnery has taken 1 day's holiday in 2010.

Assuming a Government weekly limit of £430, calculate the respective preferential and unsecured claims of the Redundancy Payments Office and Mr McEnery arising from Mr Mc Enery's claims for arrears of wages and holiday pay, gross of tax and National Insurance deductions. (6/10)

(4 marks)

5 The Directors of Be Tools Limited, a hand tool manufacturer, have contacted your principal for assistance in placing the company into creditors voluntary liquidation.

From the books and records of the company and discussion with the directors your principal has ascertained the following information.

- The Company trades from freehold factory premises in Surrey. A recent professional valuation indicates that the market value of the property is £275,000.
- The Company currently holds stocks of finished goods which are estimated to realise £30,000 at public auction and stocks of raw materials are estimated to realise 20% of their book value.
- The Company's book debts are all factored with R Star Factors Limited. The ledger presently stands at £78,000. The directors estimate that after making a provision for bad debts of £15,000, 60% of the remaining debts will be realisable. R Star Limited are owed £35,000 against the ledger.
- Agents valuations have been obtained for the remaining company assets as follows;

Motor Vehicles	£14,000
Fixtures and fittings	£8,000
Plant and Machinery	£24,000

- In addition there are two company cars that are subject to finance with J Lemon Finance Limited. These vehicles have been valued by the agents at £4,000 each with outstanding finance of £5,000 on each vehicle.
- 3 Weeks ago the Company disposed of plant and machinery with a book value of £25,000 for £10,000, details of this transaction have been fully recorded in the books and records of the Company.
- Trade creditors total £230,000.
- In additional the Company has a loan of £235,000 and an overdraft of £56,000 from Harrison Bank plc secured by a fixed and floating charge over the assets of the company created on the 1st August 2005.
- The Director Mr McCartney is owed £50,000 in respect of loans made to the Company.
- HM Revenue and Customs are owed £7,200 in respect of unpaid VAT and £14,600 in respect of unpaid PAYE/NIC contributions.
- The company has a share capital of £1,000 ordinary £1 shares, all of which has been fully paid up.
- Balance sheet extracts are as follows:

  Freehold property £180,000

  Motor Vehicles £37,000 (including £10,000 in respect of vehicles subject to finance)

  Fixture and fittings £42,000

  Plant and machinery £58,000

  Stock – finished £60,000
  – raw materials £42,000

  Balance on

  Profit and (loss) a/c £(110,000) (1st January 2009)

- Sums owed to employees on cessation of trade have been calculated as follows:

  Wages arrears – (15 employees owed 6 weeks wages) £90,000

  Redundancy pay £87,000

  Pay in lieu of notice £70,000

  Holiday pay £46,000

(a) Your principal has asked you to prepare a statement of affairs suitable for presentation at the s98 meeting. **(10 marks)**

(b) Also prepare a deficiency account for presentation at the meeting. **(5 marks)**

(6/10) **(Total 15 marks)**

---

6 According to SIP 11, when handling funds in formal insolvency appointments, which is not true? (06/08)

(a) Case funds should be maintained separately from those of the office holder or his firm

(b) Interest payable on funds held by the office holder should be credited to the account of the case

(c) Funds paid into a firm's trust account should be paid into the case account as soon as possible

(d) Cheques may be cleared through the office holders office account until a specific case account is opened

---

7 The directors of Bear Limited a Midlands based printer, have instructed your firm to assist them consider their financial position and provide them with advice about the options available to them. The directors have provided you with the following information:

- Their principal bankers are Stearn Plc., who have a fixed charge over intellectual property and certain printing presses used in the business and a floating charge over the remaining assets and undertakings of the company. The directors have produced bank statements which show an amount of £1.4m owing to Stearn Plc.
- The company has developed its own website which enables customers to place orders and review draft artwork. It has cost £300,000 to develop the website and the directors have received an offer for £125,000 from a competitor for the site.
- The company has three printing presses which were acquired on 18 March 20X7 for £2,000,000 and annual depreciation has been £100,000 per press. The presses have been valued by independent valuers at £800,000.
- The company is owed £675,000 by customers including £45,000 by a supplier who is seeking to exercise a right of set off. In addition, one customer SIV Plc, was placed into liquidation on 17 March 20X9 owing Bear Limited £12,500. Estimated realisations in the liquidation of SIV Plc are expected to be nil. The directors estimate that the net realisable value will be 66% of the net book value.
- The company has office furniture with a book value of £50,000 which is expected to realise £7,500 and other debtors of £20,000 expected to realise 5% of book value.
- The company leases its computer equipment. The equipment has a written down value of £270,000. Agents have valued the items at 50% of book value and outstanding charges owed to the leasing company, Morgan Plc, total £50,000.
- The directors have advised that two vehicles are leased. The written down value is £25,000 and the vehicles are expected to realise £12,000 at auction. The arrears owed to the leasing company total £15,000.

- The company employs 40 staff and the average weekly payroll is £15,000 gross. The directors have advised that employees are owed four weeks wages. Further investigation reveals on average, each employee is owed six weeks annual leave.
- Redundancy costs for the employees are estimated to be £45,000.
- HM Revenue and Customs are owed £10,000 in respect of PAYE deducted from employees' salaries over the last six months and £15,000 for National Insurance Contributions deducted over the last nine months.
- The company traded from leasehold premises at an annual rent of £60,000. There is approximately one quarter's rent due and there is one year left on the lease agreement.
- The creditor's ledger totals £2.7m.
- The company has issued share capital of 75,000 ordinary shares of £1 each.

Requirement

(a) Prepare a statement of affairs on Bear Limited as at 18 March 20X9. **(11 marks)**

(b) If a practitioner sells assets to a director or connected party, what information should be disclosed to creditors according to section 6.6 of SIP 13? **(4 marks)**

(06/08) **(Total 15 marks)**

---

8 Your firm has been instructed by the directors of Kili Limited to assist them in placing the company into creditors' voluntary liquidation. Meetings of members and creditors have been convened for 30 June 20X9. Notice of the proposed winding up resolution has been given to Blanc Bank plc, which has a fixed charge over property, goodwill and intellectual property, together with a qualifying floating charge over the assets of the company. Blanc Bank plc has consented in writing to the proposed resolution.

Independent valuation agents have been instructed to value the company's assets, and the directors have provided you with the following information:

1 The company's debtors ledger shows a balance of £85,000. The directors inform you that specific debts totalling £16,000 are irrecoverable, and consider that a general bad debts provision of 20% should be applied.

2 The company owns the rights to an internet domain name. No value has been ascribed to this in the company's accounts, but a competitor has offered £30,000 to purchase it.

3 The company purchased a laser printing press on 1 November 20X8 for £15,000 and on the same date scrapped old printing machinery with a book value of £8,000. The current value of the printing press is £11,000.

4 The company's other machinery and equipment currently valued at £25,000, is subject to finance agreements with Jaro Finance Limited. There is £10,000 outstanding under the agreements.

5 Stock has a book value of £65,000 and a realisable value of £15,000.

6 On 1 June 20X8 the company sold a vehicle with a book value of £5,000 for £8,000 and at the same time purchased a replacement vehicle for £15,000. It is currently valued at £10,000.

7 Sundry office furniture and equipment has a book value of £12,000 and is estimated to realise £2,000.

8 The amount outstanding to Blanc Bank plc is £65,000.

9 The company has ceased trading and its entire workforce of 15 employees has been made redundant. All staff earned more than £350 per week and are all owed three weeks wages, totalling £23,000. Additionally, there is outstanding holiday pay of £12,000 and entitlements to redundancy pay and pay in lieu of notice of £30,000 and £26,000 respectively.

10 The amounts outstanding to HM Revenue and Customs comprise three months PAYE of £30,000 and VAT of £32,000.

11 The company traded from leasehold premises at an annual rent of £30,000. There are two quarters rent outstanding and the landlord holds a rent deposit of £7,500.

12 Trade and expense creditors amount to £165,000.

13 The company has issued share capital of 20,000 ordinary shares of £1 each.

The last audited balance sheet of the company as at 31 March 20X8 is summarised below:

Kili Limited
Summarised Audited balance sheet as at 31 March 20X8

	£	£
Fixed Assets		
Machinery and equipment		60,000
Office furniture and equipment		12,000
Motor vehicle		5,000
		77,000
Current Assets		
Stock	70,000	
Debtors	100,000	
	170,000	
Current Liabilities		
Trade creditors	155,000	
Bank overdraft	60,000	
	215,000	
Net current liabilities		-45,000
		32,000
Represented by:		
Share capital		20,000
Surplus on reserves		12,000
		32,000

(a) Prepare an estimated Statement of Affairs for the company as at 30 June 20X9. **(9 marks)**

(b) Prepare a deficiency account covering the period 1 April 20X8 to 30 June 20X9, detailing the items making up the deficiency on the estimated statement of affairs. **(6 marks)**

(06/07) **(Total 15 marks)**

---

9 A partner in your firm was appointed administrator of Tacul Limited on 31 January 20X9 by the directors of the company. Tacul Limited has two divisions to its business, one manufacturing hydraulic equipment and the other servicing and repairing the equipment. Pina Bank plc, which has fixed and floating charges over the assets of the company, consented to the appointment. The debenture was duly registered at Companies House on the 19 September 20X7.

You have instructed independent valuation agents to value the company's assets, and the directors have provided you with the following information:

(1) The amount outstanding to Pina Bank plc is £750,000.

(2) The company has a full recourse factoring agreement with X Factors plc in respect of its manufacturing division debts, which stand at £200,000. X Factors plc has advanced 70% of the debts due. A major customer of the manufacturing division has entered liquidation owing £80,000 and there is no prospect of a dividend. 10% of the remaining manufacturing debts are considered doubtful, due to various disputes.

(3) The company's service division has non-factored debts of £140,000. Of these £70,000 relate to invoices raised in respect of annual maintenance contracts expiring on 30 April 20X9.

(4) The company owns its freehold trading premises which were purchased 10 years ago for £450,000. Your agents have valued the property at £600,000.

(5) The company has four vehicles, all of which were purchased three years ago for £28,000. They are currently valued at £3,500 each.

(6) The company purchased a high precision automated drilling machine four years ago for £50,000 with the assistance of a chattel mortgage with Loxley Finance Limited. The machine is now valued at £30,000 and the amount outstanding to Loxley Finance Limited is £15,000. Additionally, the company owns machinery and equipment free of finance with a book value of £40,000 and a realisable value of £15,000.

(7) Stock, raw materials and work in progress have a book value of £120,000 and a realisable value of £45,000.

(8) Sundry office furniture and equipment has a book value of £15,000 and is estimated to realise £2,000.

(9) The company has 25 staff, of which the highest paid earns £750 per week. All are owed one weeks wages, totalling £14,000. The three directors, all of whom are PAYE employees, are each owed £2,000 in respect of January's salaries. Additionally there is outstanding staff holiday pay of £15,000 and entitlements to redundancy pay and pay in lieu of notice of £32,000 and £20,000 respectively.

(10) The amounts outstanding to HM Revenue and Customs comprise two months PAYE of £43,000 and three months VAT of £65,000.

(11) Trade and expense creditors amount to £230,000.

(12) The company has issued share capital of 1,000 ordinary shares of £1 each.

Requirement

(a) Prepare the Statement of Affairs to accompany the administrator's statement of proposals. Ensure your answer sets out with supporting workings the estimated prescribed part of the company's property available for the unsecured creditors.

Do not provide for administration costs and expenses. **(11 marks)**

(b) Negotiations for the sale of the business to a third party had taken place in the period leading up to the appointment of the administrator.

Set out the matters that an administrator should take into consideration when formulating his strategy to sell a business, either:

(i) Immediately upon appointment to a previously identified purchaser, or
(ii) When appointed administrator and no immediate purchaser has been identified.

(4 marks)

(06/06) **(Total 15 marks)**

---

10 Which Statement of Insolvency Practice deals with the handling of funds in formal insolvency appointments? (06/05)

(a) SIP 8
(b) SIP 7
(c) SIP 10
(d) SIP 11
(e) SIP 13

---

11 Which section of Act provides that a prescribed part of net realisations of property subject to a floating charge shall be made available to unsecured creditors? (06/05)

(a) s175A
(b) s176A
(c) s177A
(d) s178A
(e) s182A

---

12 Dan Limited goes into Administration on 1 December 2008. The company has net property, prior to the payment of any creditors, of £440,000, and has the following creditors:

	£
▸ First qualifying charge holder	310,000
▸ Second qualifying charge holder	50,000
▸ Employee claims for holiday pay	20,000
▸ Unsecured claims	400,000

Calculate the funds available for distribution to each of the above creditors.

(06/05) **(4 marks)**

---

13 Your partner was appointed liquidator of Peg Limited, a printing company, on 31 May 20X8. State how you would deal with the following matters:

(a) A supplier, Jack, had delivered a quantity of paper to Peg Limited's factory two weeks before the company ceased trading, which he has been able to identify. He had not previously supplied to the company. He has submitted an invoice for the goods with a retention of title clause printed on the reverse. **(2 marks)**

(b) Maxine has submitted an invoice for goods supplied totalling £10,000, which fell due for payment on 30 November 2006. From documentation provided by Maxine written demand for payment was made on 31 August 20X7. Maxine is claiming interest on the debt from 30 November 20X6 at 9%. **(2 marks)**

(c) Josie has 10,000 £1 ordinary shares in Peg Limited, which are 25% paid up. Josie is also a creditor of the company for £5,000 in respect of goods supplied. **(3 marks)**

(d) Work was regularly performed for the Peg Limited by a number of freelance designers and sub-contract type setters. These individuals are creditors of the company and have sought to make claims under the provisions of the Employment Rights Act 1996. State the factors to be taken into consideration in determining whether an individual is an employee. **(4 marks)**

(e) Ricky, Katy and Gina were employed part time by Peg Limited on monthly salaries of £150, £150 and £350 respectively. These were paid out of the company's overdrawn bank account as shown in the summarised statement below.

Peg Limited

Date	*Narrative*	*Dr*	*Cr*	*Balance*
		£	*£*	*£*
01-Jan-X8	Balance b/f			-22,000
15-Jan-X8	Ricky salary	-150		-22,150
15-Jan-X8	Katy salary	-150		-22,300
15-Jan-X8	Gina salary	-350		-22,650
20-Jan-X8	Sales		3,500	-19,150
25-Jan-X8	Purchases	-7,800		-26,950
03-Feb-X8	Purchases	-8,500		-35,450
06-Feb-X8	Sales		4,000	-31,450
15-Feb-X8	Ricky salary	-150		-31,600
15-Feb-X8	Katy salary	-150		-31,750
15-Feb-X8	Gina salary	-350		-32,100
25-Feb-X8	Sales		12,000	-20,100
26-Feb-X8	Purchases	-4,300		-24,400
15-Mar-X8	Ricky salary	-150		-24,550
15-Mar-X8	Katy salary	-150		-24,700
15-Mar-X8	Gina salary	-350		-25,050
23-Mar-X8	Sales		10,000	-15,050
25-Mar-X8	Purchases	-14,100		-29,150
15-Apr-X8	Ricky salary	-150		-29,300
15-Apr-X8	Katy salary	-150		-29,450
15-Apr-X8	Gina salary	-350		-29,800
17-Apr-X8	Sales		11,200	-18,600
19-Apr-X8	Purchases	-8,800		-27,400
15-May-X8	Ricky salary	-150		-27,550
15-May-X8	Katy salary	-150		-27,700
15-May-X8	Gina salary	-350		-28,050
31-May-X8	Balance			-28,050

Requirement

Calculate the Bank's preferential claim for wages advanced, showing in your workings the principles involved. Assume all salaries have been paid in full as at the date of liquidation. **(4 marks)**

(06/05) **(Total 15 marks)**

---

14 In a creditors voluntary liquidation, date of resolution to wind up 2 January 20X9, which one of the following claims ranks as preferential? (06/04)

(a) HMRC in respect of corporation tax
(b) HMRC in respect of VAT
(c) Employees in respect of holiday pay
(d) Employees in respect of redundancy
(e) HMRC in respect of PAYE/NI

---

15 What is the maximum amount which could be available to unsecured creditors under the prescribed part provisions of the Act? (06/04)

(a) £100,000
(b) £250,000
(c) £400,000
(d) £600,000
(e) £1,000,000

---

16 In connection with the prescribed part, what is the definition of a company's 'net property'? (06/04)

(a) The amount of its property which would otherwise be available to preferential creditors

(b) The amount of its property which would otherwise be available to unsecured creditors

(c) The amount of its property which would otherwise be available to the holder of any floating charge created by the company

(d) The amount of its property which would otherwise be available to the holder of any fixed charge created by the company

(e) The surplus available to pay shareholders after payment of costs, creditors and interest

---

17 By which section of the Act is a liquidator obliged to submit receipts and payments accounts to the Registrar of Companies? (06/04)

(a) S189
(b) S190
(c) S191
(d) S192
(e) S193

---

18 To which of the following corporate insolvency procedures does the prescribed part not necessarily apply? (06/04)

(a) Company voluntary arrangement
(b) Provisional liquidation
(c) Administration
(d) Receivership
(e) Liquidation

---

19 (a) A partner in your firm has recently been contacted by the directors of Tuckers Food Suppliers Limited ('the company'), which provides food products for sale in staff canteens at various local businesses.

The company has made losses for each of the last two years and the results for the current year are also very poor. To ensure that the directors act in accordance with their obligations they have requested that your firm assist them with convening meetings of both members and creditors, to place the company into creditors voluntary liquidation.

At a meeting with the directors, you have been provided with the following information.

1 The company trades from its owned freehold premises in Barnaby Street, Camchester. An independent valuation has been carried out and values the property at £230,000. These premises were purchased by the company some eight months ago for £150,000 with the assistance of a mortgage from Best Bank Plc which is currently owed £75,000.

2 The company has three delivery vans. Two of these are on finance with Finance UK Limited. These were purchased some two years ago for £18,000, their book value, and are now valued by agents at £4,000 each with total finance outstanding of £7,500. The remaining van is on a rental agreement at a monthly cost of £400.

3 The company has outstanding book debts of £65,000 which are subject to a factoring agreement with Two Way Factors Plc. The factors have advanced 65% of the debts due to the nature of the company's business. The director has also advised that 20% of the debts will be irrecoverable due to the age of the debts concerned; they are over 150 days old.

4 The company has some further book debts which are not subject to the factoring agreement totalling £15,650. One of these debtors has proceeded into liquidation owing the company £9,665 and the liquidator has confirmed that no dividend will be paid in this regard. The balance should be collected.

5 Stock remaining has a cost value of £18,640. However as the stock is perishable it is anticipated that only 20% of its cost will be realised.

6 The company has a small amount of office furniture and equipment with a book value of £7,500. Independent agents, Deals For You Limited, estimate that the sum of £3,600 should be realised.

7 The company employs some 30 members of staff. All are owed one week's wages totalling £7,800. The highest paid employee earns £650 per week. The employees also have outstanding holiday pay totalling £12,000 and will be entitled to redundancy pay of £78,000 and notice pay of £31,200.

8 Trade and Expense Creditors total £195,000.

9 The liabilities to H M Revenue and Customs are as follows:

VAT 1 July 20X8 to 30 September 20X8 - £14,300
1 October 20X8 to 31 December 20X8 - £9,850
1 January 20X9 to 4 June 20X9 - £24,650

PAYE – 1 April 20X8 to 4 June 20X9 - £80,600

10 The company has 999 ordinary £1 shares all of which are paid up and held equally by the directors. In addition there are outstanding loans owed to directors of £25,000. There is also a share premium account shown in the last set of accounts totalling £15,000.

Requirement

Prepare the Statement of Affairs to be presented to the meeting of creditors as at 4 June 20X9 **(9 marks)**

(b) You were appointed liquidator of Tuckers Food Supplies Limited at the meeting of creditors held on 4 June 20X9. Since your appointment you have sold all of the assets of the company and are due to report to the creditors for the first time. You received authorisation from the creditors at the initial creditors meeting, held pursuant to S98 of the Act, to draw your remuneration on a time cost basis.

To date you have paid the sum of £27,500 by way of liquidator's remuneration and agent's fees of £35,000 and solicitor's costs of £2,300.

Requirement

Set out the information you, as liquidator, should provide to creditors in your report in relation to the payments made during the liquidation, which are referred to above, in accordance with Statement of Insolvency Practice 9. **(6 marks)**

(06/04) **(Total 15 marks)**

20 Which Statement of Insolvency Practice (SIP) deals with the preparation of financial information in insolvency proceedings? (06/04)

(a) SIP 3
(b) SIP 7
(c) SIP 10
(d) SIP 12
(e) SIP 14

---

21 Your principal asks you to review the amount of his specific bond on E-Bust Limited an administrative receivership which you are dealing with.

The appointing bank has fixed security over goodwill, intellectual property and freehold property. T has a floating charge over all other assets. There are no other secured lenders.

At the time of your review realisations are as follows:

	£
Freehold property	600,000
Book debts	50,000
Computer equipment	10,000
Goodwill	100,000
Office furniture	5,000
Intellectual property	95,000

The costs of the receivership are £130,000. These are charged equally against fixed and floating charge realizations. There are preferential creditors of £150,000 and unsecured creditors of £950,000. The bank is owed £475,000 including interest. No further significant receipts or payments are expected.

Requirement

Show your workings to calculate what the amount of the administrative receiver's specific bond should be at the time of your review.

(06/04) **(3 marks)**

---

22 You are trustee in a bankruptcy which commenced on 6 August 20X8. Asset realisations have been successful and on 6 May 20X9 you have £350,000 available, after settlement of petition costs and the Official Receiver's costs.

You expect to be able to pay all remaining costs, including your remuneration, in the month leading up to 6 June 20X9 and then, on that day, you will pay the balance of funds to creditors. The following facts are relevant.

Your remuneration has been fixed on a time cost basis at £25,000. You have expenses of £685.

There are agents' costs of £4,500 and solicitors' costs of £6,250.

Creditors are as follows:

	£
Preferential	8,250
Unsecured trade creditors	252,000
Bankrupt's wife	35,000
Local authority	1,000
Unsecured bank loan	12,000
Credit card debts	5,000

Requirement

Showing your workings, calculate how the amount available will be distributed (ignore any VAT issues).

(06/04) **(4 marks)**

---

23 In a Compulsory Liquidation what percentage is the Secretary of State fee on realisations in excess of £3,000, but less than £4,000? (06/02)

(a) 15%
(b) 11.25%
(c) 10.5%
(d) 10%
(e) (Realisations – £2,500) × 100%

---

24 Your firm has been instructed by the board of directors of Cromwells Limited, to assist with the convening of meetings of the company's members and creditors to place the company into creditors voluntary liquidation on 31 May 20X0. You are also instructed to assist the directors' preparation of the statement of affairs as at that date. Cromwells Limited is a company that produces cloth for the furniture industry. The company owns a freehold factory in Nottingham. The property was acquired for £500,000 in May 2006. A valuation was recently obtained in the sum of £625,000.

Following a meeting with the company's financial director, you have obtained the following additional information:

(1) Better Bank plc hold a specific legal charge over the freehold property. Current indebtedness to the bank under this charge is £450,000.

(2) The company has trade debtors totalling £670,000. 70% of these debts are factored. The company has had advances from the factoring company of 75% in respect of the factored debts. The factoring company has formally advised the company that their termination charges are £15,000. The financial director believes that a provision of 10% of total trade debtors should be made for bad debts.

(3) Plant & machinery is shown in the accounts with a book value of £475,000, of which 60% is subject to finance. Plant & machinery has been valued at £200,000 of which £125,000 is subject to finance. The outstanding finance liability stands at £200,000.

(4) Stock and work-in-progress has a current book value of £350,000. It is anticipated that only 20% of book value will be realised.

(5) There is an outstanding directors loan account with a balance of £45,000. There is every indication that this loan will be repaid to the company in full.

(6) All motor vehicles are leased.

(7) Employees' liabilities are as follows:

	£
Holiday pay	23,000
Redundancy	110,000
Notice pay	65,000

(8) The liability to HMRC is as follows:

	£
PAYE/NIC 15 months	160,000
Corporation tax	25,000

It can be assumed that the PAYE/NIC liability has accrued evenly over the period.

(9) VAT has not been paid for the following period:

	£
1/10/X9 – 31/12/X9	45,000
1/01/X0 – 31/03/X0	40,000
01/04/X0 – 31/05/X0	25,000

Again, it can be assumed that the liability has accrued evenly over the periods concerned.

(10) Trade creditors – £750,000

(11) The company has ordinary, fully paid up share capital of £15,000

(12) The balance on the company's profit and loss account as at 31.12.X8 was £125,000

(13) Your firm has received a fee for the convening of the meetings and the preparation of the statement of affairs in the sum of £7,500.

Requirement

(a) You are required to prepare a Statement of Affairs as at 31 May 20X0. **(9 marks)**

(b) You are required to prepare a deficiency account for the period 1 January 20X8 to 31 May 20X0. **(5 marks)**

(c) If Better Bank plc held security in the form of a debenture comprising a fixed and floating charge and its fixed charge purported to cover book debts, rather than the freehold property, advise in the light of recent case law, how this security should be treated. **(1 mark)**

(06/02) **(Total 15 marks)**

---

25 Your Principal has asked you to cover a meeting with a new client due to be held on 14 May 20X0. The client is a director of a limited company, Stewards Equestrian Limited, which is insolvent. The director considers the company has a viable business. He has heard of the Voluntary Arrangement procedure and considers this might be an option.

It is his intention that the company continues to trade, retaining all of its employees, and making contributions from future trading profits for the benefit of creditors.

At your meeting you obtain the following information:

1 Your firm was consulted by the company 2½ years ago and a tax partner provided some advice for which you were paid. Your firm has not acted for the company in any capacity since.

2 The company owed £45,000 to HMRC for the past 15 months PAYE and NIC. Wages are £10,000 per month of which 30% is PAYE and NIC. There is a debt due to HMRC for the last quarter's VAT of £15,000 and the current month's VAT is estimated at £5,700.

3 The company's four employees are entitled to gross weekly wages of £2,500. These are due to be paid at the end of the week as usual. Upon termination of employment the employees would currently be entitled to holiday pay of £5,000, pay-in-lieu of notice £10,000 and redundancy pay of £15,000.

4 Trade and Expense creditors total £158,898 and £75,000 is owed to a director in respect of his loan account.

5 The company estimates sales of £480,000 in year one with year on year growth of 8% per annum. The company achieves a gross margin of 30%. In addition overheads are £102,000 in year one with year on year increases of 3.5%.

6 The company has sufficient tax losses to not pay any tax until year four when corporation tax will be payable at 25% on profits. From net profit after tax the company, from year one onwards, will retain 40% of profit to fund future working capital and capital expenditure.

7 The remaining profit will be available to contribute to a Voluntary Arrangement.

Requirement

(a) Write a short note to your principal advising of any ethical considerations he should consider before accepting instructions to act as Nominee under the director's proposal for a Voluntary Arrangement. **(2 marks)**

(b) Prepare a statement showing the contributions from trading profits which the company could make to a Voluntary Arrangement in each of the next five years, based on the information given above. (Show your workings) **(5 marks)**

(c) Produce an outcome statement showing the estimated dividend to creditors which the total contributions in b) above would produce in the voluntary arrangement. You should provide an estimate of £3,000 per annum for the Supervisor's fees. You may ignore the Nominee's fee. It will have been paid before the arrangement began. **(5 marks)**

(d) Comment on how the director could assist in improving the dividend to creditors **(1 mark)**

(e) Explain the rule for requisite majority in obtaining approval for a CVA and explain how the votes of connected creditors affect this. **(2 marks)**

(06/02) **(Total 15 marks)**

---

26 Peter Gerrard has telephoned your office and spoken with one of the managers responsible for corporate recovery and asked for advice in respect of a possible Individual Voluntary Arrangement (IVA). The manager has passed a file note of his conversation to the partner who specialises in personal insolvency matters and scheduled a meeting for next week so that his affairs may be discussed in more detail.

The file note provides the following background to his position. Peter Gerrard ran an independent group of five newsagent shops. The shops traded under different names as follows:

Yelloways
Greenways
Redways
Bluejays
Brownstones

Yelloways and Bluejays were run as limited companies which were sold as a package on 12/11/X8. As part of the sale agreement Peter retained a 25% interest in a new holding company that was set up at the time. He was also entitled to a payment for loss of office of £40,000, £20,000 of which is still outstanding and is collectable. The present realisable value of the shares is £10,000.

Greenways was operated through a partnership with his brother James and on 15/12/X9 the brothers fell out and Peter served notice to dissolve the partnership. He has been advised that the amount due to him on dissolution is approximately £56,000 although James disputes the stock figures and has raised issues with regard to unauthorised drawings. In spite of this Peter thinks the full £56,000 will be paid within the next six months.

Redways and Brownstones are run as sole proprietorships and are still trading. Redways employs a full time manager whilst Peter runs the Brownstones outlet. He has only one set of books for the combined trading. Trade has been poor at Redways in recent weeks and although it has a licence to run the National Lottery, Peter is thinking of closing it down and operating solely from Brownstones.

At the subsequent meeting Peter produces a computer print out of account balances, which shows the following:

Account Name	*Debit balance*	*Credit balance*
	£	£
Freehold property	35,000	
Leasehold property	27,676	
Fixtures and Fittings	12,340	
Stock in trade	44,100	
Goodwill	12,500	
PAYE/NIC		96,000
VAT		42,000
Bank current (Western Bank Limited)		5,000
Bank loan (Western Bank Limited)		22,000
Capital	26,334	
Trade creditors		23,235
Motor vehicles	32,560	
Hire purchase (on motor vehicles)		27,668
Drawings	40,393	
Loans (due to Peter's father)		15,000
Total	230,903	230,903

You establish further information during the diagnostic interview in order to form a view as to whether an IVA can be supported:

1 Peter is currently separated from his wife. She is still living at the matrimonial home with their two children aged 11 and 13 respectively. He occupies the flat above the Brownstones shop. The matrimonial property is on the market at £225,000. A building society has a first mortgage with a current redemption figure of £137,600. The property has also been used for security purposes with the Western Bank Limited. The property is registered in joint names. Mrs Gerrard should be able to claim exoneration in respect of the Bank's indebtedness.

2 HMRC are threatening bankruptcy enforcement action in an amount of £167,000, which is made up as follows:

	£
PAYE/NIC Arrears	79,000
Income Tax	54,600
Capital Gains Tax	33,400

3 In the last two tax years he has made personal pension contributions of £25,000 and £15,000 (the second payment of which was in cash). Previously, he had only been making regular monthly contributions of £200 per month.

4 Peter has informed you that he has a portfolio of quoted stocks and shares with an approximate current market value of £22,750

5 An independent firm of valuers has been commissioned to prepare a valuation report for the purpose of providing an accurate assessment of the valuations to be used in the preparation of the Statement of Affairs and the following asset valuations are now available:

	£
Freehold property	27,000
Leasehold property	5,000
Fixtures and Fittings	2,500
Stock in trade	7,500
Goodwill	NIL
Motor vehicle	23,750

Requirement

(a) If Peter's father enters into a conditional agreement to provide a lump sum of £60,000 on approval of the IVA and waive his claim for monies he has lent, prepare an estimated outcome statement for the IVA proposal under best practice guidelines showing a comparison with the outcome in a bankruptcy. You may assume that in a bankruptcy situation a Trustee would disclaim the leasehold property without obtaining any value for it, and the stock in the trade would only realise 50% of valuation. Peter wishes to exclude all the assets of his current business from the arrangement as they will be required for the continuation of trade. All his other assets will be included. Costs are estimated at £12,000 for the IVA and £29,000 for a bankruptcy. **(11 marks)**

(b) What factors would suggest that you support the calling of a creditors' meeting in the Nominee's Report. **(2 marks)**

(c) What factors might make creditors vote against the proposals for an IVA? **(2 marks)**

(06/02) **(Total 15 marks)**

---

27 Mr Smith (a bankrupt) has liabilities to HMRC of £7,000, together with trade creditors of £15,000. The Official Receiver's remaining costs outstanding total £700 and Trustee's fees will total £4,000, with a further £300 worth of disbursements. The bankruptcy commenced after 15 September 2003.

What dividend will unsecured creditors receive from realisations of £20,000? Ignore VAT, but include Secretary of State administration fees of £3,060 in your calculations

(a) 56p/£
(b) 54p/£
(c) 70p/£
(d) 67p/£

Please show workings **(3 marks)**

(06/01)

---

28 You have recently been instructed by the directors of Lost Hope Limited to assist them to prepare a statement of affairs to be presented at that company's section 98 meeting.

You ascertain the following information from the books and records of the company and from valuations received since you were instructed.

The company has a freehold property with a book value of £350,000. However, your agents believe that the property would now realise at least £385,000 given the increase in commercial property prices in the area. At the date of the resolution to wind up, capital and interest outstanding to Slow Bank plc, which has a legal charge over the property, is £215,000.

Your own research into the company's debtor ledger shows a book value of £138,000. The directors believe that 10% of this figure is bad and doubtful. They agree with you that of the balance, it would be sensible to consider that a further 15% may be uncollectable in a liquidation.

There are no specific charges on the book debts but in order to secure a loan of £65,000 Risky Business Finance Limited were granted a floating charge over all Lost Hope Limited's assets. At the date of the resolution to wind up the amount owed to Risky Business Finance Limited was £62,000.

There are no reasons to doubt the validity of this floating charge which was granted on 1 October 2003.

Most of the company's plant and machinery is on finance. However, there is free machinery which your agents believe should realise £2,500 and which has a book value of £6,000.

The finance is provided by two separate companies. Three machines are financed by Low Cost Finance plc, with respective realisable values of £7,500, £500 and £9,500. The equivalent book values are £10,000, £5,000 and £11,000. The outstanding amounts due under each finance agreement is respectively £5,000, £3,500 and £8,000. Low Cost Finance plc does not have a consolidation clause in its agreements.

Two other machines are financed by Quick Finance Limited. They have book values of £25,000 and £15,000 and realisable values respectively of £20,000 and £6,000. The respective amounts due under the agreements are £15,000 and £12,000. Quick Finance Limited has a consolidation clause in its agreements.

The company has no work in progress but stock with a book value of £30,000 which your agents believe will realise £20,000. You are aware of valid retention of title claims of £4,000.

Unsecured trade creditors total £335,000. They include all the retention of title creditors but not the finance companies.

There is also a director's loan of £6,000 and other liabilities as follows:

£35,000 unpaid VAT for the last seven months and unpaid PAYE of £40,000 over the same period (you can assume that these liabilities have accrued evenly over the period).

There were fifteen employees who were owed the following amounts:

	£
Redundancy	25,000
Payment in lieu of notice	15,000
Holiday pay	6,000
Wages	7,500

Two employees are owed wages of £1,000 each. No other single employee is owed more than £600.

The company has paid up share capital of £25,000.

Requirement

From the figures available, prepare a statement of the company's affairs as at 30 April 20X0. Show the book values where appropriate and estimated to realise values. **(15 marks)**

(06/01)

---

29 Where in the insolvency legislation would you find details of when liquidators should pay funds into the Insolvency Services Account? (06/00)

(a) Insolvency Act 1986
(b) Insolvency Rules 1986
(c) Insolvency Practitioners Regulations 1990
(d) Insolvency Regulations 1994
(e) Insolvency Act 1994

---

30 In an administrative receivership you have paid off your debenture holder and after paying all costs, including your remuneration, you have a surplus of £20,000 in your fixed charge account.

After costs there is £18,000 in your floating charge account. There are no other secured creditors. Other creditors include the following:

(a) Six employees each owed £1,000 in salary arrears

(b) Ten employees each owed £1,500 in accrued holiday pay

(c) Managing director Andrew Evans is owed £30,000 in salary arrears and £3,000 in accrued holiday pay

State how you will payout the £38,000 available in your two bank accounts and the amount each of the preferential creditors above will receive.

Give reasons for your answers. **(5 marks)**

(06/00)

---

31 Three weeks ago (on 1 July 20X9) you were appointed joint administrative receiver of Start Again Limited. You have successfully sold the company's business and most of its assets on a going concern sale to a competitor of Start Again Limited, without having to make any redundancies.

The following amounts are realised upon completion.

	£
Assets	
Freehold property	200,000
Plant & Machinery	200,000
Stock and work in progress	160,000
Goodwill	35,000

Your solicitors advise that 30% of the plant and machinery, all the freehold property and all the goodwill are subject to the debenture holder's fixed charge which was created on 1 October 2002. The other realisations are subject to its floating charge which was created on same date.

Solicitors charged £5,000 for dealing with the sale and your agents charged £2,500. These costs are to be charged pro rata against fixed and floating charge realisations achieved in the sale.

There is a term in the sale agreement that the purchaser will deal with any retention of title claims on the stock which is sold.

In the three weeks you have traded, your sales averaged £25,000 a week and you can assume they have all been received, trading being on a cash basis.

Each of the three weeks involved purchases of £7,000, gross wages of £8,000 and a receivership trading supervision charge of £4,000 a week.

Other trading costs are utilities £750 a week and insurance £3,500 in total. Assume all these costs have been paid.

The sale did not include book debts, subject to the debenture holder's fixed charge on book debts. Total book debts at the date of appointment were £300,000. You have realised £190,000 and estimate that 50% of the balance will be collected. The remainder is old and disputed and will have to be written off.

Solicitor's costs for dealing with debt collection are estimated at £5,000. None has yet been paid.

The only remuneration you have received so far is for trading supervision. The debenture holder has agreed that you can be remunerated on a time cost basis and you estimate the total hours which will be spent on the receivership will be as follows:

Fixed charge work: Partner/manager time 50 hours at average charge out rate of £150 per hour and other staff 75 hours at average charge out rate of £75 per hour.

Floating charge work: Partner/manager time 50 hours average charge out rate of £150 per hour and other staff 200 hours at average charge out rate of £75 per hour.

You have sundry costs of £1,000 to include bonding, advertising etc and legal costs of £500 for advising on the validity of your appointment. Both these have been charged to the floating charge. In addition to the purchases stated above, you paid £2,500 to a creditor who had a valid retention of title claim. You are also aware of another such claim for £5,000 on the stock you have sold.

HMRC is owed £15,000, the Department of Work and Pensions £12,000 and HMRC (for VAT) £17,000. All of these amounts accrued equally over the last eight months.

Requirement

(a) Prepare an estimated outcome statement for the debenture holder, who was owed £800,000 at the date of your appointment. You can ignore post appointment interest and VAT. **(14 marks)**

(b) Why do you think there are no preferential claims for any employees? **(1 mark)**

(06/00) **(Total 15 marks)**

---

32 Ronald Jones is the licensee and tenant of The Bull's Head. He is experiencing severe cashflow difficulties which has culminated in a bankruptcy petition being presented. He has been advised by his accountant to put forward a proposal for an Individual Voluntary Arrangement.

Mr Jones holds the leasehold interest in The Bull's Head, the original term being 15 years and the residue being 10 years. Mr Jones paid a bond of £5,000 to the landlord and there are current rental arrears of £5,000. The rental payable is £20,000 per annum. The lease is of nil value.

Tenants fixtures and fittings have a book value of £15,000 but are expected to realise £5,000 in a forced sale situation.

Mr Jones also owns jointly with his wife, the matrimonial home 'Windy Nook'. The property is worth £100,000 and is subject to a 1st mortgage in favour of a Building Society who is owed £20,000. The mortgage is an endowment mortgage and the endowment policy has a current surrender value of £10,000.

'Windy Nook' also has a 2nd charge in favour of a Bank in relation to a business overdraft facility taken out in the sole name of Mr Jones. The Bank is owed £20,000. Mrs Jones is a partner in a solicitors firm and therefore has her own income. In a voluntary arrangement, Mrs Jones is prepared to treat all borrowings as joint as an incentive to creditors to vote in favour.

There are no other assets.

Mr Jones owed £10,000 to HMRC in relation to PAYE for the last six months and £10,000 in relation to Schedule D income tax liability.

He also owed £20,000 to HMRC for VAT which has accrued evenly over the last 12 months.

Business rate arrears total £10,000 and sundry creditors total £40,000.

In the event of ceasing to trade, three employees will have claims for redundancy and arrears of wages. Redundancy claims will total £2,000 each and each employee will be owed £200 in arrears of wages.

The arrangement will provide for a continuation of the business which will enable Mr Jones to make income contributions of £1,000 per month over a 36-month duration. The matrimonial home will be sold and Mr Jones' share of the equity will be realised.

Prepare an estimated comparative outcome statement between bankruptcy and voluntary arrangement as at 1 February 20Y0.

The following assumptions should be made.

	£
OFFICIAL RECEIVER'S COSTS	1,000
Trustee's Fees Fixed on a Time Cost Basis	5,000
Nominee's Fees	1,500
Supervisor's Fees on a Time Cost Basis	4,500
Secretary of State fees	
Petitioner's Solicitor's Costs	1,000
Agent's Costs (Bankruptcy)	1,500
Agent's Costs (VA)	750
Accountant's Fees (VA)	500
Solicitor's Costs (Bankruptcy)	3,000
Solicitor's Costs (VA)	1,000

Note: Ignore VAT

It should also be assumed that the landlord could secure a new tenant for the property after one year.

Please ensure you note any other assumptions made. **(15 marks)**

(06/00)

---

33 Berkeley Property Support Limited – Creditors Voluntary Liquidation

Below is the Liquidator's Abstract of Receipts and Payments for Berkeley Property Support Limited as at 31 May 2013.

BERKELEY PROPERTY SUPPORT LIMITED IN LIQUIDATION

LIQUIDATOR'S ABSTRACT OF RECEIPTS AND PAYMENTS ACCOUNT FOR THE PERIOD 4 APRIL 2011 TO 31 MAY 2013

RECEIPTS	Per S.A	Realised	
	£	£	
Plant & Machinery	500	485	
Motor Vehicles	7,000	7,250	
Stock	750	400	
Trade Debtors	80,000	76,435	
	88,250		84,570
LESS: PAYMENTS			
Agents' Fees & Expenses		8,207	
IT Support Services		435	
Preparation of S of A		6,000	
Statutory Advertising		305	
Specific Penalty Bond		120	
Storage		746	
Liquidator's Disbursements		577	
			16,390
Balance in Hand			68,180

The Liquidator's Remuneration has been fixed at £11,250. Ignore VAT.

Preferential Creditors have been agreed at £10,700.

The Bank is owed £113,280 and is secured by way of a fixed and floating charge debenture dated 25 September 2009. All assets are subject to the floating charge.

The Non Preferential Creditors have been agreed at £244,920.

There will be no further realisations or further costs incurred.

Requirement

(a) Calculate the Prescribed Part. **(5 marks)**

(b) Calculate the Sum payable to the Bank (expressed as p in £). **(2 marks)**

(c) Calculate the Dividend payable to the Non Preferential Creditors. **(3 marks)**

(d) Prepare a Final Outcome Statement. **(5 marks)**

(Total 15 marks)

34

(A) Your principal has been appointed Trustee of a bankruptcy estate. The bankruptcy order was made on 30 April 2012 on a petition presented to Court on 31 January 2012. The appointment of your principal as Trustee was made on 31 October 2012 by the Secretary of State.

The only asset available for the bankruptcy estate was the bankrupt's half interest in the matrimonial home. This has been valued at £400,000 and is subject to a single charge for £220,000. The mortgage is up-to-date and there are no plans by the mortgagee to commence legal proceedings for possession. The non-bankrupt spouse has made no claims for an increased share of the equity.

There are limited creditors of the bankruptcy estate. Three creditors have lodged valid proofs of debt which total £25,000. There are expected to be claims lodged in the estate for the following creditors: Eleco for £1,000, Natclays Bank for £9,000 and O3 phones for £250. No other creditor claims are expected.

The debtor and joint owner of the property cannot introduce funds to purchase the property interest which vests in the bankruptcy estate. They have agreed to sell the property on the open market with agents who will charge 1.5% of the sale price + VAT. The agents are advising that a sale at £500,000 is achievable and a sale should be concluded by 31 October 2013.

The conveyance for the sale will be carried out by solicitors for £2,000 + VAT.

The debtor and joint owner have enquired as to whether the sale of the property will pay the bankruptcy in full and have asked your principal to provide them with a calculation so that they can see if there will be sufficient funds to clear the bankruptcy so that the debtor can consider an annulment on the conclusion of a property sale.

The bankruptcy fees and expenses accrued to date are the Official Receiver's fee which is £1,715, petition costs of £2,000, agents fees for the property valuation of £100 + VAT. The case has been bonded with a bond fee of £210 and insurance has been obtained by your principal over his interest in the property at the sum of £200.

Trustees' remuneration has been agreed on a time costs basis and the current outstanding work-in-progress is £5,500 with an estimated sum of £2,000 required to finalise the bankruptcy. The Trustee has accrued an advert disbursement of £100 + VAT.

There are quarterly banking fees in respect of the ISA of £88 to date and a further 2 quarterly fees of £22 each are expected to be charged. The Secretary of State fee has been calculated at £10,300 to pay. The deposit on the petition of £700 has been paid.

The debtor is in PAYE employment and is not VAT registered.

There have been no asset realisations to date.

Requirement

Compile an estimated payment-in-full calculation for the debtor and indicate whether the estimated equity vesting in the estate will be sufficient to pay the bankruptcy debts and costs in full. (Ignore cheque fees.) **(10 marks)**

(B) The spouse is not happy about the Secretary of State fees. She wants to know what scale is used to calculate "such a large amount".

Requirement

Set out the scale that is used to calculate the Secretary of State fees for realisations for a bankruptcy estate and state what, if any, limit there is for this fee. **(2 marks)**

(C) The sale completes and the debtor has made an application to annul the bankruptcy order and notice of the annulment application has been received by your principal. He is aware that he has to file a report regarding the annulment and wants to know who he serves with his report and when he needs to serve these parties prior to the hearing.

Requirement

Provide a short memo to your principal advising who his annulment report is to be sent to and how many days before the annulment hearing he needs to ensure the report is sent to these parties.

(3 marks)

(06/13) **(Total 15 marks)**

---

4 Position of directors in insolvency situations

1 You submit an adverse D report in liquidation. Which of the following is it not necessary to append to the report? (6/11)

(a) A copy of the Statement of Affairs
(b) A copy of the resolution to wind up the company
(c) Details of the dividend prospects in the case
(d) A copy of the minutes of the Section 98 meeting

---

2 In accordance with SIP13 when should the liquidator report details to creditors of a connected party transaction occurring after the commencement of the liquidation? (6/10)

(a) 7 days prior to the proposed transaction
(b) Within 7 days of the transaction
(c) In his first report following the date of the transaction
(d) As soon as reasonably practical following the transaction

---

3 Who is not required to submit a D return on the conduct of the directors? (06/08)

(a) An administrative receiver
(b) A liquidator in a creditors' voluntary liquidation
(c) A liquidator in a members' voluntary liquidation
(d) An administrator

---

4 Which section of the Act outlines the actions that may be taken in relation to wrongful trading? (06/07)

(a) Section 212
(b) Section 214
(c) Section 216
(d) Section 218

---

5 Your partner was appointed liquidator of Global Investments Limited and is in the process of preparing the D return on the conduct of the directors. He has asked you to prepare a memorandum setting out:

(a) The factors the Disqualification Unit places particular importance on (as set out in SIP 4)? **(7 marks)**

(b) What items should be appended to every report (where information is available) **(3 marks)**

(c) Outline the issues that may be considered when assessing whether a party may be deemed to be a shadow director and the issues faced by anyone deemed to be a shadow director. **(5 marks)**

(06/07) **(Total 15 marks)**

---

6 Which Statement of Insolvency Practice deals with the acquisition of assets of insolvent companies by directors? (06/06)

(a) SIP 1
(b) SIP 7
(c) SIP 10
(d) SIP 13
(e) SIP 14

---

7 In a creditors' voluntary liquidation, the liquidator's report on the conduct of the directors of the company must be submitted in respect of: (06/06)

(a) All directors of the company since incorporation

(b) All directors of the company within one year of the commencement of the liquidation

(c) All directors of the company within two years of the commencement of the liquidation

(d) All directors and shadow directors of the company within two years of the commencement of the liquidation

(e) All directors and shadow directors of the company within three years of the commencement of the liquidation

---

8 Which Statement of Insolvency Practice deals with the reporting to the Dept BIS on the conduct of directors? (06/04)

(a) SIP 8
(b) SIP 4
(c) SIP 12
(d) SIP 3
(e) SIP 2

---

9 Against which one of the following can an action for misfeasance under section 212 of the Act not be taken? (06/04)

(a) A supervisor under the company's voluntary arrangement
(b) A liquidator of the company
(c) A former officer of the company
(d) A person who took part in the formation of the company

---

10 Which one of the following may not apply to have the conduct of an administrator, who was appointed in February 20X9, examined on an allegation of breach of fiduciary duty in relation to the company? (06/04)

(a) The official receiver
(b) A creditor of the company
(c) A liquidator of the company
(d) A director of the company
(e) A contributory of the company

---

11 Your principal, the liquidator of an insolvent company, wishes to sell the assets of that company back to the directors. Which of the following SIPs would you advise him to consult before he does so? (06/02)

(a) SIP 11
(b) SIP 12
(c) SIP 13
(d) SIP 14

---

12 Which SIP deals the matters which should be included in the content of a report on the conduct of directors? (06/01)

(a) SIP 2
(b) SIP 3
(c) SIP 4
(d) SIP 12
(e) SIP 13

---

5 Voluntary liquidation

1 Your partner has just returned from a meeting with the directors of Zep Music Limited who wish to place the Company into creditors' voluntary liquidation.

(a) Set out the sequence of statutory meetings required to place the Company into liquidation ahead of a meeting of creditors and the primary purpose of those meetings. **(2 marks)**

(b) What are the requirements to give notice of a creditors' meeting? **(4 marks)**

(c) What details should the notice to creditors contain? **(5 marks)**

(d) What information are the directors required to lay before the creditors' meeting? **(2 marks)**

(e) Under S99 of the Act a Company's statement of affairs must disclose what information? **(2 marks)**

(6/12) **(Total 15 marks)**

---

2 Which of the following powers of a liquidator is expressly exercisable with sanction? (6/11)

(a) Power to sell the company's property
(b) Power to raise money on the security of the assets of the company
(c) Power to bring legal proceedings for wrongful trading
(d) Power to appoint an agent

---

3 A partner of your firm has today been appointed at a meeting of shareholders held at short notice as Liquidator of Fresh Fruit & Veg Limited, a company which is insolvent.

Set out the requirements of providing notice of a meeting to creditors in accordance with section 98 of the Act and SIP 8. (6/11) **(4 marks)**

---

4 Table Limited was placed into Creditors Voluntary Liquidation in May 2010 and your Principal was appointed Liquidator. A creditors' committee was appointed to assist with investigations and various assets were uncovered and realised. The realisation process has now been finalised, however there are insufficient funds available to pay a distribution to any class of creditor.

(a) Set out the practical, legal and regulatory steps that need to be taken to close the case.

($^1/_2$ mark per point up to a maximum of 8 marks)

(b) Set out the items which are required by statute to be specified separately on the liquidator's summary of Receipts and Payments contained in his final report.

(6/11) **($^1/_2$ mark per point up to a maximum of 7 marks)**

---

5 Within what time period in business days following a creditors' meeting summoned under s98 of the Act must the directors' statement of affairs be filed with the Registrar of Companies? (6/10)

(a) 5 days
(b) 7 days
(c) 15 days
(d) 21 days

6 In accordance with s84 of the Act how many business days' notice of a resolution for voluntary winding up should be given to a holder of qualifying floating charge? (6/10)

(a) 2 days prior to the passing of the resolution
(b) Within 7 days following the passing of the resolution
(c) At the same time that notice of the proposed resolution is sent to shareholders
(d) 5 or more days prior to the passing of the resolution

---

7 Your firm has been instructed to assist in placing a company into members' voluntary liquidation, and the directors have raised a number of questions regarding the statutory declaration of solvency.

(a) How many directors are required to make the statutory declaration of solvency? **(1 mark)**

(b) What is the maximum period within which the directors can predict that the company will be able to pay its debts in full? **(1 mark)**

(c) Why should the directors take care to ensure they have reasonable grounds for making the statutory declaration? **(4 marks)**

(6/10) **(Total 6 marks)**

---

8 Under s99 a company's Statement of Affairs must disclose what information? (6/09)

($^1/_2$ mark per point)

---

9 Your partner has been appointed liquidator of Guppy Ltd by resolution of the members and his appointment has been confirmed at a s98 meeting of creditors, at which a liquidation committee has also been appointed.

The committee has raised concerns about certain aspects of the company's dealings and has asked you what duties the liquidator has to investigate the affairs of the company.

(a) With particular reference to SIP 2 give examples of best practice which a diligent liquidator should adopt in conducting his investigations into an insolvent company's affairs. **(3 marks)**

(b) Give three examples of the types of company records which the liquidator should seek to examine in every case? **(3 marks)**

(c) During the course of the liquidation of Guppy Ltd the liquidator incurs expenditure in connection with the following:

(i) Advertising his appointment

(ii) Allocation of the purchase costs of the firm's new time cost recording software

(iii) Photocopying of circulars to creditors by the firm's print room, calculated by reference to costs per copy

(iv) External room hire for creditors' meetings

(v) Air fare to inspect overseas property of the company

(vi) Mileage allowance of 40p per mile paid to a member of staff travelling to a meeting with the director of the company

How should the above expenses be categorised under Statement of Insolvency Practice 9? **(3 marks)**

(d) Following the realisation of Guppy Ltd's assets, it is clear that funds will be available to make a distribution to unsecured creditors. However, not all creditors have proved their claims.

What steps should the liquidator take prior to declaring a dividend? **(2 marks)**

(e) The liquidator considers the claim of Tetra Ltd lies against a director of Guppy Ltd, rather than against the company.

Outline the procedure for admitting or rejecting proofs of debt in a voluntary winding up and any recourse that is available to Tetra Ltd.

(1 mark per point up to 4 marks)

(6/09) **(Total 15 marks)**

---

10 When is a creditors' committee deemed properly constituted under s98 of the Insolvency Act, assuming the company has not previously been in administration? (06/08)

(a) The date of the certificate of constitution is sent to the Registrar of Companies
(b) The date of the creditors' meeting
(c) The date all the committee members sign notice consenting to join the committee
(d) The date of the first committee meeting

---

11 In a Creditors Voluntary Liquidation, how long does a liquidator have to file a statement of affairs once received? (06/08)

(a) 48 hours
(b) 5 business days
(c) 7 business days
(d) 21 business days

---

12 Your firm has been instructed to assist in placing a company into members' voluntary liquidation. List eight documents that should be prepared to enable the liquidation to commence. **(4 marks)**

(06/08)

---

13 If a Creditors' Voluntary Liquidation (that commenced prior to 6 April 2010) continues for more than one year within what time period within the end of the year should the liquidator summon an meeting of the company and meetings of creditors? (06/07)

(a) 21 days
(b) 1 month
(c) 2 months
(d) 3 months

---

14 What is the quorum for a meeting of the liquidation committee in a Creditors' Voluntary Liquidation? (06/07)

(a) At least two members present or represented
(b) At least one member present
(c) At least three members present
(d) At least three members present or represented

---

15 A resolution for voluntary winding up must be advertised in the Gazette within what period of the passing of the resolution? (06/06)

(a) 14 days of the passing of the resolution
(b) 8 days of the passing of the resolution
(c) 7 days of the filing of the resolution with the Registrar of Companies
(d) 15 days of the filing of the resolution with the Registrar of Companies
(e) 15 days of the passing of the resolution

---

16 Which section of the Insolvency Act 1986 provides for the acceptance of shares as consideration for the sale of company property? (06/06)

(a) s100
(b) s105
(c) s110
(d) s115
(e) s120

---

17 What matters should be included in the liquidator's report to creditors following a s98 meeting of creditors? (06/06) **(4 marks)**

---

18 Before a company passes a resolution for voluntary winding up it must give written notice of the resolution to which of the following? (06/05)

(a) HM Customs and Revenue
(b) The company's auditors
(c) The holder of a qualifying floating charge to which s72A applies
(d) The Registrar of Companies
(e) All known unsecured creditors of the company

---

19 A declaration of solvency has no effect unless it is made within which period of the passing of the resolution for winding up? (06/05)

(a) 15 days preceding the resolution
(b) 15 days following the resolution
(c) Five weeks preceding the resolution
(d) One month preceding the resolution
(e) One week preceding the resolution

---

20 Which of the following powers under Schedule 4 of the Act may the liquidator only exercise with sanction? (06/05)

(a) Power to bring legal proceedings under Sections 213, 214, 238, 239, 242, 243 or 423 of the Insolvency Act 1986.

(b) Power to raise on the security of the assets of the company any money requisite.

(c) Power to appoint an agent to do any business which the liquidator is unable to do himself.

(d) Power to pay any class of creditor in full.

(e) Power to sell any of the company's property by public auction or private contract, with power to transfer the whole of it to any person or to sell the same in parcels.

(f) Power to make any compromise or arrangement with creditors or persons claiming to be creditors, or having or alleging themselves to have any claim (present or future, certain or contingent, ascertained or sounding only in damages) against the company, or whereby the company may be rendered liable.

(g) Power to do all such other things as may be necessary for winding up the company's affairs and distributing assets.

(h) Power to do all acts and execute, in the name and on behalf of the company, all deeds, receipts and other documents and for that purpose to use, when necessary, the company's seal.

(i) Power to compromise, on such terms as may be agreed all questions in any way relating to or affecting the assets or the winding up of the company. **(4 marks)**

---

21 A company went into members' voluntary liquidation on March 24 20X8. By which date must the liquidator have given notice of his appointment to the creditors of the company? (06/04)

(a) 7 April 20X8
(b) 14 April 20X8
(c) 21 April 20X8
(d) 24 April 20X8
(e) None of these dates

---

22 What constitutes a quorum at a meeting of a liquidation committee in a winding up by the court? (06/04)

(a) Two members present or represented
(b) Two creditor members present or represented
(c) A majority of members present or represented
(d) A majority of creditor members present or represented
(e) One creditor present or represented

---

23 In an MVL commencing after 6 April 2010 under which section of the Act is a general meeting convened at the end of each year after appointment of a liquidator in a members voluntary winding up? (06/04)

(a) s91
(b) s93
(c) s105
(d) s106
(e) None of the above

---

24 Dalwood (2002) Limited, a company that trades in the food distribution industry, has ceased trading. The directors have approached your principal and have formally instructed him to assist them in calling meetings of members and creditors to place the company into liquidation in accordance with Section 98 of the Insolvency Act 1986.

A copy of the company's up to date management accounts have been made available to you as at 29 May 20X9. The balance sheet is summarised as follows:-

	£'000
Fixed Assets	
Goodwill	1
Leasehold Property	10
Leasehold Improvements	212
Research and Development	18
Refrigeration Units	184
Current Assets	
Stock	140
Debtors	420
Current Liabilities	
Trade creditors	342
Bank overdraft	85
Full on Factors	342
Other Creditors	75
Hire Purchase Outstanding	112

The following information has been made available to you:

1 The directors have indicated their interest in acquiring the assets from your principal as liquidator.

2 Their offer is as follows:

   (a) Goodwill £50,000
   (b) Stock 25% of cost
   (c) Refrigeration Units £90,000

3 The bank overdraft is with Bank of Oxford. This is secured by a fixed and floating charge. The fixed charge covers leasehold/freehold property, goodwill and intellectual property. The floating charge was created on 14/02/08.

4 The debtors are factored with Full On Factors. The amount owed to them has increased by £12,500 due to termination charges. A debenture has been taken comprising a fixed and floating charge. The fixed charge covers book debts, goodwill, leasehold/freehold property and intellectual property.

5 You have identified a Deed of Priority between Bank of Oxford and Full On Factors, from which the fixed charge of Full On Factors ranks ahead of that of Bank of Oxford.

6 One of the company's debtors has entered into liquidation leaving a debt of £78,000 that will not be paid. In addition, a further provision of 15% is to be applied to all remaining debtors.

7 The refrigeration units have been valued by independent agents in the sum of £80,000. These assets are owned outright. The hire purchase outstanding is the residual debt on assets which have been repossessed.

8 Leasehold property and related improvements have been valued in the sum of £40,000.

9 An up to date stock reconciliation shows the current cost at £85,000. The independent valuation you have received is equal to the directors' offer.

10 The total of Other Creditors is made up as follows: corporation tax of £5,000; PAYE/NIC for the two months to 31 May 20X9, totalling £8,000; VAT for the eight months to 31 May 20X9 of £30,000 and a directors loan of £32,000. PAYE and NI can be assumed to have accrued evenly over the outstanding periods.

11 Employees' claims are as follows:

	£
Arrears of Wages	700
Holiday Pay	12,000
Notice Pay	7,500
Redundancy	14,000

12 There is issued and fully paid up share capital of £10,000.

Requirement

(a) Prepare a statement of affairs of Dalwood (2002) Limited as at 29 May 20X9 **(8 marks)**

(b) Due to the perishable nature of the company's stock, it is decided that the company be placed into liquidation at short notice (re. Centrebind). What are the liquidator's powers for the period from his appointment by members up to the date of the creditors' meeting and his duties at that meeting? **(1½ marks)**

(c) What responsibilities does the officeholder have in relation to the potential sale of the assets to the directors of the company before the S98 meeting in accordance with best practice guidelines issued. **(3½ marks)**

(d) With their offer structured as it is described above, explain why the directors may end up taking on some of the liabilities of the company and state what those liabilities might be. **(1 mark)**

(e) How might the liquidator make some use from the £78,000 bad debt owed by the company in liquidation? **(1 mark)**

(06/04) **(Total 15 marks)**

---

25 You were appointed as a creditors' voluntary liquidator of Rainbow Graphics Limited, a printing company on 1 June 20X8. It is now a year since your appointment and you have realised all the assets apart from some disputed book debts, totalling £65,000, which have been passed to a solicitor for collection. You have paid preferential creditors in full and a first dividend to unsecured creditors.

Below are copies of your receipts and payments account along with a copy of your bank statement for the period of liquidation to date.

Cash Book Receipts

Date	*Detail*	*Amount*	*VAT*	*Total*
		£	£	£
9.6.X8	Sale of Colour Press	65,000.00	11,375.00	76,375.00
12.6.X8	Sale of plant and machinery	93,500.00	16,362.50	109,862.50
20.6.X8	Sale of furniture and equipment	4,782.00	836.85	5,618.85
20.6.X8	Sale of vehicles	11,500.00		11,500.00
5.7.X8	A Debtor Limited	339.36		339.36
6.8.X8	Tax Refund	3,200.00		3,200.00
5.9.X8	Freehold Property	260,000.00		260,000.00
12.9.X8	B Debtor Limited	3,100.00		3,100.00
3.11.X8	C Debtor Limited	452.36		452.36
19.12.X8	Late Debtor Limited	3,902.36		3,902.36
12.3.X9	Later Debtor Limited	444.69		444.69

Cash Book Payments

Date	*Detail*	*Cheque No*	*Amount*	*VAT*	*Total*
			£	£	£
20.6.X8	Agents R Us – Fees	100001	26,217.30	4,588.02	30,805.32
20.6.X8	Liquidators Remuneration	100002	5,000.00	875.00	5,875.00
30.7.X8	Liquidators Disbursements	100003	800.00	140.00	940.00
5.9.X8	Property Agents Fees	N/A	5,200.00	910.00	6,110.00
5.9.X8	Fixed Charge Holder re: property sale	N/A	230,000.00		230,000.00
5.9.X8	Solicitors fees	N/A	1,500.00	262.50	1,762.50
15.12.X8	Preferential div – 100p HMRC (VAT)	100004	43,654.33		43,654.33
15.12.X8	Preferential div – 100p HMRC (PAYE)	100005	62,587.99		62,587.99
15.12.X8	Preferential div – 100p DWP	100006	23,487.99		23,487.99
15.12.X8	Preferential div – 100p Dept. BERR	100007	14,537.58		14,537.58
5.3.X9	Unsec div 15p – Ink is Us Ltd	100008	2,111.36		2,111.36
5.3.X9	Unsec div 15p – Paper Ltd	100009	2,114.21		2,114.21
5.3.X9	Unsec div 15p – Ink Ltd	100010	311.10		311.10
5.3.X9	Unsec div 15p – Colours Ltd	100011	2,337.11		2,337.11
5.3.X9	Unsec div 15p – IBT Ltd	100012	2,214.58		2,214.58
5.3.X9	Unsec div 15p – F Paper Ltd	100013	4,775.28		4,775.28
5.3.X9	Unsec div 15p – HMRC (VAT)	100014	1,457.36		1,457.36
5.3.X9	Unsec div 15p – HMRC (PAYE)	100015	3,587.39		3,587.39
5.3.X9	Unsec div 15p – ABC Ink Ltd	100016	3,339.55		3,339.55
5.3.X9	Liquidators remuneration	100017	6,500.00	1,137.50	7,637.50

Bank Statement

Date	*Description*	*Debits*	*Credits*	*Balance*
10.6.X8	Bank Giro Credit		76,375.00	76,375.00
13.6.X8	Bank Giro Credit		109,862.50	186,237.50
21.6.X8	Bank Giro Credit		5,618.85	
	Bank Giro Credit		11,500.00	
	100001	30,805.32		
	100002	5,875.00		166,676.03
6.7.X8	Bank Giro Credit		339.36	167,015.39
31.7.X8	100003	940.00		166,075.39
7.8.X8	Bank Giro Credit		3,200.00	169,275.39
31.8.X8	Bank Interest – Gross		33.24	169,308.63
5.9.X8	TT – Solicitors R Us		22,127.50	191,436.13
13.9.X8	Bank Giro Credit		3,100.00	194,536.13
16.9.X8	Cheque returned unpaid	3,100.00		191,436.13
3.11.X8	Bank Giro Credit		452.36	191,888.49
30.11.X8	Bank Interest - Gross		36.99	191,925.48
22.12.X8	100007	14,537.58		177,387.90
23.12.X8	100004	43,654.33		
	Bank Giro Credit		3,902.36	137,635.93
28.02.X9	Bank Interest – Gross		27.55	137,663.48
8.3.X9	100012	2,214.58		
	100008	2,111.36		133,337.54
11.3.X9	100014	1,457.36		131,880.18
12.3.X9	100016	3,339.55		
	100017	7,637.50		120,903.13
13.03.X9	Bank Giro Credit		444.69	121,347.82

You are required to:

(a) (i) Prepare a bank reconciliation as at 13 March 20X9. **(8 marks)**

(ii) VAT returns need to be completed and filed for the quarters ending, 30 August and 30 November 20X8 and for the subsequent period to de-registration which took place on 13 March 20X9. Calculate the amount of VAT payable or receivable in relation to each return, showing your workings. **(2 marks)**

(b) Explain the duties of a liquidator in relation to monies held in hand during the liquidation and comment on how these have been dealt with in this case. **(3 marks)**

(c) Explain the duties of a liquidator in relation to the filing of his receipts and payments accounts during the liquidation (excluding his final return). **(2 marks)**

(06/04) **(Total 15 marks)**

---

26 By which of the following types of resolution is a liquidator appointed in a voluntary winding up? (06/02)

(a) General resolution
(b) Special resolution
(c) Extraordinary resolution
(d) Ordinary resolution

---

27 In a Members Voluntary Liquidation where a company has six directors, a Declaration of Solvency must be made by? (06/02)

(a) A majority of the directors
(b) One director
(c) Two directors
(d) Three of the directors
(e) All of the directors

---

28 In a voluntary liquidation after what period must the liquidator pay funds, not required for the immediate purposes of the liquidation, into the Insolvency Services Account? (06/02)

(a) One month from appointment
(b) One month, 14 days from appointment
(c) Three months from appointment
(d) Three months, 14 days from appointment
(e) None of the above

---

29 Schedule 4 of the Act states the powers of a liquidator in a winding up.

(a) State four powers for which a voluntary liquidator and a liquidator in a winding up by the court require sanction. **(½ mark for each power)**

(b) State two powers for which a liquidator in a winding up by the court requires sanction but a voluntary liquidator does not. **(½ mark for each power)**

(c) State four powers which are exercisable without sanction in any winding up. **(½ mark for each power)**

(06/02) **(Total 5 marks)**

30 Rules 4.52 and 4.53 state what business is allowed at the first meeting of creditors in a creditors voluntary liquidation. Which of the following is **not** covered by those rules? You may assume that the chairman does not think it right to allow any other resolution for special reasons. (06/01)

(a) A resolution to appoint a named insolvency practitioner to be liquidator

(b) Where two or more liquidators have been appointed, a resolution specifying whether acts are to be done by both or all of them, or by only one

(c) A resolution authorising the payment in full of a class of creditors

(d) A resolution to adjourn the meeting

(e) A resolution specifying the terms on which the liquidator is to be remunerated

---

31 The liquidator or any contributory or creditor may apply to the court for directions to determine any question in the voluntary winding up of a company. Which section of the Insolvency Act 1986 covers such applications to court? (06/01)

(a) s112
(b) s113
(c) s114
(d) s122
(e) s123
(f) s124

---

32 You are to hold a meeting of contributories in insolvency proceedings. The company has eleven contributories. How many contributories will constitute a quorum? (06/01)

(a) One
(b) Two
(c) Five
(d) Six
(e) None of these

---

33 (a) Your principal is the convening accountant for the s98 meeting of Allovertheplace Limited. He wants to hold the meeting in your firm's Birmingham office because he has a very important engagement on a golf course near that office in the afternoon.

However, you notice that many of the company's creditors, both in number and value, are suppliers from the north east of England. What should you tell him about his desire to hold the meeting in Birmingham? **(1 mark)**

(b) Which of the following rules would you mention to him in support of your argument? **(1 mark)**

(a) Rule 4.101
(b) Rule 4.223
(c) Rule 4.60
(d) Rule 4.68
(e) Rule 4.76

(c) Two days before the s98 meeting of Allovertheplace Limited your principal advises that his important engagement on the golf course has been brought forward by three hours. Therefore he cannot attend the s98 meeting.

(i) What advice would you give him? **(1 mark)**

(ii) Would your advice be any different if he had been appointed liquidator ten days before the s98 meeting? **(1 mark)**

(d) (i) Which section of the Insolvency Act 1986 would you quote to him in support of your argument? **(½ mark)**

(a) s156
(b) s166
(c) s157
(d) s167
(e) s177

(ii) Which SIP could you also use to support the same argument? **(½ mark)**

(a) SIP 3
(b) SIP 7
(c) SIP 8
(d) SIP 9
(e) SIP 14 **(Total 5 marks)**

(06/01)

---

34 An audit client has been voted on to the liquidation committee of Fallen Engineers Limited following a s98 meeting.

A number of issues were discussed at the first liquidation committee meeting after the s98 meeting and your client, not entirely satisfied with the liquidator's representations, seeks your advice on each of these.

(a) The liquidator advised the committee that he had to issue some sort of certificate of constitution at some stage. He would get round to this eventually.

Explain to your client what this certificate is and any relevance attached to the timing of when the liquidator issues it. What other formalities are relevant to the establishment of the committee. **(4 marks)**

(b) The liquidator advised the meeting that he will sell certain of the company's engineering assets to another committee member. He has been speaking to that party for the last ten days and has decided the sale will go through next week. To your knowledge the purchaser, while a creditor, is not connected to Fallen Engineers Limited.

Advise your client of the relevant issues of a sale in these circumstances. **(4 marks)**

(c) The liquidator told the first committee meeting that he would be sending reports to them whenever he had anything meaningful to report.

Your client asks you whether it is really up to the liquidator to decide when to send reports. Explain what the insolvency rules say in this regard. **(3 marks)**

(d) The liquidator advised the committee that it was for them to decide upon the level of his remuneration and that he wanted this to be approved on the basis of either a percentage of the value of the assets realised or by reference to the time properly given by the liquidator and his staff in dealing with the liquidation.

He requested that the eventual choice should be left to him. The committee had agreed to the liquidator's request. Give your comments on this situation to your client. **(2 marks)**

(e) The liquidator advises the committee that he wants to appoint agents to sell the remainder of the assets and he will contact the committee members during the next week to advise them which firm of agents he proposes to use, as he needs the committee to sanction his choice.

What would you advise your client about what the liquidator has said to the committee?
(2 marks)

(06/01) **(Total 15 marks)**

---

35 Which section of the Insolvency Act states the liquidator's duties when he is of the opinion in a members' voluntary liquidation that the company is unable to pay its debts? (06/00)

(a) s89
(b) s91
(c) s93
(d) s95
(e) s97

---

36 In a creditors voluntary winding up, within which period after he receives the statement of affairs must the liquidator deliver it to the registrar of companies? (Rule 4.34) (06/00)

(a) Forthwith
(b) 5 business days
(c) 14 days
(d) 28 days
(e) One month

---

37 In a Members Voluntary Liquidation, within what period prior to the winding up resolution must the Declaration of Solvency be sworn? (06/13)

(a) 5 weeks
(b) 4 weeks
(c) 3 weeks
(d) 6 weeks

---

38 Which power of a Liquidator in a Creditors Voluntary Liquidation requires sanction before it is exercised? (06/13)

(a) Power to make a compromise with a creditor

(b) Power to carry on the business of the company so far as may be necessary for its beneficial winding up

(c) Power to make a compromise with a debtor

(d) Power to appoint an agent to do any business which the Liquidator is unable to do himself

---

39 Your principal has been instructed to place a company into Members Voluntary Liquidation. The company holds some investment shares, which the sole shareholder of the company would like to acquire. State which resolutions should be passed at the general meeting of the company to put it into Liquidation. (06/13) **(1/2 mark per point up to 2 marks)**

---

6 Compulsory liquidation

1 Which is a power of a Liquidator exercisable with sanction? (6/12)

(a) To sell the Company's property by public auction

(b) To raise on the security of the assets of the company any money requisite

(c) To pay any class of creditors in full

(d) To do all such other things as may be necessary for winding up the company's affairs and distributing its assets

---

2 Which of the following is not a definition of a company's inability to pay its debts for the purposes of an insolvent winding up? (6/11)

(a) Failure to pay or compound for a sum exceeding £750 three weeks after the presentation of a statutory demand

(b) Failure to account to HMRC for VAT or PAYE within 30 days of the due date for payment

(c) Failure to satisfy an execution or Court judgment in whole or in part

(d) An assessment by the Court that the value of a company's assets is less than the amount of its liabilities

---

3 What is the minimum period of notice a liquidator must give when convening a meeting of creditors in a compulsory liquidation? (6/10)

(a) 7 days
(b) 14 days
(c) 21 days
(d) 28 days

---

4 In a winding up, be it voluntarily or by the court, detail four powers exercisable without sanction by the duly appointed liquidator pursuant to Schedule 4, Part III of the Insolvency Act 1986. (6/09)

(4 marks)

---

5 Within what period must the Official Receiver decide whether to summon meetings of the company's creditors and contributories for the purpose of choosing a liquidator, if not so requested by the company's creditors? (06/07)

(a) 4 months from the date of the winding up order
(b) 3 months from the date of the winding up order
(c) 12 weeks from the date of the winding up order
(d) 8 weeks from the date of the winding up order

---

6 The Secretary of State may appoint a liquidator under which section of the Insolvency Act 1986? (06/06)

(a) s100
(b) s130
(c) s129
(d) s137
(e) s146

---

7 Which of the following is not a circumstance in which a company may be wound up by the Court? (06/06)

(a) If the court considers it to be just and equitable
(b) If the company has passed a special resolution to that effect
(c) If the number of directors is reduced to below two
(d) If the company is unable to pay its debts
(e) If the company does not commence its business within a year from its incorporation

---

8 Which section of the Act provides the definition of a company's inability to pay debts? (06/05)

(a) Section 117
(b) Section 122
(c) Section 123
(d) Section 124
(e) Section 124A

---

9 For the purposes of a creditor's bankruptcy petition what is the 'Bankruptcy Level'? (06/05)

(a) £310
(b) £750
(c) The debt must be for a liquidated sum
(d) Any debt which the debtor appears unable to pay
(e) £4,000

---

10 When is a compulsory liquidation deemed to have commenced, when there has been no prior resolution passed to wind the company up? (06/04)

(a) On the presentation of the petition
(b) On the making of the winding up order
(c) On the service of the statutory demand
(d) On the advertisement of the petition in the London Gazette
(e) On the appointment of a liquidator

---

11 At any time during a winding up a liquidator may convene a meeting of creditors in order to ascertain their wishes. How much notice does he have to give to creditors? (06/04)

(a) Seven days
(b) 14 days
(c) 21 days
(d) 28 days
(e) One month

---

12 (a) A company is being wound up by the court. In what circumstances may the winding up of this company not have commenced with the presentation of the petition? **(1 mark)**

(b) Where a liquidator is appointed by the Secretary of State in a compulsory liquidation, he has to give notice of the appointment to creditors or, if the court allows, advertise the appointment in accordance with the court's directions. What should be included in the contents of that notice or advert? **(1 mark)**

(c) State two circumstances in a compulsory winding up where the official receiver will, at no time, hold the office of liquidator. **(1 mark)**

(06/04) **(Total 3 marks)**

---

13 How soon after his appointment must a Liquidator in a Compulsory Winding-Up notify the Registrar of Companies of his appointment? (06/02)

(a) As soon as reasonably practicable upon receiving his certificate of appointment
(b) Within seven days of his appointment
(c) Within 14 days of his appointment
(d) Within 21 days of his appointment
(e) Within 28 days of receiving his certificate of appointment

---

14 In a Compulsory Liquidation, what period of notice must the Liquidator give the creditors of the final meeting? (06/02)

(a) 14 days
(b) 21 days
(c) 28 days
(d) One month

---

15 A creditor's petition can only be presented in respect of a debt where the amount of the debt, or the aggregate amount of the debts, is equal to or exceeds the 'bankruptcy level'. What is the 'bankruptcy level'? (06/02)

(a) £750
(b) £2,000
(c) £5,000
(d) A liquidated debt payable immediately
(e) A debt which the debtor is unable to pay

---

16 Which of the following may not take part in the public examination of a person under s133 of the Insolvency Act? (06/01)

(a) The official receiver
(b) Any administrative receiver of the company who has been appointed by a debenture holder
(c) The liquidator of the company
(d) Any creditor who has tendered a proof
(e) Any contributory of the company

---

17 (a) You have received payment of a book debt of £4,639 on one of your compulsory liquidations. How long is it before Regulation 5 of the 1994 Insolvency Regulations requires you to pay this cheque into the Insolvency Services Account? **(1 mark)**

(b) State with reasons whether your answer would be the same if the amount of the book debt had been £5,639? **(1 mark)**

(06/01) **(Total 2 marks)**

---

18 Which of the following are not circumstances where a company may be wound up by the court? (s122) (06/00)

(a) Where the company has by special resolution resolved that the company may be wound up by the court

(b) Where the company is unable to pay its debts

(c) Where the company has ceased trading for at least three months

(d) Where the court is of the opinion that it is just and equitable that the company should be wound up

(e) Where the company does not commence its business within a year from incorporation

---

19 In a compulsory liquidation which two of the following must appear in the liquidator's report which is laid before the final meeting? (Rule 4.125) (06/00)

(a) Confirmation that the liquidator's remuneration has been approved

(b) A statement that the liquidator has reconciled his account with that which is held by the Secretary of State in respect of the winding up

(c) A statement that the liquidator has filed all the proofs of debt in court

(d) A summary of his receipts and payments account

(e) Details of time charged by the liquidator and his staff in the administration of the case

(2 marks)

---

20 At any time after the presentation of a winding-up petition, the court may appoint a Liquidator provisionally. When such a Liquidator is provisionally appointed, what are his powers? (06/13)

(a) As set out in the order appointing him
(b) The same powers as a Liquidator
(c) The same powers as a Receiver
(d) The same powers as an Administrator

---

21 What are the general functions of a Liquidator in a winding up by the Court? (06/13)

(2 marks)

---

22 You are preparing a set of minutes in relation to a general meeting of creditors in a Compulsory Liquidation. What information should be included in the minutes and what other considerations should be taken into account? (06/13) **(4 marks)**

---

7 Liquidator's investigations and antecedent transactions

1 SIP 2 dictates that an initial assessment of whether there could be any matters that might lead to recoveries for the estate should be undertaken in every insolvent Liquidation and Administration. What steps should be taken to reach a position to make this initial assessment? (6/12)

(1/2 mark per point up to a maximum of 2 marks)

---

2 What authority does a liquidator require prior to issuing legal proceedings in respect of a preference, where there are floating charge realisations but it is expected there will be a shortfall to a floating charge creditor? (6/12) **(2 marks)**

---

3 Under the Act, how may a company be an associate of another company? (6/11) **(2 marks)**

---

4 A petition for the winding up of Flog It Limited was issued by a creditor on 1 July 2010. After a number of adjourned hearings an Order for the winding up of the company was eventually made on 6 December 2010 following which a partner of your firm was appointed Liquidator of the company by the Secretary of State on 10 January 2011. In the course of your review of the affairs of the company you have identified that between June and August 2010 a number of payments were made to creditors.

What actions can the Liquidator take in respect of these payment? (6/11) **(4 marks)**

---

5 Under s235 which one of the following parties are not under a duty to co-operate with the office holder? (6/10)

(a) Officers of the company
(b) Employees of the company
(c) Shareholders of the company
(d) Anyone who has acted as administrator of the company

---

6 Under s235 which one of the following parties are not under a duty to co-operate with the office holder? (6/09)

(a) Officers of the company
(b) Employees of the company
(c) Shareholders of the company
(d) Anyone who has acted as administrator of the company

---

7 John Smith was made bankrupt on 1 May 2009. A partner in your firm was appointed his trustee on the same day and the case has been allocated to you to administer. Mr Smith has not surrendered to the proceedings and is believed to be working abroad.

There is no statement of affairs. The only information you have is that the petition debt is £66,000 for unpaid school fees and that Mr Smith is the sole registered owner of what is believed to be the family home Downyourway which the petitioner describes as 'a very smart detached property close to the school'. There are no funds in the estate.

You write to the bankrupt at Downyourway, the last known address and arrange an appointment which he does not attend, neither does he contact you. He ignores your second and third letters also. You have also tried telephoning him on the home number and left messages with a person claiming to be the housekeeper. Mrs Smith, his wife, rings you at the office to tell you to 'back off or I'll get a restraining order against you. This is intimidation. He wants nothing to do with this nonsense.'

Requirement

(a) Draft a letter to Mr Smith setting out his statutory obligations to co-operate with you as trustee and advising him of the possible consequences if he fails to do so. **(6 marks)**

(b) If the bankrupt fails to attend for interview give three examples of types of court procedure that could be invoked by the trustee to secure the bankrupt's compliance. Explain each answer. **(6 marks)**

(c) You finally obtain the information you require. The bankruptcy debts are in excess of £1million. The bankrupt also has a pension policy into which he was latterly paying £3,000 a month. Can you recover any part of the pension and if so, how? **(3 marks)**

(6/09) **(Total 15 marks)**

---

8 A partner in your firm was appointed liquidator of Fleece Limited, a company manufacturing and installing conservatories, on 1 October 20X7. The Statement of Affairs indicated a deficiency to unsecured creditors of £400,000 and the deficiency account disclosed estimated trading losses from 1 January 20X7 to 1 October 20X7 of £150,000. At the s98 meeting, numerous concerns were raised about the company's trading and the conduct of its sole director, Mr Sornoff, and a liquidation committee was appointed.

In the course of your investigations into the company's affairs, you have discovered the following:

- The company's bank account was personally guaranteed by Mr Sornoff. In the six months prior to liquidation, the bank overdraft was reduced from £80,000 to £3,000.
- The company was taking customer deposits for new conservatories in the week before your firm was instructed to convene the creditors' meeting. The funds were lodged in the company's overdrawn bank account.
- The company's filed accounts for the years ended 31 December 20X5 and 2006 indicated trading losses of £80,000 and £120,000 respectively.
- On 1 January 20X7, Mr Sornoff increased his salary from £100,000 to £130,000.
- On 1 February 20X7 the company settled in full, the account of Ice Axe Limited, a company owned by Mr Sornoff's brother.
- In March 20X6, the company had installed a conservatory at a property owned by Mr Sornoff's daughter. No consideration was received by the company.
- A six month old Range Rover and a nine month old Mercedes, both registered in the company's name, have been located at Mr Sornoff's home, Dusters Manor. These assets were not disclosed on the director's statement of affairs.
- Six customers are prepared to testify that in the two months prior to liquidation, Mr Sornoff had called at their homes and demanded early settlement of the full contract price for their partially constructed conservatories, threatening violence if payment was not made immediately.
- You have established that Dusters Manor is registered in Mr Sornoff's sole name, and there are no charges over the property.

Requirement

You are about to hold a meeting of the liquidation committee to discuss your investigations to date, and the possible action you might take as liquidator.

(a) Prepare a note for the liquidation committee detailing the possible remedies available to the liquidator to recover funds for creditors. **(10 marks)**

(b) Outline the duties of a liquidator in relation to the submission of a statutory D1 Report with specific reference to the provisions of SIP4. **(5 marks)**

(06/08) **(Total 15 marks)**

---

9 Your firm has been instructed by the directors of Scam Limited ('Scam') to assist them in placing the company into creditors' voluntary liquidation. Meetings of members and creditors have been convened for 30 April 2X09. The directors' estimated statement of affairs together with the last audited balance sheet of the company as at 31 December 20X7 are summarised below:

Scam Limited
Summarised Estimated Statement of Affairs
as at 30 April 20X9

	Book value £	*Estimated to realise* £
Freehold property	200,000	275,000
Fixtures and fittings	10,000	0
Plant and machinery	180,000	55,000
Book debts	185,000	165,000
Inter company debt	40,000	0
Office furniture and equipment	20,000	5,000
Stock	125,000	35,000
Cash at bank	45,000	45,000
Motor vehicles	40,000	15,000
	845,000	595,000
Employee claims		
Wage arrears		(20,000)
Holiday pay		(25,000)
Pension contributions		(10,000)
Pay in lieu		(30,000)
Redundancy		(25,000)
PAYE and VAT		(45,000)
Trade and expense creditors		(780,000)
Directors' loans		(100,000)
		(1,035,000)
Estimated deficiency to creditors		(440,000)
Share capital		(200,000)
Estimated deficiency to shareholders		(640,000)

Scam Limited
Summarised Audited balance sheet as at 31 December 20X7

	£	£
Fixed assets		
Freehold property		200,000
Plant and machinery		190,000
Fixtures and fittings		10,000
Office equipment		15,000
Motor vehicles		25,000
		440,000
Current assets		
Stock	100,000	
Debtors	215,000	
Cash at bank	65,000	
	380,000	
Current liabilities		
Trade creditors	530,000	
Directors' loans	100,000	
	630,000	
Net current liabilities		(250,000)
		190,000
Represented by:		
Share capital		200,000
Deficiency on reserves		(10,000)
		190,000

In preparing for the meetings you have received the following information:

- A lathe was purchased on 1 March 20X8 for £10,000. On 5 July 20X8 a lathe with a book value of £20,000 as at 31 December 20X7 was sold for £5,000.
- IT equipment was purchased on 30 June 20X8 for £10,000. IT equipment with a book value of £5,000 as at 31 December 20X7 was scrapped on 15 December 20X8.
- A motor vehicle was purchased on 30 June 20X8 for £20,000. A vehicle with a book value of £5,000 as at 31 December 20X7 was sold on 30 October 20X8 for £6,000.
- Unaudited management accounts for the six month period ending 30 June 20X8 show a trading loss of £220,000 resulting in a retained deficit on reserves of £230,000.
- In January 20X9 Scam advanced £40,000 to an associated company, Royal Limited ('Royal'). The funds extinguished an overdraft of £30,000 in Royal which was personally guaranteed by Mr Steele, the managing director of both companies. In February 20X9 Royal was placed into creditors' voluntary liquidation. There is no prospect of a distribution to creditors in that liquidation.
- Mr Steele is also a director of Scam2 Limited, a company incorporated in November 20X8, which has commenced trading in the same business as Scam.

Requirement

(a) Prepare a deficiency account covering the period 31 December 20X7 to 30 April 20X9 which details the items making up the deficiency on the estimated statement of affairs. **(7 marks)**

(b) Identify any matters above requiring investigation by the liquidator under the Act and comment on the relevant statutory provisions. Ignore any issues of wrongful trading. **(8 marks)**

(06/05) **(Total 15 marks)**

10 A liquidator requires sanction to take proceedings under all the following sections of the Act, except one. Which is the exception? (06/04)

(a) S213
(b) S214
(c) S234
(d) S238
(e) S239

---

11 Which section of the Act defines the relevant time during which a company may have given a preference? (06/04)

(a) s237
(b) s238
(c) s239
(d) s240
(e) s241

---

12 In an insolvent liquidation s216 of the Act deals with the restriction on re-use of company names. A director of a company in liquidation is precluded from re-using the name of that company if it was known by that name at any time during which period before it went into liquidation? (06/04)

(a) Six months
(b) 12 months
(c) Two years
(d) Five years
(e) 10 years

---

13 If a liquidator pursues a claim for a preference and he is unsuccessful with costs awarded against him, how are these costs recoverable? (06/02)

(a) As an expense of the liquidation, properly chargeable and incurred
(b) From the creditors of the company
(c) These costs are not normally recoverable

---

14 For a claim to be pursued by a Liquidator under Section 212 of the Insolvency Act 1986 – Summary Remedy Against Delinquent Directors, Liquidators etc. the offence must have been committed within which of the following relevant time periods? (06/02)

(a) There is no time limit
(b) Six months prior to Winding-Up
(c) Two years prior to Winding-Up
(d) Five years prior to Winding-Up

---

15 Which of the following Statements of Insolvency Practice (SIPs) deals with a liquidator's investigation into the affairs of an insolvent company? (06/02)

(a) SIP 1
(b) SIP 2
(c) SIP 3
(d) SIP 4
(e) SIP 5

---

16 (a) Which of the following office holders is not entitled to challenge a transaction at undervalue under s238?

(i) An administrator
(ii) An administrative receiver
(iii) A compulsory liquidator
(iv) A creditors' voluntary liquidator **(1 mark)**

(b) Would your answer be the same if the proceedings were:

(i) To challenge a preference under s239 and;
(ii) To take a wrongful trading action under s214 **(2 marks)**

(06/01) **(Total 3 marks)**

---

8 Asset protection regime

1 Which of the following can disclaim onerous property? (6/09)

(a) A liquidator
(b) An administrator
(c) A supervisor of a Company Voluntary Arrangement
(d) All of the above

---

2 Section 184 of the Act deals with the duties of a court enforcement officer. If the court enforcement officer receives proceeds following an execution from sale or payment to avoid sale, for what period must he hold the proceeds? (06/04)

(a) Seven days
(b) 14 days
(c) 28 days
(d) One month
(e) Three months

---

3 (a) On 25 May 20Y0 you were appointed liquidator to Phoenix Limited, in a winding up by the court, followed the making of a winding up order date 16 March 20Y0.

On 31 December 20X9 Phoenix Limited's landlord distrained on plant and machinery which was on the company's premises. The landlord has removed the assets but you are not sure whether or not he has sold them yet.

(i) What action, if any, should you, as liquidator take to recover the assets if they have not been sold?

(ii) Would your answer by any different if the assets had been sold and the landlord had received the sale proceeds?

(iii) How would you treat any resulting claim the landlord may have in the liquidation?

(6 marks)

(b) What is the main difference between execution and distress? **(1 mark)**

(c) (i) You were appointed liquidator in the compulsory liquidation of Downcast Limited on 10 May 20Y0, following a winding up order on 15 March 20Y0. A creditor presented a petition to wind the company up on 31 January 20Y0.

There has been no resolution to wind the company up.

On 16 February 20Y0 the landlord levied distraint for rent unpaid for the period to 31 December 20X9.

How do you treat the landlord's distraint?

(ii) Would you treat the distraint differently if there was no petition or winding up order but you had been appointed liquidator by a resolution to wind the company up, dated 11 February 20Y0? **(5 marks)**

(d) (i) You were appointed liquidator to Lostcause Limited on 3 May 20Y0, following a resolution to wind the company up, dated the same day.

A creditor issued execution against certain of Lostcause Limited's goods on 22 April.

What authority, if any, do you have to recover those goods?

(ii) Why might it be advantageous for a company about to go into liquidation to serve the notice calling the meeting at which the resolution to wind the company up is to be proposed on a sheriff who has levied execution? **(3 marks)**

(06/00) **(Total 15 marks)**

9 Proofs of debt in liquidation

1 Within what period following the last day for proving should a Liquidator deal with every creditor's proof by admitting or rejecting it in whole or part? (6/12)

(a) 4 months
(b) 14 days
(c) 5 business days
(d) 2 months

---

2 Set out four requirements that must be addressed for the purpose of a Notice of Intended dividend in accordance with the Rules. (6/10) **(2 marks)**

---

3 In a liquidation where the company is not in administration, what exchange rate should be used when calculating a claim for dividend purposes? (06/08)

(a) The rate at the date of liquidation
(b) The rate at the date the liquidator issues notice to declare a dividend
(c) The rate at the date of the proof of debt is accepted
(d) The average rate over the preceding 12 months

---

4 If a creditor's proof of debt is rejected for dividend purposes, how long following receipt of the Notice of Rejection has a creditor to lodge an appeal with the court? (06/08)

(a) 7 days
(b) 14 days
(c) 21 days
(d) 28 days

---

5 A creditor is owed £50,000 by a company which went into liquidation on 12 January 20X8. On 4 June 20X9, the liquidator declares a dividend. However, the £50,000 is not due to be paid until 4 September 20X9. By how much should the creditor's £50,000 proof be reduced when the liquidator pays the dividend he has declared on 4 June 20X9? (06/04) **(3 marks)**

---

6 (a) What post winding up order interest is payable on creditors' claims in a compulsory winding up where it has been possible to pay all creditors a dividend of 100p in the £ and there are further funds in the estate available for distribution? **(1½ marks)**

(b) What is the order of priority for payment of interest to the different categories of creditors? **(1½ marks)**

(06/04) **(Total 3 marks)**

7 Under which rule must an insolvency practitioner give notice to creditors that there will be no or no further dividend? (06/04)

(a) Rule 11.2
(b) Rule 11.3
(c) Rule 11.5
(d) Rule 11.6
(e) Rule 11.7

---

8 How long after receiving a liquidator's statement rejecting his proof does a creditor have to apply to court for the liquidator's decision to be reversed? (06/04)

(a) Seven days
(b) 14 days
(c) 21 days
(d) 28 days
(e) One month

---

9 Within what period after he has declared his notice of intention to declare a dividend may an insolvency practitioner cancel or postpone that dividend, if he has rejected a proof and application is made to the court for his decision to be reversed or varied? (06/01)

(a) Seven days from the last date of proving
(b) Two weeks from the last date of proving
(c) One month from the last date of proving
(d) Three months from the last date of proving
(e) Two months from the last date of proving

---

10 You are about to declare a dividend in a voluntary winding up. When given notice of the dividend, which of the following particulars relating to the insolvency, do you not need to give to creditors who have proved their debts? (06/00)

(a) Amounts realised from the sale of assets

(b) Payments the liquidator has made in the administration of the estate

(c) Details of any exercise of the liquidator's powers, with the sanction of the committee, as required by Part 1, Schedule 4, Insolvency Act 1986

(d) Provision (if any) made for unsettled claims

(e) Funds, if any, retained for particular purposes

(f) The total amount to be distributed, and the rate of dividend

---

10 Vacation of office – liquidator

1 How long after the final meeting of creditors held under s106 of the IA does a liquidator have to submit his final form to the Registrar of Companies? (06/08)

(a) 7 days
(b) 14 days
(c) 21 days
(d) 28 days

---

2 When may a company's books and records in a Creditors' Voluntary Liquidation be destroyed? (06/05)

(a) One year after the final meetings
(b) Two years after the final meetings
(c) Immediately following the final meetings
(d) At the liquidator's discretion
(e) One year after the company has been dissolved

---

3 Following a final meeting of creditors held pursuant to section 106 of the Act, within which period must the Liquidator file with the Registrar of Companies a copy of the account laid before that meeting; (06/04)

(a) One week
(b) Two weeks
(c) 21 days
(d) 28 days
(e) One month

---

4 If a vacancy occurs by death, resignation or otherwise in the office of a liquidator appointed by the company in a members' voluntary liquidation, how may the vacancy be filled? (06/01)

(a) By the company in general meeting
(b) By a creditors' meeting
(c) By resolution of the board of directors
(d) By the company in general meeting, subject to any arrangement with the creditors
(e) By resolution of the board of directors, subject to any arrangement with the creditors

---

5 In a members' voluntary liquidation, within which of the following periods must a liquidator send to the registrar of companies a copy of his account and return of the holding of the final meeting and of its date? (06/01)

(a) As soon as reasonably practicable
(b) Four days
(c) One week
(d) Two weeks
(e) One month
(f) Three months

---

11 Company voluntary arrangements

1 Who is not entitled to propose a Company Voluntary Arrangement? (6/12)

(a) The liquidator
(b) The administrator
(c) The directors
(d) The company

---

2 Where the Directors of a Company wish to obtain a Moratorium, they must supply information to the Nominee. The Nominee must then opine by submitting to the Directors a statement. Which of these are not included in the Nominee's statement? (6/12)

(a) Meetings of the Company and its Creditors should be summoned to consider the proposed voluntary arrangement.
(b) The proposed voluntary arrangement has a reasonable prospect of being approved and implemented
(c) The Directors have made a full disclosure of the Company's affairs
(d) The Company is likely to have sufficient funds available to it during the proposed moratorium to enable it to carry on business.

---

3 What are the powers of the court on a successful application to challenge the decision of a meeting of creditors to approve a CVA? (6/12) **(4 marks)**

---

4 Within how many business days following meetings of members and creditors held to consider proposals for a Company Voluntary Arrangement does the Chairman have to file his report in Court? (6/11)

(a) 4 days
(b) 5 days
(c) 14 days
(d) 2 days

---

5 Your Principal is acting as Nominee in relation to a director's Company Voluntary Arrangement proposal.

Under SIP 3 what steps should the Nominee take to satisfy himself that the value of the assets is appropriately reflected in the Statement of Affairs? (6/11)

($^1/_2$ mark per point up to a maximum of 2 marks)

---

6 Your firm has been instructed by Mr Lumley, the director of Yeti Limited, which operates as a restaurant, to assist with the preparation of a Company Voluntary Arrangement ("CVA"). Trade has been difficult in the past year, but the director has recently recruited a new chef, and turnover and profitability have improved in recent months.

The company has an overdraft standing at £50,000 with Anna Bank plc, which has a Qualifying Floating Charge over the assets of the company. The Bank has confirmed that although supportive in principle of a CVA, it is not prepared to value its security.

The company has unsecured trade creditors totalling £225,000 including a key meat supplier, Yak Limited, which is owed £38,000, and HMRC which is owed £40,000 in respect of arrears of PAYE. Additionally, Mrs Lumley, the director's mother and the major shareholder of the company, has made unsecured loans to the company totalling £200,000.

Your partner is the nominee, and is not the liquidator or administrator of the company. The directors are not seeking to obtain a moratorium for the company. The proposal and statement of affairs have been prepared and submitted to the nominee.

(a) By reference to best practice guidance, what matters should be addressed in the nominee's comments on the proposal?

(1 mark per point up to a maximum of 8 marks)

The CVA proposal is sent to creditors, and a creditors' meeting is duly convened. Chairman's proxy votes in favour of the proposal and any modifications amount to £75,000. A few minutes before the creditors' meeting is due to commence, a Mr Burnham arrives with a special proxy from Yak Limited appointing him to vote in favour of the proposal but against any modifications. Mr Burnham only produces a statement of Yak Limited's claim, for £38,000, immediately prior to the votes being cast.

Mrs Lumley has not submitted a proxy, and attends without any prior notification, bringing with her a statement of her claim for £200,000. She states she will abstain from voting on the original proposal but tables a modification reducing the term of the proposal by one year and reducing total contributions by 20%. HMRC has submitted a proxy for £40,000 voting against the proposal and any modifications.

(b) How should the claims of the following be treated for voting purposes?

(i) Anna Bank plc;
(ii) Yak Limited;
(iii) Mrs Lumley. **(3 marks)**

(c) Taking into account your answers at b) above, advise whether i) the original proposals, and ii) the modifications, should be approved at the creditors' meeting. **(4 marks)**

(6/10) **(Total 15 marks)**

---

7 Where no steps are taken to obtain a moratorium, to whom does the nominee submit his report on the prospect of a Company Voluntary Arrangement being approved and implemented? (6/09)

(a) The creditors
(b) The Court
(c) The Official Receiver
(d) The directors

---

8 In a Company Voluntary Arrangement name the persons who may apply to court to challenge the decision of the outcome of the meeting of creditors. (6/09) **(2 marks)**

---

9 Which of the following is not excluded from being eligible for a moratorium under Schedule A1 of the Insolvency Act 1986? (06/06)

(a) A company in administration
(b) A company which has a Law of Property Act receiver appointed over its assets
(c) A company in compulsory liquidation
(d) A company in provisional liquidation
(e) A company in voluntary liquidation

10 On 27 February 20X9 you were approached by Mr Becker, the managing director of Danco Limited. Danco Limited has been experiencing cash flow problems for some time, but Mr Becker is very confident that he is on the brink of signing a substantial new contract which will restore the company to profitability.

Mr Becker provides you with the following information:

	Book value	*Forced sale value*
Assets	£	£
Property	250,000	300,000
Debtors	140,000	100,000
Machinery	80,000	40,000
Stock	60,000	15,000
Vehicles	15,000	5,000
Liabilities		
Pay in lieu		30,000
Redundancy		35,000
Trade and expense creditors		600,000

Mr Becker is keen for Danco Limited to avoid liquidation and enter into a company voluntary arrangement. He proposes that Danco Limited will make contributions from profits of £5,000 a month into a company voluntary arrangement for four years.

Additionally, Mr Becker states his father is prepared to make a contribution of £100,000 from an endowment policy which matures in three years.

He states that if a voluntary arrangement is approved, Baxter Limited, a company which he also controls, will subordinate its unsecured claim of £150,000 to those of other unsecured creditors.

The following information is also relevant:

Your partner estimates that if the company is placed into liquidation, liquidator's remuneration would be £25,000, in addition to a fee of £5,000 for convening meetings of members and creditors to place the company into liquidation. Under a company voluntary arrangement, nominee's fees would be £3,000 and supervisor's fees would be £3,000 a year.

Estate agent's fee, of 1.5% would be incurred on disposing of the property, which would also give rise to a tax charge of £15,000, together with legal fees of £5,000. Chattel agent's fees would be 5% of realisations on machinery, stock and vehicles. Debt collection fees would be 10% of recoveries.

(a) Prepare an outcome statement comparing the estimated outcome in a creditors' voluntary liquidation with that in a company voluntary arrangement. **(5 marks)**

(b) During your initial discussions with Mr Becker, the following matters are disclosed:

(i) In December 20X8, the company repaid a loan to Lend Bank plc for £30,000. The loan was unsecured and was personally guaranteed by Mr Becker.

(ii) On 5 April 20X7 the company sold a property to Hunter Limited, a company in which Mr Becker has a 75% shareholding, for £200,000. The property had been professionally valued at the time at £300,000.

(iii) In August 20X8 the company made a one-off repayment of a loan of £60,000 to Thompson Finance Limited, a company unconnected with Danco Limited. The loan was originally advanced in 1998.

(iv) In May 20X8 the company granted a floating charge to High Street Bank PLC. The existing bank overdraft on that date was £25,000 and it has now been repaid in full.

(v) In January 20X6 the company transferred a freehold property into the ownership of Mrs Becker, Mr Becker's former wife as part of a divorce settlement. No consideration passed to the company.

Outline the possible causes of action available in respect of the above matters and how they might influence the creditors when considering Mr Becker's company voluntary arrangement proposal. **(10 marks)**

(06/06) **(Total 15 marks)**

---

11 Within what period of being given notice of a proposal for a Company Voluntary Arrangement (subject to extension by the court) must a nominee report to the court whether meetings of the company and its creditors should be called to consider the proposal? (06/05)

(a) 31 days
(b) 14 days
(c) One month
(d) 21 days
(e) 28 days

---

12 Who is the appropriate authority to whom company officers suspected of an offence in connection with a Company Voluntary Arrangement should be reported? (06/05)

(a) The Official Receiver
(b) The Registrar of Companies
(c) The Secretary of State
(d) A subsequently appointed liquidator
(e) The police

---

13 For how long can members and creditors agree to extend a small company's moratorium under the Insolvency Act 2000? (06/04)

(a) Up to 14 days from the date of the first meetings
(b) Up to 21 days from the date of the first meetings
(c) Up to 28 days from the date of the first meetings
(d) Up to one month from the date of the first meetings
(e) Up to two months from the date of the first meetings

---

14 When a moratorium comes into force prior to the calling of meetings to approve a company voluntary arrangement the nominee is required to advertise the fact that a moratorium is in force. When must the nominee place this advertisement? (06/04)

(a) Forthwith
(b) As soon as is reasonably practicable
(c) Within four business days of the moratorium coming into force
(d) Within four days of the moratorium coming into force
(e) Within seven days of the moratorium coming into force

---

15 A partner in your office has recently been contacted by Cleaning and Dusting Services Limited (the company), a local business cleaning company. The company has a number of small business contracts. Business has been quiet and although a small profit is being achieved, the company is experiencing cash flow problems and is unable to meet its debts as and when they fall due.

The company has recently won a tender to clean a chain of 15 hotels which will ultimately alleviate the company's problems but in the meantime it needs to address the current cash flow difficulties and has requested your advice in relation to a company voluntary arrangement.

The company has been issued with a statutory demand from a supplier of cleaning products, Kill Germs Fast Limited in the sum of £30,000 and is unable to pay this. Further pressure is being received from two other trade creditors and HMRC who are all threatening to apply to court for a winding up order to be made.

The company is anxious to resolve matters as quickly as possible and to secure its position so that creditors cannot continue with their threatened actions and so the new contract can be commenced.

Requirement

Draft a memo to your partner advising him of the following:

(a) The reasons why a company voluntary arrangement (CVA) would be beneficial to the company if it could obtain a moratorium under the provisions introduced by the Insolvency Act 2000 and the conditions which must apply to the company to enable it to obtain such a moratorium **(4 marks)**

(b) The steps to be taken to obtain a moratorium and, when obtained, the effect it has on creditors and the company **(9 marks)**

(c) The duties of the nominee in connection with monitoring the company's performance during the moratorium **(2 mark)**

(06/04) **(Total 15 marks)**

---

16 Under section 6 of the Act it is possible to make an application to the court to challenge the decision of the meetings held pursuant to section 3 of the Act. Such application shall not be made after: (06/03)

(a) A period of 7 days after the chairman's report of the meeting is sent to court
(b) A period of 14 days after the chairman's report of the meeting is sent to court
(c) A period of 28 days after the chairman's report of the meeting is sent to court
(d) A period of one month after the chairman's report of the meeting is sent to court

---

17 Optimistic IT Limited is a company specialising in writing bespoke software packages. Following the loss of a major customer 18 months ago the last two financial years have shown combined losses of £250,000.

The directors have made staff reductions and surrendered the lease to expensive premises. Redundancy payments remain outstanding together with the reverse premium payable to the landlord for surrendering the lease.

Budgets still predicted a trading loss for the following twelve months of £20,000 even with overhead cuts. With forecast losses and a cash crisis, the directors had almost reached the decision to liquidate the company when they won a major five-year contract with a bank which would enable the company to make a profit of £100,000 per annum.

Cash flow forecasts indicate that continued trading including this contract can be financed within the existing bank overdraft facility of £60,000, provided existing creditors are not paid.

The bank's security consists of a fixed charge over book debts and goodwill and a floating charge over all other assets. You may assume that the floating charge pre-dates 15/09/03.

The directors have approached your firm to seek advice on the possibility of obtaining a company voluntary arrangement (CVA).

The company's balance sheet as at 31/03/X9 reflects the following.

	£
Fixed Assets	
Office furniture and equipment	200,000
Motor vehicles	40,000
	240,000
Current Assets	
Book Debts	150,000
Work in progress	20,000
	170,000
Current liabilities	
HMRC – PAYE & NIC (eight months)	80,000
HMRC – VAT (nine months)	72,000
Trade and expense creditors	200,000
Bank overdraft	50,000
Landlord – reverse premium	75,000
Redundancy costs	50,000
Directors loans	200,000
	727,000
Net current assets	(557,000)
Total assets less liabilities	(317,000)

In addition you find the following.

(a) Office furniture and equipment consists mainly of computers and software and in forced sale scenario should achieve 20% of it's book value.

(b) The realisable value of motor vehicles is estimated at £30,000 and the directors consider that all debtors are collectable although a 20% provision would be prudent.

(c) Work in progress will have no value in a liquidation.

(d) From continued trading the company could realistically make contributions to a CVA of £50,000 per year for five years.

(e) The directors are anxious for the company to survive and are prepared to defer their loans to rank behind unsecured creditors if a voluntary arrangement is accepted.

(f) The company will need to retain all its assets if trading continues under the voluntary arrangement.

(g) The VAT liability has accrued evenly over nine months outstanding.

(h) In addition to the redundancy costs already incurred, if trading was to cease there would be additional redundancy and pay in lieu of notice claims of £75,000.

Requirement

This matter has been referred to your principal by another firm and he has advised the company that a voluntary arrangement is indeed a possibility. On his behalf you are required to do the following:

(a) Produce an estimated outcome statement comparing the position in a voluntary arrangement to that in a creditors voluntary liquidation. The voluntary arrangement is to be based on five years' annual contributions of £50,000 as stated above. Assume the nominees fee to be £7,500 and the statement of affairs fee to be £5,000. The costs and expenses of the supervisor will amount to 10% of realisations as compared to those of a liquidator at 20%. The statement must show the estimated dividend to creditors in each procedure. You must give reasons for any assumptions you make about the bank's security. **(10 marks)**

(b) Advise your principal how a voluntary arrangement affects the bank and its security and how you would suggest dealing with the bank. **(1 mark)**

(c) What information must be divulged to creditors about the firm which referred this matter to your principle and where should this information appear? **(2 marks)**

(d) If the voluntary arrangement fails and the company goes into liquidation, what is the effect on any trust created by the company voluntary arrangement? **(2 marks)**

(06/04) **(Total 15 marks)**

---

18 In a Company Voluntary Arrangement which creditors are bound by the terms of the approved arrangement? (06/02)

(a) All creditors included and scheduled within the proposal

(b) Creditors that attended the creditors meeting

(c) Creditors that received notice of the meeting and were entitled to vote

(d) Creditors that were entitled to vote at the meeting or would have been so entitled if they had had notice of it

---

19 In which of the following corporate insolvency procedures are there no provisions in the legislation covering the operation of committees? (06/01)

(a) Administrations
(b) Administrative receiverships
(c) Creditors voluntary liquidations
(d) Compulsory liquidations
(e) Company voluntary arrangements

---

20 Which insolvency rule requires the chairman of a s3 meeting of creditors to prepare a report on the meeting and send it to the court? (06/01)

(a) R1.24
(b) R1.29
(c) R5.24
(d) R5.29
(e) R5.30

---

21 S234 may assist certain office holders in obtaining the property, books or papers of a company from persons who have possession of those items. Which of the following may not be assisted by s234? (06/01)

(a) An administrator
(b) An administrative receiver
(c) A compulsory liquidator
(d) A creditors' voluntary liquidator
(e) A supervisor

---

22 (a) Your principal has just returned from a meeting with the directors of Not Too Late Limited. He believes that the company, while insolvent, should be able to trade out of its current situation if it can come to an arrangement to pay 50p in the pound to its unsecured creditors.

Your principal gives you the financial details of a proposal he wants you to draft and he says that he wants you to complete the proposal by including all the matters which are required to be stated in rule 1.3(2).

What are these matters? **(8 marks)**

(b) After the meetings of creditors and members have appointed your principal as supervisor you are asked to prepare a report on the meetings. Within what period after the meetings must your report be sent to court and what details should be included in your report? **(3 marks)**

(c) Thirteen months after your principal was appointed supervisor of the above arrangement, your diary tells you that you have to report to creditors soon. By which time does this report have to be sent out and, to whom does it have to be sent as well as the creditors? **(3 marks)**

(d) Within what period after final completion of the arrangement should the supervisor send to all creditors a notice that the arrangement has been fully implemented? **(1 mark)**

(06/01) **(Total 15 marks)**

---

23 In all the following insolvency proceedings, the chairman of creditors' meetings (other than a s98 meeting) has to be nominated by the office holder, if the office holder is not able to chair the meeting him/herself. In only one of the proceedings does that person not have to be nominated in writing. Which one? (06/00)

(a) Creditors' voluntary liquidation (other than the s98 meeting)
(b) Administrative receivership – s48 meeting
(c) Administration – s23 meeting
(d) Company voluntary arrangement – s3 meeting

---

24 Which of the following does not have to be included in the report of the s3 meetings in the company voluntary arrangement proceedings? (06/00)

(a) A statement as to whether the proposal for the company voluntary arrangement was approved or rejected, and if approved, with what, if any, modifications

(b) Details of the resolutions taken at the meeting and the decision on each one

(c) A list of creditors and members (with their values) who were present or represented at the meetings and how they voted on each resolution

(d) Such information, if any, as the chairman thinks it appropriate to make known to the court

(e) A statement as to how the chairman voted with the general proxies in his favour

---

25 You are nominee in a company voluntary arrangement and are looking for guidance on what type of matters you should include in your nominee's report. Which Statement of Insolvency Practice gives you this advice? (06/00)

(a) SIP 3
(b) SIP 4
(c) SIP 5
(d) SIP 6
(e) SIP 7

---

26 Which one of the following may not propose a Company Voluntary Arrangement? (06/13)

(a) Directors
(b) Administrative Receiver
(c) Administrator
(d) Liquidator

---

27 Shelley's Shoes Ltd

Your principal has been appointed Nominee in relation to a Company Voluntary Arrangement for Shelley's Shoes Limited. According to the director, sales have recently seen an increase and it is intended that the company will pay contributions from continued trading and the director will inject some personal funds into the Arrangement. The company owns an investment property and it is the intention to sell this and inject the net proceeds into the Arrangement. The director has had favourable discussions concerning continued trading with its key suppliers, most of whom are based in the Netherlands. The director has provided a list of creditors and has also advised you that one customer recently came into the premises threatening to sue the company as their shoes had caused them to have an accident whilst running.

Requirement

(a) With reference to the facts and in accordance with SIP 3, what matters should be included/covered in the director's Proposals? **($^1/_2$ mark each, maximum of 10 marks)**

(b) In the event that the Proposals are approved, what matters should be detailed in the Chairman's report following approval? **(1 mark each, maximum of 5 marks)**

(06/13)

---

12 Introduction to administrations

1 Which of these is not one of the objectives of Administration in accordance with Paragraph 3(1) of Schedule B1? (6/12)

(a) realising property in order to make a distribution to one or more secured or preferential creditors

(b) to enable a sale of the business as a going concern

(c) rescuing the company as a going concern

(d) achieving a better result for the company's creditors as a whole than would be likely if the company were wound up

---

2 Your firm has been consulted by the directors of Piton Limited ('the Company'). The Company distributes sports equipment. It trades from office and warehouse premises which are subject to a 25 year lease at an annual rental of £120,000. The Company has 25 employees.

The Company has a bank overdraft with Crampon Bank Plc, currently standing at its limit of £100,000, secured by fixed and floating charges created on 1 February 2005 over the Company's assets and undertakings.

The Company has experienced a bad debt from a significant customer for £50,000. The remainder of the sales ledger is considered good, and the majority of the Company's customers are well known high street stores.

The Company has experienced a 10% increase in stock prices and general overheads in the last 12 months which has not been passed on to customers. Turnover has reduced by 10% in the same period as a result of competition on the internet.

The Company has recently invested £150,000 developing its own internet sales service and mail order business, which has now been launched and early trading results from this source have significantly exceeded forecasts.

The Company has three months' unpaid PAYE, amounting to £25,000 and HM Revenue and Customs has visited the Company's premises in the last week. HM Revenue and Customs has given notice that it will enter into walking possession over the stock in the Company's warehouse if the outstanding debt is not paid within 21 days. Stock is sourced from numerous suppliers, the majority of which incorporate reservation of title clauses into their contractual terms.

The Company has not paid the current quarter's rent, and the quarter rent day falls due next week; the Company is not in a position to pay the rent for the forthcoming quarter.

A supplier of equipment has an unpaid debt of £15,000 and has petitioned for the compulsory winding up of the Company. The petition has been advertised and is due to be heard in two weeks.

Using information provided by the directors at the meeting, there appears to be a current deficiency to creditors in the region of £400,000.

The directors have informed you that a number of competitors have expressed interest in the past six months in a possible purchase of the Company. The directors have also expressed a desire to preserve, and invest in, the business.

(a) What are the two standard tests of a company's insolvency? **(2 marks)**

(b) Identify briefly the possible insolvency procedures available to Piton Limited **(2 marks)**

(c) In the circumstances, which parties can cause an administrator to be appointed in respect of Piton Limited, and by what procedure? **(3 marks)**

(d) What effect would an administration have on:

(i) the winding up petition
(ii) HM Revenue and Customs' ability to enter into walking possession
(iii) the landlord's right of forfeiture
(iv) the directors' powers and duties **(2 marks)**

(e) Setting out your reasons, what do you consider to be the most appropriate strategy to achieve a going concern disposition of the business of Piton Limited, and what key steps should the appointee take in implementing this strategy? **(6 marks)**

(06/08) **(Total 15 marks)**

---

3 Under Paragraph 3(1) to Schedule B1 of the Act, what is the primary objective of the Administrator of the company? (06/07)

(a) To achieve a better result for the company's creditors as a whole than would be likely if the company were wound up

(b) To make a distribution to one or more secured or preferential creditors

(c) To achieve a going concern sale of the business

(d) To rescue the company as a going concern

---

4 You have been asked by your partner to attend a meeting in two hours time with a director of a company who is asking for advice about Administrations. The partner has asked you to prepare a memorandum setting out:

(a) The relevant steps and factors for the directors to consider when considering placing the company into administration **(10 marks)**

(b) The processes by which an Administration may be terminated **(5 marks)**

(06/07) **(Total 15 marks)**

---

5 Which of the following may not make an application to the Court for an Administration Order? (06/05)

(a) A contingent creditor of the company
(b) An administrative receiver of the company
(c) The directors of the company
(d) The holder of a qualifying floating charge
(e) The liquidator of the company

---

6 Under which paragraph of Schedule B1 of the Act may an administrator be appointed by a company or by the directors of a company? (06/05)

(a) Para. 10
(b) Para. 14
(c) Para. 17
(d) Para. 22
(e) Para. 26

---

7 Which Schedule to the Act deals with the powers of an administrator? (06/04)

(a) Schedule 1
(b) Schedule 2
(c) Schedule 3
(d) Schedule 4
(e) Schedule 6

---

8 Thorney Construction Limited (the company) was incorporated on 20 November 20X0 as ABC Limited and changed its name to its current style on 30 November 20X0.

The principal objects since incorporation have been general construction and maintenance works. The company has worked mainly for one large customer, Mainline Plc under a blanket order at its two plants in London and Manchester. The company's turnover for the year ending 30 March 20X8 was £7.5 million. The company has 120 full time employees. At present, the company is owed the sum of £800,000 by Mainline Plc and has ongoing contracts at the two plants, which have a potential value of £1.9 million.

Several months ago, the company tendered for and won a contract with Yorks Plc which is valued at £1.1 million. The contract has run for three months and invoices raised total £425,000.

The company operates an overdraft facility with Lees Bank Plc (the bank). The bank holds a debenture comprising a qualifying floating charge over the whole substantially or the whole of the company's property. This charge is dated 20 November 20X8.

The directors have become increasingly concerned by the financial position of Yorks Plc and have recently received notification that the company has entered into administration and have been advised to cease works on the contract.

Owing to this development, the company has come under pressure from its trade suppliers and a creditor is threatening winding up proceedings.

The directors are aware that if the company ceases trading it will severely impact upon the monies due from Mainline Plc and the future value of the contracts at Mainline's two plants.

Requirement

(a) Briefly describe the insolvency procedures available to a limited company. Give reasons why each procedure may or may not be appropriate for Thorney Construction Limited, based on the facts of the question. **(4 marks)**

(b) Outline the purposes of an administration order assuming no winding up petition has been presented, outline the statutory requirements to be considered and steps to be taken by the company or directors in placing the company into administration. **(9 marks)**

(c) If a winding up petition has been presented against the company, explain how the position differs for the company or the directors obtaining the appointment of an administrator compared with the holder of a qualifying floating charge obtaining such an appointment. **(1 mark)**

(d) If the company is in compulsory liquidation how would the position differ in respect of the liquidator and a qualifying floating charge holder applying for the appointment of an administrator? **(1 mark)**

(06/04) **(Total 15 marks)**

---

9 Which of the following powers is only available to an administrator following a court order: (06/04)

(a) Power to raise or borrow money and grant security therefore over the property of the company

(b) Power to refer to arbitration any question affecting the company

(c) Power to sell or otherwise dispose of the property of the company by public auction or private auction or private contract

(d) Power to use company's seal

(e) Power to dispose of or otherwise exercise his powers in relation to any property of the company which is subject to a fixed charge

---

10 Who of the following may not make an application for an Administration Order? (06/02)

(a) The directors
(b) A creditor or creditors
(c) The company
(d) The liquidator
(e) The shareholders

---

11 Which of the following is not a purpose for whose achievement an administration order may be made (para 3(1))? (06/00)

(a) Sale of the business as a going concern

(b) Rescuing the company as a going concern

(c) Achieving a better result for the company's creditors as a whole than would be likely if the company were wound up

(d) Realising property in order to make a distribution to one or more secured or preferential creditors

---

13 Procedure for administration

1 Within how many days are an Administrator's proposals deemed to have been accepted following the circulation of the statement of his proposals and where no creditors' meeting has been convened or such a request for a meeting has been received? (6/12)

(a) 7 days
(b) 28 days
(c) 8 business days
(d) 5 business days

---

2 When is an Administrator required to send a progress report to creditors? (6/12)

($^1/_2$ mark per point up to a maximum of 2 marks)

---

3 Who may not represent a member of a Creditors' Committee in an Administration? (6/12)

(4 marks)

---

4 Rainbow Ltd

You are appointed Administrator in respect of Rainbow Limited. At the initial meeting to consider the Administrator's Proposals, a creditors' committee is formed comprising of 5 members.

Requirement

(a) What are the Administrator's duties with regard to convening meetings of the committee? **(4 marks)**

After the Proposals have been approved, the director of Rainbow Limited makes an offer for some of the assets of the company. His offer falls between the best case and worst case valuations that your professional advisers have indicated should be achievable and therefore you decide to seek formal approval to the sale from the Committee by way of a postal resolution.

Requirement

(b) Set out the necessary procedure which should be followed. **(4 marks)**

(c) The assets are sold to the director and you decide to make a full disclosure in your next report to creditors. What matters should creditors be advised of in this regard? **(4 marks)**

(d) A member of the committee subsequently resigns. What options are available to the Administrator? **(3 marks)**

(6/12) **(Total 15 marks)**

---

5 Within how many business days following the directors' filling Notice of Intention to Appoint Administrators do the directors have to file Notice of Appointment of Administrators? (6/11)

(a) 5 days
(b) 7 days
(c) 10 days
(d) 14 days

---

6 You intend to publish your Administrators' Proposals on a website to discharge your duties under Paragraph 49 of Schedule B1 of the Insolvency Act 1986.

What information must be included in the relevant notice to creditors specifically with regard to accessing the information? (6/11) **($^1/_2$ mark per point up to a maximum of 2 marks)**

---

7 On what basis may an Administrator dispense with the requirement to call an initial meeting of creditors? (6/10)

(a) Where the consent of more than 75% in total of creditors has been obtained
(b) The Administrator considers it uneconomical to convene a meeting
(c) That neither the objective of (a) or (b) of Paragraph 3(1) can be achieved
(d) The business and assets of the Company were sold via a pre-packaged Administration

---

8 Your partner has been approached by the directors of Peak Limited. From the information provided, it is clear that the company is insolvent. There will be insufficient funds to pay salaries at the end of the month, and the quarterly rent is overdue. A number of creditors have stopped supplying the company. One creditor, Serac plc, has a Court judgment and has distrained over the company's property for a debt of £15,000, and another creditor is threatening to petition for winding up. The company's bank, Mount Bank plc, has fixed and floating charges over the assets of the business.

The directors feel the business is viable, and have received an offer of funding for a new company, Peak II Limited, owned and controlled by the directors, through which they hope to purchase the business.

(a) Set out the process by which the directors of Peak Limited may appoint an administrator. (1/2 mark per point) **(6 marks)**

The business of Peak Limited is subsequently transferred to Peak II Limited via a pre-packaged administration sale.

(b) In order that creditors can be satisfied that the administrator has acted with due regard for their interests, what information should the administrator provide to creditors following the sale to Peak II Limited? (1/2 mark per point.) **(6 marks)**

The administrator forms the view that there is no prospect of a distribution to the unsecured creditors of Peak Limited.

(c) What are the administrator's obligations regarding the summoning of an initial meeting of the creditors of Peak Limited? **(3 marks)**

(6/10) **(Total 15 marks)**

---

9 What steps must an administrator take to announce his appointment? (6/09) **(4 marks)**

---

10 A partner in your firm was appointed administrator of Mera Ltd on 30 April 20X9 by the directors of the company. Mera Ltd manufactures and installs double glazing products. Island Bank plc, which has fixed and floating charges dated 30 June 20X4 over the assets of the company, consented to the appointment.

You have instructed independent valuation agents to value the company's assets and the directors have provided you with the following information:

- The overdraft with Island Bank plc stands at £950,000
- The company has a full recourse factoring agreement with Monch Factors Ltd, which has advanced 65% of the debts due. The balance on the factored debtor's ledger stands at

£350,000. This includes known bad debts of £30,000. The directors consider that 15% of the remaining debts are doubtful.

- The company also has non-factored debts of £100,000. Of these, £40,000 relates to invoices raised in respect of annual cleaning and maintenance contracts expiring on 30 June 20X9. The directors consider that 25% of the remaining non-factored debts are doubtful.
- Stock, raw materials and work in progress have a book value of £130,000 and a realisable value of £35,000.
- The company owns a plastic extrusion machine purchased for £95,000 by means of a chattel mortgage from Belay Finance Ltd. The machine is now valued at £25,000 and the amount outstanding to Belay Finance Ltd is £10,000.
- The company also owns machinery and equipment free of finance with a book value of £50,000 and a realisable value of £10,000.
- Sundry office furniture and equipment has a book value of £10,000 and is estimated to realise £2,000.
- The company owns its freehold trading premises which were purchased for £500,000. Your agents have valued the property at £700,000.
- The company has five vehicles, which cost in total £50,000 and have been valued at £4,000 each.
- Amounts outstanding to HM Revenue & Customs comprise three months' PAYE of £85,000 and three months VAT of £75,000.
- Trade and expense creditors amount to £450,000.
- The company has 35 staff, of which the highest earns £780 per week. All are owed one week's wages, totalling £21,000. Additionally the four directors are also PAYE employees and are each owed £3,500 in respect of March's salaries. Additionally, there is outstanding staff holiday pay of £20,000 and entitlements to redundancy pay and pay in lieu of notice of £55,000 and £30,000 respectively.
- The company has issued share capital of 4,000 ordinary shares of £1 each.

Requirement

(a) Prepare the Statement of Affairs to accompany the administrator's statement of proposals.

(10 marks)

(b) What matters should be included in the administrator's statement of proposals for achieving the purpose of the administration?

($^1/_2$ mark per point up to 5 marks)

(6/09) **(Total 15 marks)**

---

11 In an administration, how many creditors may join a creditors' committee? (06/08)

(a) Two or less
(b) Between three and five inclusive
(c) At least five
(d) As many as want to be involved

12 A holder of a qualifying floating charge may not appoint an Administrator under paragraph 14 of schedule B1 to the Act unless he has given how many days written notice to the holder of any prior floating charge? (06/08)

(a) One business day
(b) Two business days
(c) Five business days
(d) Seven business days

---

13 How many days does a court appointed administrator have to file notice of his appointment with the Registrar of Companies? (06/08)

(a) 7 days
(b) 14 days
(c) 21 days
(d) 28 days

---

14 Where an Administration order has been made, within what period (other than a longer period as the court may allow) should an Administrator present his proposals to a meeting of creditors? (06/07)

(a) Less than 2 weeks
(b) Less than 3 weeks
(c) Less than 8 weeks
(d) Less than 10 weeks

---

15 Where an Administrator serves the prescribed notice on a person to submit a statement of affairs within what period (subject to any requests for an extension of time) must the person submit the statement of affairs? (06/07)

(a) Before end of 7 days
(b) Before end of 10 days
(c) Before end of 11 days
(d) Before end of 14 days

---

16 Which of the following would not give rise to an automatic termination of membership of a Creditors Committee in an Administration? (06/07)

(a) Person found to be a shadow director of the company
(b) Person becomes bankrupt
(c) Person fails to attend three consecutive meetings
(d) Person ceases to be a creditor

---

17 An Administrator appointed by Administration Order shall send a notice of his appointment to the Registrar of Companies within what period? (06/07)

(a) 7 days of the date of the order
(b) 10 days of the date of the order
(c) 10 days of receiving notice from a qualifying floating charge holder
(d) 7 days of receiving notice from the directors of the company

---

18 An appointment of an administrator by the directors of a company must be made within what period of the filing of the notice of intention to appoint? (06/06)

(a) 2 business days
(b) 20 business days
(c) 10 business days
(d) 5 business days
(e) 15 business days

---

19 The Administrator shall send a copy of the statement of his proposals to creditors before the end of which period after the company enters administration? (06/05)

(a) 8 weeks
(b) 3 months
(c) 28 days
(d) 12 weeks
(e) 4 months

---

20 A qualifying floating charge holder may appoint an administrator. However he may not appoint an administrator until he has given how many days written notice to any prior qualifying floating charge holder? (06/04)

(a) Two days
(b) Two business days
(c) Five days
(d) Five business days
(e) Seven days

---

21 An administrator, appointed 2 January 20X9, sends notice to each person to whom he considers it appropriate, requiring them to prepare and submit a statement of affairs. The notice is required to inform each of those persons of all the following, except one. Which one? (06/04)

(a) The names and addresses of all the others to whom the same notice has been sent
(b) The time within which the statement must be delivered
(c) The penalty for non-compliance with the notice
(d) The purposes for which the statement is to be used, as stated in the Act
(e) The application to each person to whom the notice applies of S235 of the Act

---

22 How many days' notice does the committee have to give to an administrator if it requires him to attend before it? (06/04)

(a) Seven days
(b) 14 days
(c) 21 days
(d) 28 days
(e) One month

---

23 How long after the para 51 creditors' meeting must an administrator send notice of the meeting result to creditors who received notice of the meeting? (06/02)

(a) Immediately
(b) As soon as reasonably practicable
(c) Seven days
(d) 14 days

---

24 Directors who are intending to apply for an administration order in respect of their company have approached you. They seek your advice on the content of the application.

(a) Which of the following must be specifically included within the witness statement supporting the application? **(½ mark for each correct answer)**

(i) A statement of the company's financial position
(ii) The last audited accounts of the company
(iii) Details of any insolvency proceedings in relation to the company
(iv) Name and address of the auditors
(v) A list of all the company's creditors
(vi) Details of any security known or believed to be held by creditors of the company

(b) Advise the directors which three of the following must be notified as soon as reasonably practicable after the making of an application for an administration order? **(½ mark for each correct answer)**

(i) The Registrar of Companies
(ii) The unsecured creditors of the company
(iii) Any person who has or has the power to appoint an Administrative Receiver
(iv) The bankers to the company
(v) The shareholders
(vi) Any Administrative Receiver appointed
(vii) The person proposed as Administrator **(3 marks total for question)**

(06/02)

---

25 Where an application is made to the court for an administration order by the directors or the company, a witness statement must be prepared and sworn. Which of the following parties can make this witness statement? (06/01)

(a) A director of the company
(b) A shareholder of the company
(c) The proposed administrator
(d) The auditors of the company
(e) None of the above

---

26 Upon which of the following need an administration application not be served? (Rule 2.6) (06/00)

(a) The person proposed as administrator

(b) Any administrative receiver who has been appointed

(c) Anyone who has appointed or who is able to appoint an administrative receiver or administrator under para 14

(d) Any creditor seeking to recover goods under a retention of title claim

(e) The petitioner if a petition for a winding up order is pending

---

27 How long after his appointment must an administrator convene a meeting of creditors in order to consider his proposals? (06/00)

(a) Three months
(b) One month
(c) 28 days
(d) Eight weeks
(e) 10 weeks

---

28 What conditions must exist in order for the director of a company to apply to Court for an Administration Order under Paragraph 12, schedule B1 of the Act? (06/13)

(2 marks)

---

14 Implementation of administration

1 Your Principal has been appointed Administrator of Jeans Limited by the company's Bank, which has fixed and floating charges over the company's assets. The Administrator intends to continue to trade the business for a period of at least two weeks in order to seek a sale of the business as a going concern. The company trades from five retail outlets, all of which are subject to formal leases with quarterly rent payable in advance on the usual quarter days. Each of the leases has more than two years left to run.

Set out the Administrator's responsibility following their appointment for rent and rates in respect of occupation of the company's premises. (6/11) **(4 marks)**

---

2 Your partner was recently appointed as Administrator of Sabbath Records Limited which is still trading in administration. Since your appointment you have received a number of calls from creditors claiming Retention of Title ('ROT') to stock supplied to the Company. List four basic principles to deal with any stock subject to ROT and/or ROT claims. (6/10)

(2 marks)

---

3 What are the statutory purposes of an administration and where are they set out in the legislation? (6/09) **(2 marks)**

---

4 Your partner has recently been instructed by Easy Money Factors Ltd ('Easy') to conduct a review of the affairs of Sparse Scaffolding Ltd ('the Company'). Following your review you have established that the company is insolvent and under severe creditor pressure. You have also learnt that wages are due to be paid to staff by the end of the week and there are no funds to meet these payments. HM Revenue & Customs is the Company's largest unsecured creditor and have threatened to issue a petition to wind up the business if they do not receive full payment within the next two weeks. The directors have provided unlimited personal guarantees to Easy for all sums due.

As part of your discussions with the directors they have indicated that they have heard through the grapevine that a pre pack administration is a good vehicle to deal with the company debt and be able to buy the business back. However in an article run in the local Wormley Gazette they have read that there are complications to this process and it did not appear as straightforward as they first thought.

In anticipation of buying the business back last week they set up Sparse Scaffolding 2009 Ltd ('Newco'), of which the shareholders and directors are the same as the Company. Easy has advised you that whilst it is not prepared to fund an administrator's trading period it will, however, fund a successor business to provide continuity, thus preserving the value of the sales ledger and assets of the Company.

You have prepared an estimated outcome statement which shows if the sale proceeds to Newco, the value of the assets will be significantly enhanced and Easy will be paid in full, resulting in a surplus on the ledger enabling a dividend to be paid to the unsecured creditors within 12 months from the commencement of the proceedings. You are aware from discussions with HM Revenue & Customs that it has a desire for the Company to be placed into liquidation within six months following the Para 51 meeting.

Requirement

(a) With particular regard to SIP 16, advise your partner as to his conduct during the period prior to his appointment in preparation of a pre-packaged sale of the business.

(1 mark for each point up to 3 marks)

(b) On the basis that a pre-packaged sale is completed to Newco, detail the information to be disclosed in the first notification to creditors following the sale.

(1 mark for each point up to 8 marks)

(c) HM Revenue & Customs have requested that steps be taken to place the Company into liquidation within six months of the Para 51 meeting. On this basis explain how the directors can resolve any issues in relation to s216 without the need for an application to court. **(4 marks)**

(6/09) **(Total 15 marks)**

---

5 A partner of your firm has been appointed Administrator of Rangers Limited, a manufacturing company. The supplier of lease manufacturing equipment has arrived on the premises threatening to distrain.

What is the legal position of the lease creditor and the Administrator and what action should you take? **(4 marks)**

(06/07)

---

6 Your partner was appointed administrator of Blanc Limited on 31 January 20X8. He has sold the business and assets of the company as a going concern, including equipment subject to a hire purchase agreement.

(a) Set out the procedure under which an administrator may dispose of property subject to a hire purchase agreement. **(3 marks)**

(b) Following the sale of the business and assets there are net funds in the administration estate of £100,000. There are no secured creditors. There are preferential claims of £25,000 and unsecured claims of £150,000.

Set out the procedure under which the administrator may make a distribution to creditors. Include details of any information the administrator is required to provide to creditors. **(9 marks)**

(c) By what other processes could the funds in the administration be distributed to creditors? **(3 marks)**

(06/06) **(Total 15 marks)**

---

7 (a) Set out the matters required to be dealt with in an administrator's statement of proposals. **(8 marks)**

(b) Draft a memo to your partner setting out the means by which an administration may be terminated. **(7 marks)**

(06/05) **(Total 15 marks)**

---

8 A company entered administration on 13 March 20X9. Before paying a court sanctioned dividend, how long after the last date for proving must the administrator of that company state that it is his intention to make a distribution to creditors? (06/04)

(a) 21 days
(b) 28 days
(c) One month
(d) Two months
(e) Four months

---

9 (a) You are advising a number of creditors who intend to vote at the para 51 meeting in a large administration. Explain what, if any, amount of their overall claim, the following creditors will be allowed to vote for.

(i) A secured creditor **(1 mark)**
(ii) A creditor with retention of title **(1 mark)**
(iii) A hire purchase creditor **(1 mark)**

You are also advising an individual creditor who, together with his family has a 30% shareholding in the company in administration. Neither he nor any member of his family are directors or employees of the company in administration.

(iv) Explain how, if at all, the shareholding affects the creditors vote at the para 51 meeting. Give reasons for your answer. **(3 marks)**

(b) You are administrator of Mainly Properties Limited and wish to sell a property over which a clearing bank has a fixed charge. The clearing bank has refused you permission to sell the property.

(i) What rights do you have to override the wishes of the clearing bank and how would you seek to put these into action? **(2 marks)**

(ii) Assuming you are able to sell the property, what would you do with the sale proceeds? **(1 mark)**

(iii) What would have been the position if the clearing bank had only had a floating charge over the property? **(1 mark)**

(c) Schedule 1 to the Insolvency Act 1986 gives the administration 23 separate powers. Name 10 of them. **(5 marks)**

(06/00) **(Total 15 marks)**

---

15 Introduction to receivership

1 What must be included in the Notice of Appointment of an Administrative Receiver? (6/12)

(4 marks)

---

2 Whose agent is an Administrative Receiver? (06/07)

(a) The company's
(b) The creditors'
(c) The directors'
(d) The shareholders'

---

3 The definition of an administrative receiver is contained within which section of the Insolvency Act 1986? (06/06)

(a) s27
(b) s40
(c) s29
(d) s33
(e) s43

---

16 Effect of administrative receivership and duties of receiver

1 Which Schedule of the Act deals with the powers of an administrative receiver? (6/10)

(a) Schedule 1
(b) Schedule 4
(c) Schedule 6
(d) Schedule 10

---

2 Within what period must an administrative receiver deliver an abstract of receipts and payments to the registrar of companies? (6/09)

(a) Within one month after the end of 12 months from the date of his appointment and every subsequent period of 12 months

(b) Within two months after the end of 12 months from the date of his appointment and every subsequent period of six months

(c) Within one month after the end of 12 months from the date of his appointment and every subsequent period of six months

(d) Within two months after the end of 12 months from the date of his appointment and every subsequent period of 12 months

---

3 In an administrative receivership, when are directors required to submit a statement of affairs? (06/08)

(a) Within 21 days of being requested to
(b) Within 28 days of being requested to
(c) Within 6 weeks of being requested to
(d) Within 2 months of being requested to

---

4 An administrative receiver is not required to send an abstract of his receipts and payments to which of the following? (06/06)

(a) The Court
(b) The creditors' committee
(c) The company
(d) The Registrar of Companies
(e) The appointor

---

5 Which of the following matters does not have to be included in a report by an Administrative Receiver under Section 48 of the Act? (06/05)

(a) The events leading up to his appointment

(b) The disposal by him of any property of the company

(c) Amounts of principal and interest payable to the debenture holder and the amounts payable to preferential creditors

(d) Names, addresses and debts of the unsecured creditors

(e) An estimate of the value of the prescribed part available for unsecured creditors

---

6 An administrative receiver must file with the Registrar of Companies an abstract of his receipts and payments. After what periods of time must he file this abstract? (06/04)

(a) Within one month of every 12 months following his appointment

(b) Within two months of every 12 months following his appointment

(c) Within one month of every six months following his appointment

(d) Within one month of the anniversary of his appointment and then within one month of the expiry of each six months thereafter

(e) Within two months of every six months following his appointment and then within two months of the expiry of each six months thereafter

---

7 Who of the following may an administrative receiver **not** require to submit a statement of affairs? (06/01)

(a) Anyone who is or has been an officer of the company

(b) Anyone who is or who has been a shareholder of company at any time within one year before the date of appointment

(c) Anyone who has taken part in the company's formation at any time within one year before the date of appointment

(d) Anyone who was in the company's employment, or has been in its employment within that year and are in the administrative receiver's opinion capable of giving the information required

(e) Anyone who in that year has been an officer of or in the employment of a company which is or within that year was an officer of the company

---

8 In administrative receivership, if the company goes into liquidation two weeks after the receiver's appointment, the receiver need not call a creditors' meeting if, within three months of his appointment, he does which of the following? (06/00)

(a) Obtains approval from his appointer

(b) Obtains approval from the liquidator

(c) Sends to the liquidator a copy of his report within seven days of sending his report to the registrar of companies

(d) Obtains approval from more than 25% in value of the creditors

(e) Obtains approval from more than 15% in value of the creditors

---

9 Which Statement of Insolvency Practice details an administrative receiver's duty to preferential creditors? (06/00)

(a) SIP 8
(b) SIP 10
(c) SIP 11
(d) SIP 12
(e) SIP 14

---

10 Within what period after the anniversary of an Administrative Receiver's appointment must he file his statutory account of receipts and payments? (06/13)

(a) 2 months
(b) 1 month
(c) 28 days
(d) 6 weeks

---

17 Administrative receivership: practical aspects and closure

1 According to SIP 17, which is not a power of an administrative receiver in respect of books and records? (06/08)

(a) Power to destroy pre appointment records
(b) Power to return pre appointment records to directors
(c) Power to change the registered office
(d) Power to take possession of statutory records for safekeeping

---

2 You have been appointed administrative receiver over a company. Which Statement of Insolvency Practice (SIP) gives guidance on how you should deal with the company's books and records? (06/02)

(a) SIP 1
(b) SIP 2
(c) SIP 3
(d) SIP 4

---

3 A partner in your office has recently been appointed as administrative receiver of First Class Fashions Limited, a clothing manufacturer in the West End, providing stock to the local high street shops. That partner has requested your assistance in this matter.

The administrative receiver has been negotiating for the sale of the business for the last week and you are dealing with the negotiations. You have decided that in order to preserve the value of the business you should continue to trade the company during the short term.

However, during your first few days of trading, you have been faced with the following difficulties:

(a) You trade from leasehold factory premises where the annual rent is £84,000. The rent is due to be paid quarterly in advance. The current quarter has not been paid.

You are required to advise what potential problems you may be faced with, as administrative receiver if the ongoing rent is not paid as a matter of urgency and how you would overcome this. **(3 marks)**

(b) The company has some 25 employees who are paid on a weekly basis. All of the employees are owed one week's wages for the period prior to your appointment and have outstanding holiday. All employees have worked for the company for several years.

You are required to list the points you would include in a note to your partner outlining the administrative receiver's obligations to the employees. **(3 marks)**

(c) The company has not paid its last two electricity bills and you have now received a disconnection notice. You have contacted the electricity company who have advised that they require full payment of all outstanding bills and a deposit for the future supply from the administrative receiver.

You are required to list the points you would include in a note to your partner outlining any rights and obligations he has in this situation. **(2 marks)**

(d) Two of the major fabric suppliers have notified you that they have a retention of title claim. The first is with Bargain Fabrics Ltd who are owed the sum of £6,000. They have visited the factory and have identified fabric with a value of £1,500. The second supplier is Tafatta Ltd who are owed £9,000. They have also visited the premises and identified their fabric which has been cut and incorporated into dresses. Both suppliers have standard 'all monies clauses' in their terms of trading.

You are required to state how you would deal with each of the suppliers concerned. **(3 marks)**

(e) You have now been trading for three weeks and you are close to agreeing a sale of the business to a potential purchaser. However, it has recently come to your attention that a major supplier has presented a petition for the compulsory winding up of the company. You have contacted the petitioner but have failed to dissuade them from continuing with the petition.

You are required to explain what effects this will have on the administrative receiver.

(3 marks)

(f) The appointed administrative receiver has a duty to not only his appointer but also the preferential creditors. He must ensure that he allocates the costs appropriately between fixed and floating charge asset realisations.

Requirement

In which Statement of Insolvency Practice is this defined? **(1 mark)**

(06/02) **(Total 15 marks)**

---

4 To whom of the following does the administrative receiver **not** have to give 5 business days notice before resigning his office? (06/01)

(a) The person by whom he was appointed
(b) The company, if no liquidator was appointed
(c) The liquidator, if appointed
(d) The creditors
(e) The members of any creditors' committee

---

18 Bankruptcy

1 What insolvency options are available for a creditor to pursue who has an unpaid debt due from a partnership business (not an LLP)? (6/12) **(4 marks)**

---

2 Provided a debtor is domiciled in England & Wales and is not an undischarged bankrupt or subject to any IVA or bankruptcy proceedings, name four other conditions to be met for a debtor to be granted a Debt Relief Order. (6/12) **(4 marks)**

---

3 Rachel, aged 27, has come to see you for advice about her current financial circumstances. She explains that she has incurred a range of debts with various credit card and loan companies, totalling approximately £40,000 which she is in no position to pay as she has recently lost her job as a legal executive. She is struggling to find a new job but hopes she will find something soon. She owns a residential property jointly with her partner, Craig, who unfortunately has been out of work himself for some months. There is currently no equity in the house as it was purchased with a 100% mortgage shortly before property prices fell. The couple's borrowing has primarily been in Rachel's name because her job was better paid and was thought to be more secure. Craig has no significant liabilities in his name and neither of them have any other assets of any consequence.

Advise Rachel on her main personal insolvency options. In particular you should comment on bankruptcy, IVAs and Debt Management Plans. Also comment on whether a Debt Relief Order may be an appropriate option. Compare and contrast the different insolvency solutions, taking into account Rachel's financial circumstances.

(6/11) **(15 marks)**

---

4 Which one of the following is not included in the contents of a creditor's bankruptcy petition? (6/09)

(a) The name in which the debtor carries on business, if any
(b) The debtor's residential address
(c) The debtor's date of birth
(d) The debtor's occupation, if any

---

5 Which one of the following statements is true in relation to a statutory demand? (06/08)

(a) A statutory demand is a written demand for repayment within 10 days
(b) A statutory demand is a written demand for repayment within 28 days
(c) A statutory demand is issued by the court
(d) A statutory demand is issued by a creditor

---

6 How much is the deposit payable on a debtor's petition for bankruptcy? (06/08)

(a) £235
(b) £300
(c) £525
(d) £50

---

7 (a) Under what circumstances might the court dismiss a creditor's petition against a debtor? **(2 marks)**

(b) Once a bankruptcy order has been made, the court may order a stay of proceedings.

(i) What is meant by the term 'stay of proceedings' in relation to a bankruptcy order? **(1 mark)**

(ii) Under what circumstances might the court stay bankruptcy proceedings against a debtor? **(1 mark)**

(06/08) **(Total 4 marks)**

---

8 Mark Boyle (aged 33) has come to see your principal. He is worried about his financial position having got into credit card debt eighteen months ago on expenditure which his wife knows nothing about. He now owes £25,000 on six cards on which he is paying minimum payments only totalling £425 a month. He had been managing the payments by switching to lower rate cards but has been unable to transfer any balances (he thinks because some direct debits were not met last month) and is now locked in at high interest rates on all of the cards. He wants help now before things spiral out of control.

The debtor takes home £3,000 per month salary from his job as manager of a local high end estate agency. This month he also received a bonus of £950 (the bonus is payable annually on 1 May) and commission on sales for the previous month on related products of £250 and is likely to remain at that level.

The debtor pays £1,400 a month to the mortgagee on a 15 year repayment loan of £175,000. The rate is fixed at 5% until November 20X9. He has direct debits to various utilities as follows – gas and electricity £150; water £120; council tax £125; phone/ internet £40. He pays £90 a month on term life assurance, £60 a month joint gym membership, £100 a month covenanted giving to his local church and £200 a month to his son at university in Aberdeen. He pays £1,000 a month into a joint account with his wife into which she also pays her income of £300 from her ironing service.

Analysis of spending on the joint credit card shows they spend £1,000 a month on food, wine and entertaining and £250 a month on petrol and car costs. This card is paid for out of the joint bank account which is with a different bank from Mr Boyle's personal account.

The jointly owned home 1 Well Walk is worth £250,000. It is in good repair.

They have one car a four year old Honda CRV which is free of finance charges and registered in his wife's name, given to her last year by her parents. He has the use of a company car for which he pays his own petrol.

Mr Boyle has thought about remortgaging but is worried about his job given the weak housing market. He doesn't want to lose the house and is reluctant to involve his wife.

Requirement

(a) Prepare an Income and Expenditure statement for Mr Boyle based on the above information. **(5 marks)**

(b) Outline what options Mr Boyle has to deal with his credit card debt bearing in mind his uncertainties and requirements. Your answer should cover both statutory and non statutory debt solutions. **(10 marks)**

(06/08)

(Total 15 marks)

---

9 John Smith is a final year economics student. He graduates this term. He is 22 and has no dependants. He is to take up a placement with a top ten law firm in January after a six month break to be spent travelling and doing voluntary work in South America. His starting salary will be £25,000. He wants to go into politics. He is coming to meet you today.

John has fallen out with his parents who have not supported him financially for at least the past 21 months. This coincided with his purchase of a terraced house on a 100% mortgage, his parents having paid the associated costs of purchase. He rents three bedsitting rooms to fellow students - using tenancy agreements obtained via the Student Union. The house has just been valued at £120,000, effectively no increase in value (he paid £118,000) probably because the internal conversion work into three bedsits and a ground floor flat has been botched. A local builder said it would cost about £3,000 to put the house in order and then it would fetch a higher price of around £130,000.

Without his parent's support he has relied on credit cards and the bank to fund his lifestyle, incurring £23,500 of debt, inclusive of a student loan of £3,500. He has little to show for his spending, a significant proportion of which was spent on visits to New York to see his girlfriend, who is moving here to live with him.

He exploited low interest balance transfer deals to manage his debts, but these have now expired leaving him with accumulating interest in excess of his contributions. He does not want to get deeper into debt.

He is keen to resolve this situation but wants to avoid any later repercussions given his political ambitions. He would also like to keep the house; his girlfriend will help out with expenses as she has a job lined up with a local advertising company. He is concerned about coming to see you as he fears that you will make him bankrupt and that wouldn't go down well at his local branch of the Clean Party.

His financial situation is as follows:

	£
Assets	
Three Bed Terraced House (per recent valuation by agent – in current state as four way student let)	120,000
Liabilities	
Store cards (seven)	3,500
Credit cards (five)	14,500
Student loan	3,500
Bank overdraft	2,000
Mortgage (interest only)	118,000
Income/monthly	
Rent – three students/month	600
Bar work/month – average	400
Outgoings/monthly	
Mortgage	750
Utilities	100
Food etc	100
Travel and entertainment	200
Card minimum repayments	450

(a) How would you allay John's concerns about your initial meeting and what he sees as the prospect of being made bankrupt by you? **(2 marks)**

(b) Outline the formal insolvency options available to John, clearly explaining the advantages and disadvantages of each option. **(10 marks)**

(c) Using the information available, and having regard to John's wishes, advise John which is the best course of action for him and why. **(3 marks)**

(06/07) **(Total 15 marks)**

10 What information would you expect to be contained in a debtor's petition for his own bankruptcy (not his statement of affairs)? (06/05) **(4 marks)**

---

11 How long does a debtor have to comply with or set aside a statutory demand? (06/04)

(a) 7 days
(b) 10 days
(c) 14 days
(d) 21 days
(e) 28 days

---

12 When does the bankruptcy of an individual commence? (06/04)

(a) The day on which a bankruptcy order is made
(b) The day on which a trustee in bankruptcy is appointed
(c) The day on which a statutory demand is served
(d) The day on which a bankruptcy petition is presented

---

13 In accordance with the general duty of the Official Receiver how often after the making of the bankruptcy order should a report and statement of affairs be submitted to creditors? Is it: (06/00)

(a) At least once
(b) Every three months
(c) Every six months
(d) Every 12 months
(e) None of these

---

14 Following what type of appointment is it necessary to receive the court's directions to advertise a trustee's appointment? Is it: (06/00)

(a) Bankruptcy following a voluntary arrangement
(b) Appointment by meeting following a creditor's petition
(c) Appointment by meeting following a debtor's petition
(d) Appointment by the Secretary of State

---

15 Who may appoint an interim receiver? Is it: (06/00)

(a) The director
(b) Official Receiver
(c) Trustee
(d) Supervisor
(e) The Court

---

16 Mr Careless owns a small second hand car dealership in Southbridge. The dealership has experienced a downturn in trade due to a large Car Supermarket opening in Borchester. Mysteriously, £10,000 in cash representing three weeks trade and retained for the purpose of settling a number of accounts, including a local hire purchase company, has gone missing from his office.

The hire purchase company has recently issued a petition for a bankruptcy order.

Mr Careless, concerned that he can no longer pay his liabilities or continue to trade, contacts your Partner and requests advice on the role of the Court in bankruptcy proceedings. In particular, Mr Careless requests information on the grounds for adjournment and the possibility of annulment.

Mr Careless has heard from a friend, who is an undischarged bankrupt, that his assets could be seized and his premises broken into.

Your Partner has requested that you prepare notes for a forthcoming meeting with Mr Careless on the following issues:

(a) On what grounds will an order from the Court be avoided

(b) What are the grounds for an annulment

(c) By whom and by what process can assets be seized and on what authority can premises be broken into

(d) What control can the Court exercise over the trustee and in what circumstances can the bankrupt or others challenge the acts of the trustee **(15 marks)**

(06/00)

---

17 For a successful application for a Debt Relief Order, the maximum allowable monthly surplus income that an individual may have must be less than what amount? (06/13)

(a) £50
(b) £100
(c) £10
(d) £0

---

18 Debt solutions

James is a solicitor aged 27 and his wife Sally is a doctor aged 28. They have a problem in repaying their debts. Their creditors are unwilling to negotiate and there are significant arrears.

You establish that they have 2 loans in joint names totalling £9,000. Sally also has various credit cards with outstanding balances totalling £9,450 and she owes £10,000 on a student loan taken out in 2007. James has various other credit cards and loans totalling £27,200.

You review their budget and after taking into account all their essential expenditure you establish that they have a joint surplus of £390 per month available for their creditors. Individually James would have £140 and Sally would have £250 but they tell you that they would prefer to manage their debts together. They live together in rented accommodation, Sally is expecting a significant promotion soon and James is hoping to be considered for partnership before he is 30.

Requirement

(a) Send a letter to James and Sally summarising possible general debt solutions available, briefly explaining why some of the solutions would not be suitable for one or both of them, without duplicating your answer to part (b) below. **(4 marks)**

(b) Explain how bankruptcy, individual voluntary arrangements and debt management plans might resolve their debt problems providing reasons for and against each solution. **(9 marks)**

(c) Provide a conclusion of the advice that you would give to them. **(2 marks)**

(06/13) **(Total 15 marks)**

19 Post bankruptcy order procedure

1 Your principal has been appointed as trustee in bankruptcy of the estate of Rupert Woods. You are aware that Mr Woods is in employment and also owns a property jointly with his wife. You are asked to write a memo setting out the main statutory and practical matters which the trustee should attend to within the first few days following his appointment.

(6/09) **(15 marks)**

---

2 Within what time period must the Trustee supply a copy of his latest receipts and payments account on request from any creditor or the debtor? (06/07)

(a) 7 days
(b) 14 days
(c) 21 days
(d) 28 days

---

3 A trustee shall prepare and keep separate financial records for each bankrupt. How long should those records be retained by him, where he is not succeeded by another trustee? (06/06)

(a) Six years following his date of appointment as trustee
(b) Two years following his date of appointment as trustee
(c) Six years following his vacation of office
(d) One year following his vacation of office

---

4 Which of the following is not a bankruptcy offence? (06/05)

(a) Fraudulent disposal of property
(b) Rash and hazardous speculation
(c) Concealment/ destruction of books and record
(d) Absconding with assets
(e) Making false statements

---

5 You have been appointed trustee in a bankruptcy. Which of the following is not one of your duties to the official receiver (OR)? (06/04)

(a) A duty to furnish the OR with such information as the OR may reasonably require

(b) A duty to attend upon the OR as the OR may reasonably require

(c) A duty to produce and permit inspection of such books, papers and records as the OR may reasonably require

(d) A duty to give the OR such other assistance as the OR may reasonably require

---

6 You are appointed trustee in bankruptcy by the Secretary of State. In accordance with the Dear IP guidance issued, within what period of time, following the effective date of your appointment, should you send notice of your appointment to creditors? (06/04)

(a) You are only required to advertise your appointment
(b) As soon as reasonably practicable
(c) Five days
(d) 28 days
(e) One month

---

7 To which of the following bankruptcy offences is the 'defence of innocent intention' not available? (06/02)

(a) Bankrupt failing to disclose property or disposals to official receiver or trustee

(b) Bankrupt failing to deliver property to, or concealing property from, official receiver or trustee

(c) Bankrupt failing to deliver books, papers and records to official receiver or trustee

(d) Bankrupt absconding with property he is required to deliver to official receiver or trustee

(e) Bankrupt obtaining credit or engagement in business without disclosing his status or name in which he was made bankrupt

---

8 Where a Bankrupt continues to trade through Bankruptcy, how often should he submit an account of his trading to his Trustee (as a bare minimum)? (06/01)

(a) Annually
(b) At the end of the three year bankruptcy period
(c) Monthly
(d) Not less than six monthly
(e) When required by the trustee

---

9 When asking for credit, in excess of what level of credit is it an offence to not disclose that you are undischarged bankrupt? Is it: (06/00)

(a) £250
(b) £500
(c) £750
(d) £1,000
(e) None of these

---

20 Meetings of creditors – bankruptcy

1 If a Trustee is unable to chair a meeting of creditors, who is able to act as chairman in accordance with the Rules? (6/10) **(2 marks)**

---

2 Which one of the following statements is NOT true in relation to a Creditors' Committee in a Bankruptcy? (06/07)

(a) A creditors' committee can be established in a general meeting of the bankrupt's creditors

(b) Where the official receiver is trustee the functions of the creditors' committee are vested in the Secretary of State

(c) If there is no creditors' committee and the official receiver is not trustee, the functions of the committee are vested in the court

(d) A fully secured creditor cannot be a member of the creditors' committee

---

3 The notice period for a final creditors meeting in bankruptcy proceedings (excluding days for postage) is: (06/05)

(a) 28 days
(b) 21 days
(c) 1 month
(d) 14 days
(e) 7 days

---

4 A creditor wishes to requisition a general meeting of creditors in bankruptcy proceedings. What level of creditor claims (including the value of the requisitioning creditor's claim) would be required to convene a meeting? (06/04)

(a) 10% by value of the bankrupt's creditors
(b) 25% by value of the bankrupt's creditors
(c) 50% by value of the bankrupt's creditors
(d) 25% by value of the bankrupt's creditors whose claims have been admitted by the trustee
(e) 10% by value of the bankrupt's creditors whose claims have been admitted by the trustee

---

5 A trustee in bankruptcy has certain reporting obligations to a creditors' committee, which are set out in the Insolvency Rules. Which one of the following statements is not reflected in the rules? (06/02)

(a) The trustee should report all matters as appear to him to be of concern to the members of the creditors' committee with respect to the bankruptcy

(b) The trustee should report as and when directed by the committee, but not more often than once every two months

(c) The trustee should report to the committee if it has come into being more than 14 days after his appointment

(d) The trustee need not comply with any request for information where it appears to him that the request is frivolous or unreasonable

(e) The estate is without funds sufficient to enable the trustee to comply with the request for information

---

6 According to rule 12A.21(2)(a) what constitutes a quorum at a creditors' meeting in insolvency proceedings? (06/01)

(a) Seven creditors entitled to vote
(b) Five creditors entitled to vote
(c) Three creditors entitled to vote
(d) One creditor entitled to vote
(e) Two creditors entitled to vote

---

7 Within what period must the official receiver decide to summon the first meeting of creditors in a bankruptcy? Is it: (06/00)

(a) 14 days
(b) 21 days
(c) 28 days
(d) 12 weeks
(e) Four months

---

8 Whenever a meeting of creditors is summoned, what notice must the convenor give to the bankrupt? Is it: (06/00)

(a) At least seven days
(b) At least 14 days
(c) At least 21 days
(d) At least 28 days
(e) None of these

---

21 Bankruptcy estate and antecedent transactions

1 What is the 'relevant time' period for a transaction that may be challenged as a preference under S340 of the Act against an associate of the bankrupt? (6/12)

(a) 2 years immediately preceding a bankruptcy order
(b) 2 years immediately preceding a bankruptcy petition
(c) 6 months immediately preceding a bankruptcy order
(d) 6 months immediately preceding a bankruptcy petition

---

2 Gail has been working on a self-employed basis as a horse dealer but as a result of purchasing horses which then failed vet checks when she tried to arrange sales has run into financial difficulty. She has incurred a number of debts with suppliers of feedstuffs, equipment, her farrier and vet. She has also used a number of credit cards and personal loans to pay for the rent for the yard from which she trades, vehicle hire, fuel costs, competition entry fees and also to help fund cash payments for horses she intended to sell on. She has been struggling to make ends meet for a couple of years now and realised some time ago that she had little prospect of being able to pay all her debts and faced the prospect of bankruptcy. The saddler for her business obtained a county court judgment for £10,000 four months ago and is threatening further proceedings. HMRC has also been threatening bankruptcy proceedings in respect of unpaid VAT and PAYE/ NIC. She has therefore taken steps to arrange her affairs to protect herself in the event that she is made bankrupt.

Her house was jointly owned with her husband but he agreed to the property being transferred into his sole name and took sole responsibility for the £150,000 mortgage. The total equity in the property at the time of transfer about a year ago was in the region of £120,000. Gail was not paid for her share of the equity as this was a transaction between husband and wife.

Gail transferred ownership of six horses worth between £2,000 and £10,000 each to two creditors who she wanted to make sure were not owed money if she ended up being made bankrupt. One of these was her mother who had made a personal loan of £15,000 to Gail several years ago and the other was the saddler who had obtained judgment, who was previously a friend who had supplied her with saddles and other equipment and with whom Gail had built up a debt of over £10,000. She transferred ownership of three horses to her mother about a year ago and the other three to the saddler three months ago.

Gail was served with a bankruptcy petition by HMRC following which she formed a limited company and transferred her remaining business assets, a horse box, equipment and four horses, to that company (without any payment being made) to avoid them falling into the hands of a trustee in bankruptcy. The total estimated value of these assets was £30,000. Because she will be made bankrupt it was agreed that her husband would be the sole director and shareholder of the company. The company has become the trading vehicle for Gail's business and she is an employee. After the bankruptcy is over, Gail believes the shares could be transferred to her so she would have the benefit of the company assets.

Requirement

(a) At the hearing of the bankruptcy petition a bankruptcy order was made and your principal has now been appointed trustee. You are reviewing the handover documents received from the Official Receiver and have been asked to prepare a note for the trustee setting out what assets could be claimed for the bankruptcy estate. You should state what types of claims may be made in each of the circumstances set out above, commenting on relevant timescales and matters which would need to be demonstrated to bring successful claims.

(13 marks)

(b) How might the claims be pursued in the absence of funds in the estate?

(2 marks)

(6/12) **(Total 15 marks)**

3 Certain types of assets are excluded from a bankrupt's estate such as tools, books, vehicles and equipment required for work or personal use.

Set out four other types or categories of assets which do not from part of a bankrupt's estate. (6/11) **(4 marks)**

---

4 Which one of the following assets would be included in a bankruptcy estate? (6/10)

(a) Property held by the bankrupt on trust for a third party
(b) A car of modest value to enable the bankrupt to commute to work
(c) Rights under a personal pension policy
(d) An inheritance from the bankrupt's late mother's estate

---

5 What is the maximum length of time for which a bankrupt may be subject to an Income Payment Order? (6/10)

(a) 3 years from the date of the bankruptcy order
(b) 5 years from the date of the bankruptcy order
(c) 3 years from the date of the income payment order
(d) 5 years from the date of the income payment order

---

6 If a Trustee wishes to claim an after-acquired asset for the bankruptcy estate, who does written notice have to be given to and what is the time-limit for the issuing of this notice? (6/10) **(2 marks)**

---

7 Bob Bobbins was declared bankrupt on 1st April 2010 on a petition presented to Court by H M Revenue & Customs on 1 December 2009. Your principal was appointed as Trustee on 1st June 2010 at a meeting of creditors held that day. Bob traded as a painter and decorator but ceased to trade on the making of the bankruptcy order and now works at a large DIY store. The following matters are disclosed in the hand-over of papers received from the Official Receiver.

- Bob previously owed money to his father and to his friend Paul. His father had lent him £10,000 in November 2007 in respect of his former business to replace a van that had failed an MOT. Paul had loaned Bob £3,000 in April 2008 to pay off a tax bill which was the subject of legal recovery proceedings. Bob repaid both his father and Paul in full in May 2009 from cashing in shares which were owned by him.

- Bob owned a life policy which had a surrender value of £15,000. Bob surrendered the policy on 1 March 2010 and received the proceeds on 31 March 2010. He put the proceeds in trust for his children.

- Bob lives in a 3 bedroom property which has an estimated value of £250,000. There is a single charge registered against the property and Bob has advised the Official Receiver that the balance outstanding is £100,000. The property is held at HM Land Registry in the sole name of Bob's wife and has been since August 2006. Bob and his wife have lived at the property since the early 1990's and it was previously in joint names. Bob has said he transferred his share to his wife for £1 as she had just cleared a bill of £10,000 to a trade supplier who was threatening legal proceedings and his wife was 'concerned about losing the property'.

- Bob previously owned a second property which he sold to his brother in January 2005 for £10,000. The property was not in good repair at the time but had an estimated value of £40,000 at the date of transfer.

- Bob has total debts of over £300,000 - the largest debt is to HM Revenue & Customs for VAT that started to accrue from the quarter commencing November 2005 and further debts were incurred from May 2006 onwards and remain unpaid.

Your Principal has asked you to review and consider the above details and to provide him with a memo to advise him as follows:

(a) In respect of each transaction described above, comment on whether the trustee may be able to overturn the transaction and, if so, identify the type of antecedent transaction which appears to be involved. **(7 marks)**

(b) In accordance with the Act, what criteria would have to be demonstrated to the Court by the trustee to successfully overturn each transaction. **(8 marks)**

(6/10) **(Total 15 marks)**

---

8 Who would be an associate of a bankrupt within the meaning of s435? (6/09)

(1 mark per grouping or type up to 4 marks)

---

9 Which one of the following persons is not an associate for the purposes of the Insolvency Act 1986 s435? (06/08)

(a) The individual's reputed civil partner
(b) The individual's former business partner
(c) The individual's former accountant
(d) The individual's former employee

---

10 In which one of the following cases would a payment made by a debtor to a supplier (and which was not also a transaction at undervalue) five months before the debtor filed the petition on which he was made bankrupt, be caught by s340 of the IA (preference provisions)? (06/08)

(a) The payment was made in the ordinary course of business
(b) The recipient made no more supplies to the debtor
(c) The debtor was not insolvent at the time
(d) The debtor was insolvent at the time

---

11 Peter Pang, interior designer, has come to see you. He was made bankrupt last Thursday (on a petition presented two months ago by HM Revenue and Customs) and Miss Dodge, his trustee, was appointed the following day. Peter is upset and wants your advice.

(a) Flat 1, Curtin Close, Peter's flat had been on the market for months. Finally he found a willing purchaser but at less than the asking price. They exchanged and completed contracts last Wednesday, the day before he was made bankrupt. Peter was aware of his bankruptcy hearing but had failed to understand its significance, and, anyway, thought it better to get on and deal with the flat than lose his purchaser.

The trustee, Miss Dodge, has notified Peter and the purchaser that the sale amounted to a 'void disposition' under section 284 of the Insolvency Act. She asked Peter to contact her agents with a view to commencing marketing immediately.

You establish the following:

The purchaser's solicitors had spotted that a bankruptcy petition had been presented but assumed it must be being resolved. The sale price was £145,000. After settling the mortgage, £142,000 and costs of sale, there was a surplus of £500, held by Peter's solicitors. The mortgagees tell you that the redemption figure will increase by around £700 per month, which means Peter could very easily end up with a debt, not a surplus, on the sale.

You contact Miss Dodge who confirms her action and her intentions stating that she wants to 'test the market for a few weeks with a proper agent' although of course will sell to Peter's purchaser if his is the best offer. Peter's purchaser is genuine, and keen to go ahead but needs to act fast as he has tenants lined up to move in next week-end.

(i) Explain to Peter what is meant by a void disposition of property as defined by s284. **(2 marks)**

(ii) Assuming that the contract for the sale of Flat 1 might be caught by s 284 advise Peter what remedy would be available to him or to his purchaser. **(1 mark)**

(iii) What evidence would be needed to support any application that either party might make? **(2 marks)**

(b) Peter is also furious that his new bank account has been frozen. He opened it four months ago (when he realised bankruptcy was inevitable) with £13,500 transferred on closure of his old business account at a different bank. Basically, he stopped taking on new work six months ago and concentrated on finishing all of his existing jobs and collecting in all monies owed to him, raising £25,000 in total. Of that money, £9,000 was used to clear his business overdraft and loan (both unsecured) at his old bank, £2,500 to pay back his mum before she moved to Spain and the other £13,500 was used to open the new account. There is about £4,000 left in the account. He didn't tell Miss Dodge about the account and can't see what it has to do with her as it is his only source of income.

Peter's estate has scheduled liabilities of £40,000 of which £35,000 is claimed by HMR&C (for estimated assessments of tax for last four years) and the balance to two trade suppliers. There are no scheduled assets other than the £500 surplus on the sale of his flat and held by his solicitor. There is no bank debt.

Peter says he is a victim and that Miss Dodge has no right to 'meddle in his affairs'. He has no intention of working with her as 'she obviously works for the tax man'. He says he doesn't owe the tax people any money - they owe him but no one cares about that. He asks you to take over as trustee.

(i) Explain to Peter his duties and obligations to his trustee, Miss Dodge, and in particular his duty of disclosure. **(2 marks)**

(ii) Explain to Peter the functions of the trustee and outline what rights he might have to ensure the trustee be held accountable for his or her actions. **(2 marks)**

(iii) Explain to Peter why the bank account has been frozen, indicating which transactions Miss Dodge might want to examine and why. **(5 marks)**

(iv) Explain to Peter what action he might take to resolve his tax position **(1 mark)**

(06/07) **(Total 15 marks)**

---

12 An Income Payment Agreement entered into by a bankrupt with his trustee shall not last longer than? (06/06)

(a) Three years after the date of the agreement
(b) Beyond the bankrupt's discharge
(c) Five years after the date of the bankruptcy order
(d) Three years after the date of the bankruptcy order

---

13 What are the main criteria that are required to exist for a transaction which took place before a bankruptcy order to amount to a preference under s 340 Insolvency Act 1986? **(4 marks)**

(06/06)

---

14 If execution is levied upon land belonging to a bankrupt it is not excluded from the estate if: (06/05)

(a) Execution was levied post commencement
(b) A final charging order has been made pre-commencement
(c) A receiver has been appointed pre-commencement
(d) Execution has been completed by seizure pre-commencement
(e) The land was sold before the bankruptcy order was made

---

15 Which of the following time limits is not correct? (06/05)

(a) Transaction at an undervalue – five years pre-petition for bankruptcy
(b) Preference to associate – six months pre bankruptcy order
(c) Transaction defrauding creditors (S423) – No limit
(d) Disposition of property – Between petition and appointment of trustee
(e) Excessive pension contributions – No limit

---

16 If a trustee in bankruptcy becomes aware that the bankrupt has acquired some valuable property, how long does the trustee have to claim the property as 'after-acquired'? (06/05)

(a) 14 days
(b) 28 days
(c) 42 days
(d) Three months
(e) No time limit

---

17 Which of the following statements is not true? (06/04)

A trustee in bankruptcy may disclaim any onerous property even if:

(a) He has taken possession of the property

(b) He has tried to sell it on the open market

(c) He has collected rent due to the estate in respect of the property

(d) He has not disclaimed within 28 days of receipt of a notice requiring a decision as to whether he should disclaim or not

(e) He has sought relief against forfeiting the lease

---

18 Any disposition of property is void (unless ratified by the Court) if it takes place between what dates? (06/04)

(a) The date of the presentation of the petition and the date of the appointment of the trustee
(b) The date of the bankruptcy order and the appointment of the Official Receiver
(c) The date of the bankruptcy order and the appointment of the trustee
(d) The date of the presentation of the petition and the date of the bankruptcy order
(e) The date of the presentation of the petition and the date of the discharge of the bankrupt

---

19 (a) Your principal has been appointed as trustee in bankruptcy of a Mr Jonathon Depp. The official receiver has advised you that Mr Depp has entered into a number of transactions that may not have been in the best interests of the general body of creditors.

Requirement

Set out the steps you would take to make further enquires both of the bankrupt and others in order to uncover as much information as possible about these transactions. **(5 marks)**

(b) From your enquires you establish the following facts:

Mr and Mrs Depp purchased their first house as joint tenants for £100,000 in 1997. They put down a deposit of £10,000 from their joint savings account with the balance being funded by way of a mortgage of £90,000 from the Doubloon Building Society.

In 20X2, Mr Depp went into business on his own account. He obtained a loan for his business of £30,000 from Black Pearl (the Bank). The Bank insisted on taking a charge on Mr and Mrs Depp's house, which Mrs Depp consented to after obtaining independent legal advice. At this time the house was valued at £200,000 and the balance outstanding to Doubloon was £80,000. Mortgage payments were made from the Depps' joint resources.

In 20X6, the Bank borrowing (secured on the house) had increased to £50,000. Mr Depp had other liabilities to various creditors of £50,000 in addition to income tax assessments of some £100,000, although he believed these to be excessive. The house was now worth £300,000 with £70,000 remaining outstanding to Doubloon. Mrs Depp, a lady of independent means, was concerned about her husband's indebtedness and asked him to agree to the house being conveyed into her sole name, in consideration for which she would take on responsibility for the first mortgage and the second charge in favour of the Bank. Mr Depp, (who had no other significant assets), agreed and the house was duly conveyed in accordance with Mrs Depp's wishes. Mr Depp continued to live, with Mrs Depp at the house.

On 22 January 20X9 HMRC presented a bankruptcy petition against Mr Depp and on 5 March 20X9, a bankruptcy order was made. Your principal was subsequently appointed trustee. You have established that the balance outstanding to the first mortgagee is now £50,000, (with all payments since 20X6 solely being made by Mrs Depp), and she also reduced the indebtedness to the bank to £30,000. The house has now increased in value to £350,000.

Requirement

Produce an estimated outcome statement, working from the current property value, setting out what, if anything, you would expect the trustee in bankruptcy to be able to recover from any claim(s) he may have. State the nature of any claim(s) and attach supporting notes to explain your conclusions and any assumptions made. You should not incorporate details of costs. **(7 marks)**

(c) The bankruptcy estate has no funds with which to pursue any claim. Assuming that your firm would not risk funding the proceedings how might funding be arranged to enable any claim to be pursued? **(3 marks)**

(06/04) **(Total 15 marks)**

---

20 A debtor made substantial contributions to his approved pension arrangement some time before being made bankrupt. His trustee is now arguing that the contributions are excessive given the debtor's circumstances at the time the contributions were made and should be recovered for the bankruptcy estate. With reference to the time at which the debtor made the contributions, what 'excess contributions' may the trustee seek to recover? (06/04)

(a) Excess contributions made within the five years preceding the relevant bankruptcy petition
(b) Excess contributions made within the two years preceding the relevant bankruptcy petition
(c) Excess contributions made within the six months preceding the relevant bankruptcy petition
(d) Excess contributions which the debtor made at any time on his own behalf

---

21 As trustee in bankruptcy you have received notice of a debtor's intention to propose an IVA, from the debtor's nominee. You have realised £15,000 from the surrender of a life policy belonging to the debtor's estate. What should you do with the money? (06/04)

(a) Release it to the debtor
(b) Hold it on a designated client account pending the outcome of the IVA creditors meeting
(c) Pay it into the Insolvency Service Account
(d) Forward it to the nominee

---

22 Which of the following is **not** an 'associate' of a bankrupt: (06/04)

(a) An aunt
(b) The wife of a business partner
(c) A cousin
(d) An employee
(e) A former wife

---

23 Your principal has been appointed Trustee of Michael Adams who was made bankrupt on 3 July 20X9. Your principal was appointed on 1 September 20X9. You have obtained the following information:

(a) Michael is married to Denise and they have two young children. Together, they purchased their first home 10 years ago. Despite Michael contributing a greater proportion of the deposit payable towards the purchase price, they agreed that they should own the property, named 'Greystones', as tenants in common in equal shares. The purchase price of Greystones was £75,000, funded by a mortgage with the Cherry & White Building Society of £60,000. Michael contributed £10,000 to the deposit and Denise £5,000.

(b) Michael set up his own business about eight years ago as a sports physiotherapist. Shortly afterwards, he obtained a lucrative contract with a local rugby club in addition to general private client work. He needed to re-equip and decorate his rented premises and obtained a bank loan from Barts Bank of £20,000 for this purpose. The bank insisted on taking a charge on Greystones to secure this borrowing. Denise consented to the granting of the legal charge on the property after taking independent legal advice.

(c) Two years before the bankruptcy order, Michael lost the contract with the rugby club as part of a cost cutting exercise by the club. Following this his business went downhill and he was eventually made bankrupt on a petition presented (on 4 June 20X9) by HM Revenue and Customs.

(d) Denise is a qualified accountant and worked full-time in this career until 20X5. She then reduced her hours to enable her to look after the children who were born in 20X5 and 20X7.

(e) The marriage failed and the couple were permanently separated in September 20X8 when Michael moved out of Greystones. He was unable to contribute towards the mortgage payments to Cherry & White, although he did keep up the payments of loan interest to Barts Bank. Denise returned to full-time work in September 20X8 and paid the interest element of the mortgage with Cherry & White, totalling £2,000 to the date of the bankruptcy order and £2,500 since then. The children have remained at Greystones and Denise has had to pay childcare costs of £100 per week.

(f) In January 20X9, Denise inherited £25,000 from her late mother's estate. She reduced the capital outstanding to the first mortgagee from £60,000 to £50,000. She also paid for a conservatory and patio costing £15,000. Your agents have advised that this had the effect of increasing the value of the property by £8,000, which has been agreed by Denise.

(g) Michael and Denise have just started divorce proceedings. Denise is intending to apply for a property adjustment order seeking the transfer of Greystones into her sole name. There have been no court hearings yet but Michael has indicated he will contest the application.

(h) Denise has made it clear to your principal that she will not agree to a voluntary sale of the property, nor will she be able to buy-out the trustee's interest. In any event, she believes she has a 100% beneficial interest in the property in view of all the payments she has made and the proposed property adjustment order.

Requirement

Part one

(a) Prepare a financial statement showing the respective estimated outcomes for the bankruptcy estate and Denise following possession and sale proceedings by the trustee, taking account of the above and the following information:

(i) The court orders that Denise pays half the legal costs of the trustee's possession proceedings from her interest in the sale proceeds. The costs total £2,500.

(ii) Estate agent's fees will be 2% of the sale price.

(iii) The property sells for £150,000.

(iv) The balances outstanding at the time of sale to the first mortgagee and second chargeholder respectively are £50,000 and £20,000.

(v) There has been no property adjustment order

(vi) Ignore any taxes and Dept BIS fees **(5 marks)**

(b) Prepare supporting notes to explain how you arrive at your conclusions, and state any assumptions that you are making. **(5 marks)**

(c) According to the provisions of the Insolvency Act 1986 what matters should the court have taken into account in deciding whether or not to grant an Order for Possession in respect of Greystones, in accordance with the trustee's application? **(2½ marks)**

Part two

Your principal is trustee of the bankruptcy estate of Bryan Adams who jointly owns a property with his wife, in which they both reside, (and did so since prior to the presentation of the bankruptcy petition). The bankrupt's interest in the property forms part of the bankruptcy estate and has been agreed at 50% of the equity. The total equity has been estimated at £5,000 based on an open market valuation but nothing if the property was to be sold following proceedings by the trustee for possession and sale. Your principal wishes to obtain his release from office without realising the interest in the property, as he does not believe it will be cost effective to do so.

Prepare a memo to your principal setting out the main options available to him as trustee to enable him to obtain his release. **(2½ marks)**

(06/04) **(Total 15 marks)**

---

24 A bankruptcy order was made on 29 May 20X9. Which one of the following assets will not be automatically excluded from the bankruptcy estate? (06/02)

(a) The bankrupt's personal pension policy (benefits will not become payable for at least five years)

(b) Tools of trade necessary for use by the bankrupt personally in his business

(c) Property held by the bankrupt on trust for another person

(d) A car (not of 'excess value') required by the bankrupt for his own use for domestic (not business) purposes

(e) None of the above

---

25 What is the relevant period for restrictions on dispositions of property by a person who is adjudged bankrupt (s284 of the Act)? (06/02)

(a) The period of six months immediately preceding the date of the presentation of a petition for a bankruptcy order

(b) The period of six months immediately preceding the date of the making of a bankruptcy order

(c) The day of the presentation of the petition for a bankruptcy order to the date of the bankruptcy order

(d) The day of the presentation of the petition for a bankruptcy order to the date of the vesting of the bankruptcy estate in a trustee

(e) The date of the bankruptcy order to the date upon which the bankrupt obtains his discharge from bankruptcy

---

26 Assuming a bankrupt was insolvent at the time of, or became insolvent as a consequence of, entering into a transaction at an undervalue, the 'relevant time' for a transaction at an undervalue is which of the following? (06/02)

(a) The period of six months ending with the day of the presentation of the bankruptcy petition on which an individual is adjudged bankrupt

(b) The period of six months ending with the day of the making of the bankruptcy order

(c) The period of two years ending with the day of the presentation of the bankruptcy petition on which an individual is adjudged bankrupt

(d) The period of five years ending with the day of the presentation of the bankruptcy petition on which an individual is adjudged bankrupt

(e) The period of five years ending with the day of the making of the bankruptcy order

---

27 (a) James Cannon was made bankrupt following a creditors petition on 2 March 20X9. He was a director of a UK subsidiary of a US parent company. The company is engaged in manufacturing chemical products.

James earns £2,500 per month (net of PAYE & NIC) and it is understood that the parent company are happy to provide him with an employment contract as Sales Manager at the same rate of pay notwithstanding he can no longer act as a director. He will continue to have the use of an all expenses paid company car.

He is also paid commission at the rate of £1,000 (gross) per month by a Belgian company for consultancy fees. This is paid into an account in his name in Belgium.

James has provided the Official Receiver with an estimate of his monthly outgoings as follows:

	£
Mortgage	1,250
Life insurance	175
Pension	250
Council tax and Utility Bills	1,000
Motor expenses	100
Insurances	100
Housekeeping	500
School fees	1,000

Your principal has accepted the appointment as James Cannon's Trustee in Bankruptcy following an application to the Secretary of State on the basis that there is equity in matrimonial property and he may be able to make voluntary contributions out of income.

Since appointment, you ascertain that Mrs Cannon has earnings of £2,000 per month (net of PAYE & NIC) from a limited company in which she hold 100% of the shares.

Requirement

(i) Advise your principal of the detailed steps to be taken to obtain an Income Payments Order and the likely level that might be determined **(5 marks)**

(ii) The Official Receiver advises your office that the bankrupt has not cooperated with him and that he intends to make application to suspend the discharge period. What steps could you take as Trustee to obtain more information regarding his affairs? **(3 marks)**

(b) You are Trustee in Bankruptcy in a case where an amount of £32,000 is available for distribution to unsecured creditors. A number of creditors have not submitted claims and you have queries on a number of proof of debt forms which have been submitted. It is understood that the bankrupt disputes certain claims.

Requirement

(i) Explain the steps to be taken to clarify the position to enable you to finalise the creditor schedule. **(3 marks)**

(ii) Provide your principal with a closing checklist of the procedures to be carried out to conclude the administration of the case, following the settling of the creditor schedule, thereby enabling the Trustee to obtain his release from office. **(4 marks)**

(06/02) **(Total 15 marks)**

---

28 A Bankruptcy Order was made against Mr Powell on 27 July 20X9 following the presentation of a petition on the 10 June 20X9. Your principal has been appointed Trustee in bankruptcy. Mr Powell has contacted your office and requested a meeting with you to discuss his affairs.

At the meeting you ascertain certain information. Mr Powell, is a self-employed long distance lorry driver and is 55 years old. It is Mr Powell's intention to continue working as a lorry driver.

Mr Powell's assets comprise of the following:

	£
Pension fund	150,000
Box Van (L Reg)	2,000
Cash at Bank	1,256
Matrimonial home – Jointly owned	150,000
(Mortgage of £55,000)	
(Business loan of £20,000)	

The following transactions occurred in the twelve months to the date of the presentation of the petition:

Payment of £50,000 to the pension scheme following the disposal of Mr Powell's fleet of articulated lorries.

A diamond ring costing £5,000 for his wife's 50th birthday

Payment of £20,000 in respect of his daughter's wedding.

Payment of £15,000 to Mr Elliott, a creditor and cousin of Mrs Powell. Mrs Powell has indicated that since paying the money to Mr Elliott, Mr Elliott has been noticeable by his absence and neither she, nor Mr Powell, had spoken to him for several months.

(a) Advise Mr Powell as to the assets which will comprise his estate in Bankruptcy and why assets may be excluded. **(3 marks)**

(b) What factors should be taken into consideration in calculating the Trustee's interest in the matrimonial home? **(4 marks)**

(c) In respect of the transactions referred to above briefly describe what remedies are available to the Trustee and what investigations you would undertake? **(8 marks)**

(06/01) **(Total 15 marks)**

---

29 Within what period must a bankrupt notify his trustees in relation to after acquired property? (06/00)

(a) Seven days
(b) 14 days
(c) 21 days
(d) 28 days
(e) Two months

---

30 Which of the following can be done, without leave of the court, after an application for administration has been made, but before an administration order is granted or dismissed? (06/00)

(a) A resolution be passed or order made for the winding up of the company
(b) Security be enforced over the company's property
(c) The appointment of an administrator by a QFC holder
(d) Execution be continued against the company's property

---

31 Within what period to the date of the bankruptcy may a trustee make application to the court in relation to an extortionate credit transaction? Is it: (06/00)

(a) Three years
(b) Five years
(c) Seven years
(d) 10 years

---

22 Bankrupt's home

1 Mike, who has been running a business on a self-employed basis as a motorbike mechanic, has recently been made bankrupt and your principal has been appointed Trustee. You have been asked to administer the case and have ascertained the following information:

- The bankruptcy order was made on 1st March 2011 on a creditor's petition presented by HM Revenue & Customs in respect of unpaid schedule D tax going back to 2006/07. The amount of the petition debt is in the region of £126,000, some of it based on assessments as Mike has not been good at submitting his accounts and tax returns.
- The petition was presented on 27 November 2010 and there were two adjournments before the bankruptcy order was made.
- Mike has other unsecured debts totalling £183,000.
- Mike is married to Tracey. Before they were married, Mike and Tracey decided that they would sell their own properties and pool their resources to buy a new house to set up home. The new house cost £180,000 and they put down £30,000 each from the sale proceeds of their own properties. Tracey was serving overseas in the forces at the time of the purchase and they decided that the property would be put in mike's name to make life easier. However it was always intended that they would own the property jointly although they did not make a formal declaration of trust in favour of Tracey. The house was purchased on 30 July 1995 with the balance of the sale price (£120,000) being funded by a mortgage in Mike's name.
- On Tracey's return from overseas a few months later, the couple married. They set up a joint bank account and all their income was paid into that account. Their household expenses and the mortgage payments were all met from this account. Although their earnings fluctuated from time to time, they both earned similar incomes.
- In 2007 Mike's mother died and he inherited approximately £160,000 from her estate. The couple had always wanted a holiday home in Devon and this was their chance. Mike ignored the fact that he was in arrears (as usual) with his tax affairs and in October 2008, after he had received his inheritance and using that money, together with Tracey he purchased a small terraced cottage for £150,000. He was able to take advantage of the depressed housing market and got a 'good deal'.
- It was the couple's intention that the property be owned by them together and accordingly it was purchased by them as joint tenants. They have let the property (through an agent) for much of the time since they bought it and that income (net of all letting costs) has been paid into their joint bank account.
- Mike and Tracey do not have any other significant assets apart from £6,000 in their joint bank account. You are aware that the current value of the property is in the region of £260,000 and the balance outstanding to the mortgagee is £110,000.

(a) Prepare a memo to the Trustee stating with reasons what interest you believe Mike has in the matrimonial home. Clearly state any assumptions. **(6 marks)**

(b) Advise the Trustee on Mike's interest in the holiday home. Its value remains in the region of £150,000 and it is free of mortgage or any charges. Is there any way in which the value of Mike's interest which now vests in the Trustee can be enhanced for the benefit of Mike's creditors? If so, state how this could be achieved. **(7 marks)**

(c) If there is £6,000 in the joint bank account, comment on whether, and if so how, the Trustee might be able to claim more than a half share of that balance for the estate. **(2 marks)**

(6/11) **(Total 15 marks)**

2 Where a trustee intends to claim an interest in a dwelling house what information should be included in a S283A notice issued to the bankrupt, his spouse or partner or former spouse or partner? (6/10)

(4 marks)

---

3 Which one of the following statements concerning the effect of a s313 'charging order' is false? (6/09)

(a) A charging order secures a trustee's interest in a dwelling house on behalf of the bankruptcy estate

(b) A dwelling house means a property which is occupied by the bankrupt or by his spouse or former spouse or by his civil partner or former civil partner

(c) Once a charging order is obtained the property will remain vested in the trustee on behalf of the bankruptcy estate

(d) The amount secured by the charging order is the value of the bankrupt's interest in the property as at the date of that order (plus interest thereafter)

---

4 Which ONE of the following assets would fall under the three year time limit provisions imposed by s283A? (6/09)

(a) Interest in a dwelling house occupied as the main residence by the bankrupt's former common law partner

(b) Interest in a dwelling house occupied as the main residence by the bankrupt's former spouse

(c) Interest in a building plot purchased for the family home

(d) Interest in an investment property

---

5 Frederick Smith was made bankrupt yesterday and your principal was appointed his trustee at the request of the petitioner and major creditor, ABC Builders. The handover note from the Official Receiver advises that there is a possible interest in property.

Your principal has left a further file note from the petitioners stating 'He (Mr Smith) has more than he's letting on – he gave his ex the lot and without any fuss. His girlfriend's house, where he lives, is worth a bit – surely there must be some interest there?'

There are no hard assets of any note (£30 premium bonds, 100 ordinary shares in a telecoms company and his works van, a Ford Dodge 2004) and from the income and expenditure account supplied, Mr Smith doesn't have any spare cash either.

Your principal has asked you to find out whether there is any likelihood of any recovery in this case.

You call Mr Smith in for interview. He tells you:

- He is a self employed builder/plumber and has been in business on his own account for the whole of his working life (23 years – he is now 43)
- He has debts of £50,000, (£35,000 of which is owed to ABC) which all relate to a failed building project in 20X5 on which he was contracted to carry out all the structural work and plumbing for the developers, HomesInc. HomesInc went into liquidation in mid 20X6 at which point ABC started to pressure him for payment. The only asset in Homes Inc was the property which was finally sold this January by the liquidator at a small shortfall. Mr Smith said that as soon as ABC realised there would be no dividend they issued a bankruptcy petition against him, at the end of January.

- The financial strain put an end to his marriage and he was divorced at the end of 20X6. He consented to the matrimonial home, 1 Old Way, being transferred into his wife's sole name to speed things up with the divorce and ensure that his family would keep a roof over their heads. He said that he'd lost enough already and was not going to let the house go too. His ex wife lives there still with their three children aged 18, 16 and 10 who are all in full time education. The house is worth £150,000 and was purchased in their joint names in 19X6 using the surplus on the sale of their first home as a deposit. The mortgage is now around £50,000 and has been paid by his ex wife since he left the house two years ago. She has paid off about £2,000 capital in that period.
- He lives at 1 New Road with his partner of two years, Mary Wright. He has no legal interest in the house which is in Ms Wright's sole name and which she bought 18 months ago, using her own funds for the deposit. Mr Smith pays all the bills (utilities and telephone) which amount to an average £400 a month in lieu of rent. They share costs for food and general living expenses. Ms Wright pays the mortgage and related insurances out of her income as a financial adviser.

Requirement

(a) In relation to 1 Old Way:

(i) How might the trustee claim an interest in the former matrimonial home 1 Old Way? **(2 marks)**

(ii) Using only the information above, estimate the value of the trustee's interest in 1 Old Way clearly explaining your reasons. **(1 mark)**

(iii) Outline how the trustee could protect his interest in 1 Old Way. **(2 marks)**

(iv) Outline what steps the trustee might take to realise his interest in 1 Old Way. **(2 marks)**

(v) Outline what arguments the ex wife might have to defeat or reduce the trustee's claim against 1 Old Way. **(2 marks)**

(b) In relation to 1 New Road

(i) How likely is it that the trustee could successfully pursue a claim to an interest in 1 New Road? Give your reason(s). **(2 marks)**

Giving your reasons, explain whether either of the following facts might create an interest for the trustee in relation to 1 New Road:

(ii) Mr Smith had built a conservatory (at her expense but using his labour) onto the property and which had increased its value by £5,000. **(2 marks)**

(iii) Mr Smith had contributed to the deposit on the purchase of the property. **(2 marks)**

Give reasons for your answers.

(06/08) **(Total 15 marks)**

---

6 Under Section 283A of the Act, the trustee in Bankruptcy in a post Enterprise Act case has how long to deal with his interest in the debtor's dwelling house? (06/07)

(a) One year from the date of the bankruptcy
(b) One year from the date of his appointment
(c) Three years from the date of the bankruptcy
(d) Three years from the date of his appointment

7 The principle of equity of exoneration enables which one of the following results? (06/07)

(a) A person to claim an interest in a property through direct contribution

(b) A person to claim an interest in a property through indirect contribution

(c) A person to marshal all or part of a secured debt against another person thus increasing their own share in the equity

(d) A person to treat a secured debt as unsecured thus increasing the available equity in the property

---

8 (a) Give four examples of information or documentary evidence that a court might require when asked to consider an application by a trustee in bankruptcy for an order for sale of an interest in a dwelling house. **(2 marks)**

(b) Give four examples of action that a trustee might take to prevent s283A(2), the re-vesting of an interest in a dwelling house, coming into play, before the relevant time limit expires. (06/07) **(2 marks)**

(Total 4 marks)

---

9 A trustee is required to give notice that a dwelling house is subject to the provisions on ceasing to form part of a bankrupt's estate after three years (unless otherwise dealt with). By when should this notice be served on the bankrupt or spouse/ civil partner? (06/06)

(a) Six months after the trustee's appointment
(b) One year after the trustee's appointment
(c) Not later than six months prior to the expiry of the three year period
(d) Not later than 14 days prior to the expiry of the three year period

---

10 A trustee wishes to apply for a charge on an interest in a jointly owned dwelling house which forms part of the bankruptcy estate with which he is dealing. How much will the charged value normally be? (06/06)

(a) The value of the bankrupt's interest in the property as at the date of the charging order together with interest from that date at the prescribed rate

(b) The value of the bankrupt's interest in the property as at the date of the bankruptcy order together with interest from that date at the prescribed rate

(c) The open market value of the property as at the date of the charging order together with interest from that date at the prescribed rate

(d) The total amount of the unsecured creditors claims as at the date of the bankruptcy order together with interest from that date at the prescribed rate

---

11 Your principal is acting as trustee in bankruptcy of a bankrupt's estate and asks you to advise him on his options in relation to dealing with the bankrupt's interest in a property.

The property is the dwelling house of the bankrupt, his wife and their three children. The bankrupt and his wife own the property jointly and have done so for a number of years. The bankrupt presented his own bankruptcy petition on 25 May 20X7 and he was duly made bankrupt on that date.

Your principal was appointed trustee by the Secretary of State on 3 August 20X8. Initial attempts to realise the bankrupt's interest in the property have been resisted by the bankrupt and his wife.

Your principal says he has heard about something called the three year 'use it or lose it' rule and wonders if this should be of any concern to him.

Part one

Write a memo to your principal to advise him on the following:

(a) The key practical steps involved in establishing the extent and value of the trustee's interest in the property. **(5 marks)**

(b) The statutory options which are open to the trustee in dealing with his interest in the property and what he should do to avoid the property re-vesting in the bankrupt in accordance with the 'three year' provisions as set out in s. 283A of the IA 86. **(7 marks)**

Part two

If the trustee's interest in a dwelling house is of no realisable value (eg the balance outstanding to the mortgagee exceeds the property value), how may a trustee abandon his interest back to the bankrupt if he doesn't wish to wait for the property to re-vest in the bankrupt in accordance with the 'three year' provisions? Why might this be advantageous? **(3 marks)**

(06/06) **(Total 15 marks)**

---

12 The 'prescribed amount' below which the court will not grant a possession order in respect of a bankrupt's matrimonial home is: (06/05)

(a) £20,000
(b) £5,000
(c) £2,000
(d) £1,000
(e) No limit

---

13 In accordance with the principle of 'equitable accounting' where the property is jointly owned by the bankrupt and spouse, the non-bankrupt spouse may be credited with payments made for which one of the following? (06/05)

(a) 50% of the costs of improvements (or half the increase in value if lower)
(b) 100% of any repayments of the capital element of the mortgage liability
(c) 50% of any repayments of the interest element of the mortgage liability
(d) Occupational rent

---

14 Mr and Mrs Lea reside in a semi-detached house in Chelbury. They have one child, a daughter of 14 called Rosie.

Mr Lea is made bankrupt on 29 May 2009 and your principal has been appointed trustee at the first meeting of creditors.

You are currently aware of the following information:

- Mr Lea has estimated the value of the property to be in the region of £150,000
- The property is subject to one mortgage in favour of the Chelbury Building Society to secure borrowings of £80,000. The mortgage payments are up to date.
- Mr Lea believes the property insurance was arranged through the mortgagee.
- Mr Lea advises that the property was purchased (five years ago) by him and his wife as joint tenants in equal shares.

Requirement

You are required to prepare a memo to your principal setting out the key steps for protecting, establishing and realising his interest in the property. You should briefly comment on the different options that may be available to realise the trustee's interest.

(06/05) **(15 marks)**

---

15 Mr Green (a discharged bankrupt) has a property at 10 Gertrude Gardens, which he values at £100,000, and claims that charges on the property total £110,000. He requests that the Trustee release his interest in the property upon payment of the Trustee's legal fees, due to the absence of equity in the property.

What **two** things **must** be independently ascertained prior to consideration of Mr Green's offer?

(i) Mr Green's date of birth.
(ii) The value of the property.
(iii) The level of the outstanding charges upon the property.
(iv) Whether any dependants live in the property.

(a) (i) and (iv)
(b) (iv) and (ii)
(c) (iv) and (iii)
(d) (ii) and (iii) **(2 marks)**

(06/01)

---

23 Powers of the trustee

1 Who may be ordered to attend a private examination under S366 of the Act? (6/10)

(4 marks)

---

2 (a) Give two conditions that must be satisfied to enable the trustee in bankruptcy to exercise his power to appoint the bankrupt to assist him in the carrying out of his functions as trustee. **(2 marks)**

(b) Give two circumstances in which a trustee is prevented from disclaiming property **(2 marks)**

(06/08) **(Total 4 marks)**

---

3 A trustee in bankruptcy has a general power to disclaim onerous property under which section of the Act? (06/06)

(a) s314
(b) s315
(c) s313
(d) s322
(e) s324

---

4 From which section of the Act does a trustee in bankruptcy take his power to disclaim onerous property? (06/04)

(a) s314
(b) s315
(c) s316
(d) s317
(e) s318

---

5 Schedule 5 to the Act sets out the powers of a Trustee in Bankruptcy. Name four powers which are set out in this Schedule under the category of General Powers. (06/13)

(4 marks)

---

24 Proofs of debt – bankruptcy

1 Which one of the following are not entitled to view the proofs of debt lodged with a Trustee? (6/12)

(a) A creditor who has submitted a proof
(b) A person acting on behalf of a creditor who has submitted a proof
(c) The debtor
(d) A creditor who has a claim but has not yet lodged a proof

---

2 Which one of the following is a provable debt in bankruptcy proceedings in accordance with the Rules? (6/11)

(a) A parking fine
(b) Monthly maintenance assessment payments
(c) A confiscation Order under the Proceeds of Crime Act 2002
(d) A maintenance assessment lump sum award

---

3 Don Brown consulted your firm when a bankruptcy petition was served on him. As an accountant he can't risk bankruptcy. He has appointed a partner in your firm as his nominee. An interim order has been obtained and a meeting of creditors called to approve proposals for an individual voluntary arrangement under s257.

You have been asked to prepare the voting schedule for the meeting.

Indicate the value at which you would admit the following claims for voting purposes and give your reasons.

(a) Claim of Zehan Butar for 60,000 yen for goods supplied.

Exchange rate as at date of presentation of bankruptcy petition 100 yen/£
Exchange rate as at date of interim order 200 yen/£
Exchange rate as at date of s257 creditors' meeting 300 yen/£

(b) Big Bank plc – hold a mortgage over Mr Brown's house. The house is on the market for sale (voluntarily) at £200,000, a realistic price to achieve as quick a sale as possible. Big Bank are owed (as at today's date) £192,000. On the face of it they are fully secured but they feel that in this market they will almost certainly have a shortfall, although the amount cannot be ascertained until such time as a sale is concluded.

They want to vote at the meeting and have tabled some modifications.

(6/09) **(4 marks)**

---

4 Which one of the following statements is true in relation to the distribution of a dividend by the trustee? (06/08)

(a) The trustee must declare a dividend within four months of the first meeting of creditors

(b) The trustee must declare a dividend whenever he has sufficient monies in hand for the purpose and after allowing for likely expenses of the bankruptcy;

(c) The trustee may declare a dividend at any time and is not obliged to make any provision for creditors who have not yet proved their debts

(d) The trustee may recall a dividend if creditors come to light who had not proved before the declaration of that dividend

---

5 A trustee gives notice of his intention to declare a dividend. Within what period of time should the trustee declare that dividend? (06/06)

(a) Within the period of two months from the date of the notice
(b) Within the period of two months from the last date for proving specified in the notice
(c) Within 21 days from the date of the date of the notice
(d) There is no time limit

---

6 No member of a partnership being wound up under The Insolvent Partnerships Order 1994 may prove for a debt due to him in competition with the joint creditors unless certain circumstances apply. Which of the following is a valid circumstance for this purpose? (06/06)

(a) The debt has arisen as a result of an obligation for maintenance under the Child Support Act 1991

(b) The debt has arisen in the ordinary course of a business carried on separately from the partnership

(c) The debt has arisen as a result of a damages claim against the partnership

(d) The debt does not fall due for payment until a future time

---

7 Which of the following is a provable debt? (06/04)

(a) A fine imposed for a driving offence
(b) A claim for maintenance under the Child Support Act 1991
(c) A debt payable at a future time
(d) An obligation from a confiscation order under the Drug Trafficking Offences Act 1986

---

8 As trustee you have just paid a first dividend. A creditor notices he has not proved for all of the debt due to him and now wishes to do so. Advise what, if anything, the creditor can do to pursue the related dividend on the balance of his claim and the effect any possible payment would have on any further dividend. (06/04) **(3 marks)**

---

9 **Part One**

Your principal has been appointed trustee in bankruptcy and has asked you to assist him with adjudicating on the following claims for dividend purposes. The bankruptcy order was made on 26 May 20X9 pursuant to a creditor's petition presented on 17 April 20X9. Explain how you would deal with each of the following claims:

(a) A creditor submits a proof of debt in respect of a liability incurred by the debtor on 15 May 20X3. The creditor has not issued legal proceedings to recover the debt. The debtor has included the debt in his statement of affairs, marked as 'disputed'. **(1 mark)**

(b) A claim which includes interest which was not provided for in the original contract. Attached to the proof is a copy of a letter to the debtor advising that as the debt had not been paid the creditor was going to charge interest at 10% from the date the debt was incurred until payment. The interest on the proof has been calculated at that rate from the date of the debt, to the date of the bankruptcy order. **(1 mark)**

(c) A claim by a creditor in respect of goods ordered on 1 June 20X9, with payment falling due 30 days thereafter. **(1 mark)**

(d) The debtor's spouse has lodged a proof of debt in respect of a personal loan made to her husband before they were married. They were married three months before the date of the bankruptcy order. **(1 mark)**

(e) A creditor has lodged a proof of debt in respect of goods supplied. The creditor had an arrangement with the bankrupt whereby the bankrupt supplied various finished products to him. In this respect the creditor owes money to the bankruptcy estate which the trustee has been seeking to collect as a book debt. **(1 mark)**

Part one total 5 marks

Part Two

The trustee wishes to convene a general meeting of creditors to consider a resolution to approve the basis of his remuneration.

(a) What matters should the trustee have regard to when convening the meeting and what should be stated in the notice of the meeting to creditors? **(2 marks)**

(b) At the meeting, you are required to advise the trustee on the adjudication for voting purposes of the following proxies/creditors claims:

- (i) A proxy in favour of the chairman supported by a proof of debt for an estimated sum but the value of the claim has yet to be ascertained. The proxy directs the chairman to vote in favour of the remuneration resolution. **(1 mark)**
- (ii) A proxy in favour of the chairman directing the chairman to vote against the resolution, supported by a proof of debt disclosing that the creditor holds security (valued by him) in respect of part of the debt. **(1 mark)**
- (iii) A proxy in favour of the chairman giving discretion to the chairman on how to vote on the remuneration resolution. **(1 mark)**
- (iv) A creditor, who is a sole-trader, attends the meeting in person without lodging a proxy. He has previously lodged a valid proof of debt. He wishes to vote against the remuneration resolution. **(1 mark)**
- (v) A company officer attends the meeting in person on behalf of his company without lodging a proxy. The company has previously lodged a valid proof of debt. He wishes to vote in favour of the remuneration resolution. **(1 mark)**
- (vi) A properly completed faxed proxy in favour of the chairman is received (by the deadline for the meeting) from a creditor. The original proxy has not been received by the time of the meeting. The proxy directs the chairman to vote in favour of the remuneration resolution. **(1 mark)**

(c) If the chairman of a meeting is in doubt whether a proof should be admitted or rejected, what should he do and what may subsequently happen? **(1 mark)**

(d) What constitutes a quorum for the purposes of a general meeting of creditors? **(1 mark)**

Part two total 10 marks

(06/04) **(Total 15 marks)**

10 Who in a bankruptcy, from the following list, has the right to review proof of debt forms? (06/01)

(i) The debtor.
(ii) Proving creditors with claims admitted.
(iii) Creditors with rejected claims.
(iv) The agents of (i) and (ii).

(a) (i) only
(b) (ii) and (iii) only
(c) All the above
(d) (i), (ii) and (iv) only

---

11 Which one of the following is not a non-provable debt in a bankruptcy? (06/13)

(a) A fine imposed for any offence
(b) An obligation to pay a lump sum arising under an Order in family proceedings
(c) An obligation to make monthly payments under an Order in family proceedings
(d) An obligation arising under a confiscation order make under the Drug Offences Act

---

12 What are the required contents of a proof of debt form to be lodged by a creditor in bankruptcy proceedings in accordance with the Rules? (06/13) **(4 marks)**

---

25 Discharge and annulment

1 On what grounds may the Court annul a bankruptcy order under S282 of the Act? (6/12)

(2 marks)

---

2 Where an IVA is approved after a bankruptcy order has been made at a time when the debtor is an undischarged bankrupt, the Court may order the following, apart from which one? (6/11)

(a) Annul the bankruptcy order

(b) Give directions on the conduct of the bankruptcy

(c) Give directions on the administration of the bankrupt's estate to facilitate the implementation of the IVA

(d) Grant the bankrupt's discharge from bankruptcy

---

3 A Bankruptcy Restrictions Order may be made only on the application of which one of the following? (06/08)

(a) The Secretary of State
(b) The Trustee, other than the Official Receiver
(c) The Official Receiver in his capacity as Trustee
(d) The petitioning creditor

---

4 Which one of the following statements is false? (06/08)

(a) The individual insolvency register is maintained by the Secretary of State

(b) The individual insolvency register contains information on bankruptcies and on individual voluntary arrangements

(c) Bankruptcy restrictions orders are recorded in the bankruptcy restrictions register

(d) Bankruptcy restrictions orders are recorded in the individual insolvency register

---

5 Discharge from Bankruptcy has the effect of? (06/07)

(a) Releasing the estate back to the debtor
(b) Releasing the debtor from bankruptcy debts
(c) Releasing the Trustee from his obligations
(d) Terminating a creditor's rights to prove in the bankruptcy

---

6 Which one of the following statements relating to annulment of a Bankruptcy order is NOT true? (06/07)

(a) A bankruptcy order cannot be annulled after the date of discharge

(b) The court may annul a bankruptcy order at any time

(c) There is no requirement to advertise an order of annulment

(d) If the Official Receiver has notified creditors of the bankruptcy order, he must forthwith notify them of the annulment

---

7 A Bankruptcy Restrictions Order may be made for how long? (06/05)

(a) Between two and 15 years
(b) 12 months
(c) Up to five years
(d) Between one and 10 years
(e) Between one and 15 years

---

8 When a bankrupt is discharged, all the following statements are true except one. Which one? (06/04)

(a) Discharge does not affect the rights of a secured creditor to enforce his security

(b) Discharge has no affect on the functions of the trustee

(c) Discharge does not release the debtor from any bankruptcy debt which was incurred by the debtor by way of a fraud

(d) Discharge releases the debtor from orders made in matrimonial proceedings

(e) Discharge does not release any person who acted as surety for a debt incurred by the debtor

---

9 Who/which of the following maintains a register of individual voluntary arrangements? (06/04)

(a) The district court in which the relevant debtor resides
(b) The Secretary of State
(c) The Official Receiver
(d) The High Court
(e) None of the above

---

10 An undischarged bankrupt proposes an IVA which is approved by creditors following the making of a bankruptcy order on 2 February 20X9. When can the court consider an application for annulment following the approval, when no appeal against the outcome of the meeting has been lodged? (06/04)

(a) Forthwith after the filing of the chairman's report to court on the outcome of the meeting

(b) Not less than 14 days after the date on which the IVA was approved

(c) Not less than 28 days after the filing of the chairman's report to court on the outcome of the meeting

(d) Not less than 28 days after the date on which the IVA was approved

(e) Forthwith following the Supervisor's final report advising that the arrangement has been successfully completed

---

11 On what grounds may the court annul a bankruptcy order, which is not superseded by an IVA? (06/02) **(2 marks)**

---

12 A bankruptcy order was made on a creditor's petition and a trustee appointed at the first meeting of creditors convened by the Official Receiver. No assets have been realised yet. You are advising the debtor and come to the conclusion that it would be advantageous to both the debtor and his creditors for an IVA to be proposed and for the bankruptcy order to be annulled. What costs or other liabilities would you expect to be met out of the first assets to be realised? (Ignore the nominee's and supervisor's fees.) (06/02) **(3 marks)**

---

13 A Bankruptcy Order was wrongly issued against Mr Block on a debt owed by a third party, which he did not guarantee. He applies to court for an order annulling his Bankruptcy.

What **must** a Trustee report to court in the debtor's subsequent Section 282(1)(a) annulment application? (06/01)

(a) The bankrupt's conduct
(b) All assets, liabilities and costs of the estate
(c) Both of the above
(d) None of the above

---

26 Vacation of office – trustee

1 You have convened a final meeting of creditors to resolve that you be released as trustee. Only one creditor votes, representing less than one-tenth of the value of the bankrupt's creditors. This creditor votes against you receiving your release so how do you now obtain this? (06/04)

(a) Release deemed effective as less than one-tenth of bankrupt's creditors have voted against
(b) Apply to the Official Receiver for the release
(c) Apply to the Court for release
(d) Apply to Secretary of State for release
(e) Reconvene final meeting, having resolved issues with creditor who voted against

---

2 If no creditors attend a final meeting, in person or by proxy, what must the Trustee do to obtain his release from office? (06/01)

(a) Give all creditors notice of an inquorate meeting, and notice that he resigns as trustee.
(b) Report to the Court that a final meeting was summonsed but that no quorum was present.
(c) Write to the Official Receiver to obtain sanction for his release.
(d) Apply to the Secretary of State.
(e) None of the above.

---

27 Individual voluntary arrangements

1 In a protocol compliant IVA what do the standard conditions state is the discretion given to the Supervisor with regard to the admission of claims in an Arrangement? (6/12) **(2 marks)**

---

2 If an Interim Order is in place for a proposed IVA, how many days prior to its expiry should the Nominee lodge his report to Court? (6/11)

(a) 5 business days
(b) 2 business days
(c) 2 days
(d) 5 days

---

3 Which one of the following statements in relation to a debtor who has deliberately omitted assets or creditors in order to gain approval of his proposals for a voluntary arrangement is true? (06/08)

(a) The debtor will have committed a civil offence preventing him from entering into this or any other arrangement for 12 months

(b) The debtor will have committed a civil offence terminating any approved voluntary arrangement

(c) The debtor will have committed a criminal offence (with a maximum penalty of seven years imprisonment and fine) only where the proposals have been approved

(d) The debtor will have committed a criminal offence (with a maximum penalty of seven years imprisonment and fine) whether or not his proposals are approved by creditors

---

4 How much is the Individual Voluntary Arrangement Registration Fee? (06/08)

(a) £5
(b) £10
(c) £15
(d) £20

---

5 Write a memo to your principal setting out what should be included in a proposal for an individual voluntary arrangement commenting on both practical and statutory matters. **(15 marks)**

(06/06)

---

6 Which of the following is not an advantage of an IVA? (06/05)

(a) Flexibility, proposals can be tailored to suit the particular circumstances of the debtor
(b) Interim Order protects assets while proposals are considered
(c) Debtor not formally subject to bankruptcy restrictions, eg on obtaining credit
(d) The debtor's interest in his house is automatically exempt
(e) May be possible to preserve professional status

---

7 You and your principal are preparing for a meeting with a Mr Bob Bodgit who was the director and main shareholder of a limited company which carried on business as general builders. The company has gone into creditors voluntary liquidation with a local firm of Insolvency Practitioners who have referred him to you for advice on his personal financial circumstances. They have indicated to you that he may wish to enter into an Individual Voluntary Arrangement (IVA) with his creditors.

Mr Bodgit has personal guarantee liabilities resulting from the failure of his company totalling £60,000. In addition he has incurred substantial personal loan and credit card liabilities in his name as a result of not drawing his salary from the company as well as paying certain of the company suppliers from his own funds. These debts total approximately £100,000.

Mr Bodgit is married with two young children. His house is worth approximately £100,000 and there is a mortgage of £85,000. The property is owned in the joint names of himself and his wife.

Mr Bodgit generally has a good reputation in the local building industry. In reliance on this he is in the process of setting up a new building company with a handful of employees. He has secured a new contract with a major local developer in the company's name which he believes will enable him to draw a salary of about £30,000 a year from the company.

Mrs Bodgit has part-time earnings of about £16,000 a year as a teacher.

Mr Bodgit owns a Porsche Boxster motor car worth approximately £15,000 which he apparently needs to commute to work. The car, which is his pride and joy, is free of finance.

Requirement

Set out in a memo to your principal the main advantages and disadvantages of a voluntary arrangement for Mr Bodgit and his creditors, as compared to bankruptcy proceedings.
(06/05) **(15 marks)**

---

8 Describe the various roles and duties of an insolvency practitioner (IP) when an individual approaches him/her with a view to proposing an individual voluntary arrangement with the individual's creditors, paying particular attention to the following:

(a) The IP's initial contact with the debtor
(b) The position of any third parties who may be affected
(c) Consideration of the need for an Interim Order
(d) The Statement of Affairs **(15 marks)**

(06/04)

---

9 If a debtor has acted to the detriment of his creditors in disposing of his assets for less than their value, yet still wishes to propose an Individual Voluntary Arrangement, what is the correct course of action for him/her? (06/01)

(a) Not reveal the dealings unless creditors enquire

(b) Make himself bankrupt in order to allow a trustee to challenge the transaction

(c) Disclose these dealings to his creditors, openly addressing the matter

(d) Sue the third party for recovery of the assets, in order to include them in the arrangement

---

28 Individual voluntary arrangement procedures

1 Where an Interim Order is in force, which one of the following statements is not true? (6/12)

(a) No bankruptcy petition may be presented against the debtor
(b) No possession proceedings may be commenced against the debtor's property by a mortgagee
(c) No execution or legal process may be commenced or continued without leave of Court
(d) No landlord may exercise any right of forfeiture by peaceful re-entry without leave of Court

---

2 Which of the following is not a formal requirement of the Act which the Court must be satisfied with before making an Interim Order for a proposed IVA? (6/11)

(a) The debtor intends to make a proposal to his creditors

(b) On the day of the application the debtor was an undischarged bankrupt or able to petition for bankruptcy

(c) The major creditor(s) have indicated its/their willingness to consent to the proposed IVA

(d) No previous application for an Interim Order has been made in the preceding 12 months

---

3 In IVA proceedings, who may chair the creditors' meeting to consider the debtor's proposals? (6/11) **(2 marks)**

---

4 Where an Interim Order is obtained in respect of IVA proceedings, what specific matters should be included in the nominee's report to Court under S256(1)? (6/10) **(2 marks)**

---

5 At a creditors' meeting to approve a debtor's proposal for an IVA, what is the requisite majority to pass a modification to the proposals? (6/09)

(a) three-quarters in value of the creditors voting on the resolution
(b) one half in value of the creditors voting on the resolution
(c) three-quarters in number of the creditors voting on the resolution
(d) one half in number of the creditors voting on the resolution

---

6 A debtor's proposal for an IVA under s256A (no interim order) was rejected. The debtor is not subject to any formal insolvency proceedings and wants to put forward revised proposals for an IVA to his creditors. How long must he wait before he can do so? (6/09)

(a) No time restriction
(b) 12 months from date of the creditors' meeting
(c) 12 months from the date of the proposals
(d) 12 months from the date of filing the chairman's report at court

---

7 Name the four parties on whom notice of an Interim Order must be served by the applicant where the debtor is an undischarged bankrupt. (6/09) **(2 marks)**

---

8 In accordance with SIP 3 and the case of *Re: A Debtor, Greystoke v Hamilton Smith and Others*, state two out of the three conditions that should be met when preparing the nominee's report to court and when considering whether a meeting of creditors should be convened to consider the debtor's proposal for an IVA. (6/09) **(2 marks)**

---

9 Which one of the following statements in relation to the effect of an Interim Order under IA s252 is false? (06/08)

(a) An Interim order will prevent a HCEO from completing execution on behalf of a judgment creditor

(b) An Interim Order will prevent the enforcement of a criminal compensation order

(c) An Interim Order will prevent a landlord from distraining for arrears of rent

(d) An Interim Order will prevent a creditor from petitioning for the debtor's bankruptcy

---

10 Which one of the following statements is false in relation to a so called Fast Track Voluntary Arrangement under Insolvency Act s263A? (06/08)

(a) An interim order must be applied for
(b) An interim order is not needed
(c) Only the Official Receiver can act as nominee
(d) Only undischarged bankrupts can use this procedure

---

11 Where no Interim Order is to be obtained, within what period must the Nominee lodge his report at court? (06/08)

(a) 7 days from receipt of the proposal from the debtor
(b) 14 days from receipt of the proposal from the debtor
(c) 21 days from receipt of the proposal from the debtor
(d) There is no requirement to lodge the report at court

---

12 What change to the IVA process was implemented by the Insolvency Act 2000 with effect from 1 January 2003? (06/07)

(a) Requisite majority for passing all resolutions reduced to 'in excess of 50% in value'

(b) The meeting may be adjourned for up to 28 days with sanction of the court

(c) An interim order is no longer required

(d) An interim order is no longer required where the debtor is already an undischarged bankrupt

---

13 Within what time period must a dissenting creditor who had notice of the meeting apply to court under Section 262 of the Act to challenge the meeting's decision? (06/07)

(a) 14 days from the date of the meeting
(b) 14 days from the date of filing the meeting report at court
(c) 28 days from the date of the meeting
(d) 28 days from the date of filing the meeting report at court

---

14 Conversion from bankruptcy into an IVA will not be available to a debtor in which ONE of the following circumstances? (06/07)

(a) Where the debtor is an undischarged bankrupt
(b) Where the debtor is a discharged bankrupt
(c) Where no interim order has been applied for
(d) Where the Official Receiver is the proposed nominee

---

15 A chairman of a creditors meeting to consider a debtor's proposal for an IVA with an I.O. shall file a copy of his report on the outcome of the meeting at Court within what period following the meeting? (06/06)

(a) 14 days
(b) Forthwith
(c) 28 days
(d) 4 business days

---

16 Which of the following persons may not apply for an interim order where the debtor is an undischarged bankrupt? (06/06)

(a) The debtor
(b) The Official Receiver
(c) The Nominee (if not Trustee)
(d) The Trustee (if there is one)

---

17 Which of the following persons may not apply to court to challenge a decision made at a meeting of creditors to approve a voluntary arrangement? (06/06)

(a) The debtor
(b) The Official Receiver if the debtor is an undischarged bankrupt
(c) A creditor whose claim is fully secured
(d) The Nominee

---

18 What is the effect of an Interim Order made pursuant to s252 of the Insolvency Act 1986? (06/06) **(4 marks)**

---

19 Which SIP governs the content of a nominee's comments on an IVA proposal? (06/05)

(a) SIP 1
(b) SIP 2
(c) SIP 3
(d) SIP 4
(e) SIP 5

---

20 For the purposes of an IVA, what statutory requirements must the debtor comply with to enable him to apply for an Interim Order? (06/05) **(4 marks)**

---

21 Where a debtor is an undischarged bankrupt and subsequently has applied for an interim order because he intends to propose a voluntary arrangement, for the purposes of assessing a pre-bankruptcy order creditor's entitlement to vote, which of the following statements is correct?

The claim is calculated by reference to: (06/04)

(a) The amount of the debt owed at the date of the interim order
(b) The amount of the debt owed at the date of the creditors' meeting
(c) The amount of the debt owed at the date of the bankruptcy order
(d) The amount of the debt owed at the date of the proposal
(e) The amount of the debt owed at the date of the bankruptcy petition

---

22 The effect of an approved proposal for a voluntary arrangement is to bind various parties. Which of the following will not be bound: (06/04)

(a) Those who were entitled to vote at the creditors' meeting
(b) Those who would have been entitled to vote if they had received notice of the meeting
(c) A creditor whose debt is fully secured
(d) The debtor
(e) A creditor with a claim for unliquidated damages

---

23 Under rule 5.6, a nominee may call upon a debtor to provide more information to assist him with the preparation of his report to court. Which one of the following is not included in this rule? (06/04)

(a) Further and better particulars of why the debtor has become insolvent

(b) Whether the debtor has been concerned in the affairs of any company that has become insolvent, where so ever in the world incorporated

(c) Whether the debtor has previously been adjudged bankrupt or entered into an arrangement with his creditors

(d) Particulars of any business with which the debtor's spouse has been concerned

(e) Particulars of any previous proposals for a voluntary arrangement which the debtor has made

---

24 When delivering his proposal to the nominee, a debtor has also to deliver to the nominee a statement of his affairs. Which of the following does not have to appear in that statement? (06/02)

(a) A list of his assets, divided into such categories as are appropriate for easy identification, with estimated values assigned to each category

(b) Particulars of any debts owed by or to the debtor by persons who are associates of his

(c) The names and addresses of the debtor's preferential creditors with the amounts of their respective claims

(d) The names and addresses of the debtor's unsecured creditors with the amounts of their respective claims

(e) The names and addresses of any third parties who are claiming title to or an interest in any of the debtor's assets and details of any such claims

---

25 The creditors meeting to consider Mr Jones' proposal for an Individual Voluntary Arrangement is to be held on 29 May 20X9. If the requisite majority for approval of the arrangement is not obtained on that date, what is the latest date on which an adjourned meeting could be held? (06/02)

(a) 7 June 20X9
(b) 10 June 20X9
(c) 12 June 20X9
(d) 21 June 20X9
(e) 28 June 20X9

---

26 Of the following, who may not apply to court for an interim order to enable a proposal to be made for an IVA? (06/02)

(a) A debtor who is not bankrupt
(b) A debtor who is an undischarged bankrupt
(c) A debtor's trustee in bankruptcy
(d) A creditor who has presented a bankruptcy petition in respect of a debtor
(e) The Official Receiver

---

27 How many voluntary arrangements with an interim order can a debtor propose? (06/01)

(a) As many as he/she likes

(b) One at a time

(c) One per year

(d) One every three years

(e) One IVA per set of creditors: once rejected, no further proposal should ever be made to the same creditor

---

28 If a debtor falsely misleads creditors in his IVA proposal in order to obtain creditors consent to it, what is the maximum punishment that the debtor may receive? (06/01)

(a) A five year bankruptcy period
(b) Seven years in prison and a fine
(c) Disqualification from being a director
(d) A fine of up to £20,000

---

29 The Nominee's report must reach court in respect of an Individual Voluntary Arrangement (06/01)

(a) With the application for the interim order
(b) On the day the interim order ceases
(c) Two days before the interim order ceases
(d) Seven days before the interim order ceases
(e) 14 days before the creditors' meeting

---

30 Within what period may an application be made under section 262 to challenge a creditors meetings decision in relation to an individual voluntary arrangement? (06/00)

(a) Seven days
(b) 14 days
(c) 21 days
(d) 28 days
(e) None of these

---

31 In a situation where a debtor intends to apply to court pursuant to section 256(3) for the nominee to be replaced. What is the minimum notice he should provide to the nominee? Is it: (06/00)

(a) 5 business days
(b) 14 days
(c) 21 days
(d) 28 days
(e) None of these

---

32 In submitting his report to the Secretary of State following approval of the voluntary arrangement at a creditors' meeting, what should the report include? Is it: (06/00)

(a) Extent of preferential creditor claims
(b) The name and address of the debtor
(c) The date on which the arrangement was approved by the creditors
(d) Copy of the proposal document
(e) Copy of nominee's report
(f) The name and address of the supervisor
(g) The court in which the chairman's report has been filed
(h) Sealed copy of the interim order **(2 marks)**

---

33 Where the debtor provides a statement of affairs with his/her proposal for an Individual Voluntary Arrangement, the statement of affairs shall be made up to a date not earlier than how long before the date of the notice to the nominee? (06/13)

(a) 5 days
(b) 7 days
(c) 2 weeks
(d) 1 month

---

29 Post approval matters

1 In certain circumstances application may be made to the Court to review the actions or decision of a Supervisor of an IVA.

Who may make such an application and what type of order may the Court make? (6/11) **(4 marks)**

---

2 A supervisor of an IVA may not challenge any antecedent transactions apart from which one of the following? (6/10)

(a) Transactions defrauding creditors
(b) Extortionate credit transactions
(c) Preferences
(d) Transactions at an undervalue

---

3 Following the approval of an IVA what matters should be reported to the Secretary of State in accordance with the Rules. (6/10) **(4 marks)**

---

4 Which one of the following statements in relation to the Supervisor of an IVA is NOT true? (06/07)

(a) The supervisor may apply to court for directions on any matter

(b) The supervisor may only apply to court for directions where an interim order was first obtained

(c) The court may appoint a person to replace the existing supervisor

(d) The court may appoint a person to act as supervisor alongside the existing supervisor

---

5 You are Supervisor of an IVA. The debtor's direct debit was unintentionally cancelled as a result of which the debtor defaulted on four, monthly, contributions, a fact that went undetected until now due to failure of your own internal reporting system. The debtor has apologised and tells you that he took the family on holiday with the surplus cash as every one was at breaking point and was then too afraid to contact you. He has sent you this month's payment and tells you that he will pay the arrears out of his bonus due in the next couple of months. The proposal directs you to fail the arrangement on missing three consecutive payments. The proposal was for five years and has one year left to run. It has otherwise been successful.

(a) What are your obligations as supervisor given the facts above? **(2 marks)**

(b) What discretion if any do you have and how and under what circumstances might you exercise that? **(2 marks)**

(06/07) **(Total 4 marks)**

---

6 Where a voluntary arrangement has been approved but it appears to the supervisor that the debtor may have committed a criminal offence in connection with the arrangement, the supervisor has certain duties. Which of the following is not a statutory obligation of the supervisor? (06/06)

(a) Report the matter to the Secretary of State

(b) Forthwith apply to the court for the revocation of the arrangement

(c) Provide the Secretary of State with information

(d) Give access to the Secretary of State to documents in the supervisor's possession

---

7 What obligations does the nominee or supervisor of an individual voluntary arrangement have if he/she discovers that the debtor has been guilty of any offence in connection with the arrangement for which he is criminally liable? (06/04) **(3 marks)**

---

8 Under Rule 5.31A, the supervisor of an individual voluntary arrangement (IVA) must produce an abstract of his receipts and payments and a progress report at least once every 12 months. Of the following, to whom does he not need to send this progress report? (06/02)

(a) All creditors bound by the arrangement
(b) The Secretary of State
(c) The debtor
(d) The court

---

9 Mr Pownell's Voluntary Arrangement was approved on 12 October 20X9. A summary of his Statement of Affairs reveals the following:

W POWNELL

Statement of affairs

	£
Marital home	50,000
Mortgage	25,000
Wife's half share	(12,500)
	12,500
Pension fund	40,000
Motor vehicles (excluded)	10,000
Shares (excluded)	5,000
Tools of trade (excluded)	4,000
	71,500

The significant points to his Proposal stated the following:

- That he was to carry on trading as an electrician to enable monthly contributions from ongoing profits of £1,000 per month for a period of 48 months.
- The re-mortgage of his property within 36 months of approval to release his beneficial interest, valued at approximately £12,500.
- His only other obligation was to draw the lump sum benefit from his personal pension at the conclusion of the Arrangement at which time he would be 50 years old.

It is now 12 January 20Y0 and a review of the file has shown that the debtor is three months in arrears with his contributions. A modification to the proposal states that the Supervisor must fail the Voluntary Arrangement should contributions fall two months in arrears.

Mr Pownell has advised that he does not believe his business can return to profitability. He also advises that he has post-Voluntary Arrangement creditors of £26,000.

(a) Confirm what steps the Supervisor must take to fail the Arrangement and what considerations must be taken into account in dealing with the funds in hand at present. Ensure that the position of preferential creditors is not prejudiced. **(10 marks)**

(b) Confirm which assets would be available to a Trustee in a subsequent Bankruptcy. **(4 marks)**

(c) How would your answer to question b) differ if the Arrangement had not failed but a petition was presented by a post-Arrangement creditor? **(1 marks)**

(06/01) **(Total 15 marks)**

---

10 If a debtor subject to a Protocol compliant IVA has an emergency item of expenditure and is unable to make the usual monthly contribution, the Supervisor can agree a payment holiday without the need to convene a variation meeting. What conditions must be met to allow the payment holiday?

(2 marks)

---

11 Where a debtor is subject to a Protocol compliant IVA, what steps should he take in accordance with the Protocol if he is made redundant? (06/13) **(4 marks)**

Part B:
Exam Solutions

1 The IP: Key professional issues

1 B

2 A Rule 12A.12(4)

3 Rule 6.138 (6)

- The trustee's remuneration must be fixed by either the creditors' committee or a meeting of creditors within 18 months after the appointment of the trustee.
- If not so fixed within 18 months rule 6.138A will apply to fix the remuneration as follows:
  - By first applying the realisation scale set out in Schedule 6 to the monies received by him from the realisation of the assets of the bankruptcy (including any VAT, but after deducting any sums paid to secured creditors in respect of their securities) and any sums spent out of money received in carrying on the business of the bankrupt; and
  - Then by adding to this, the sum arrived at by applying the distribution scale set out in Schedule 6 to the value of assets distributed to creditors of the bankrupt (including sums paid in respect of preferential debts.

4 (a) Reporting requirements

The progress report must cover the period of 6 months commencing on the date on which the company entered administration and every subsequent period of 6 months ending with the date that an administrator ceases to act.

The administrator must, within 1 month of the end of the period covered by the report, send:

- A copy to the creditors attached to Form 2.24B, and
- A copy to the registrar of companies;

The court may, on the administrator's application, extend the period.

If the administrator makes default in complying with this Rule, he is liable to a fine and, for continued contravention, to a daily default fine.

The content of the report is set out in rule 2.47 and must include:

- Details of the court where the proceedings are and the relevant court reference number;
- Full details of the company's name, address of registered office and registered number;
- Full details of the administrator's name and address, date of appointment and name and address of appointor;
- Details of any extensions to the initial period of appointment;
- Details of the basis fixed for the remuneration of the administrator (or if not fixed at the date of the report, the steps taken during the period of the report to fix it);
- If the basis of remuneration has been fixed, a statement of:
  - The remuneration charged by the administrator during the period of the report
  - Where the report is the first to be made after the basis has been fixed, the remuneration charged by the administrator during the periods covered by the previous reports together with a description of the things done by the administrator during those periods in respect of which the remuneration was charged, irrespective in either case of whether payment was made in respect of that remuneration during the period of the report;
- A statement of the expenses incurred by the administrator during the period of the report, irrespective of whether payment was made in respect of them during that period;

- Details of progress during the period of the report, including a receipts and payments account;
- Details of any assets that remain to be realised;
- A statement of the creditors' right to request information under Rule 2.48A and their right to challenge the administrator's remuneration and expenses under Rule 2.109; and any other relevant information for the creditors.

(b) Creditors' rights to challenge remuneration and expenses.

Any: secured creditor; or unsecured creditor with the support of at least 10% in value of the creditors (including his/herself); or unsecured creditors with the permission of the court may make application to the court to challenge the remuneration/expenses of the administrator.

Any application must be made within 8 weeks of receipt of the progress report in which the level of remuneration/expenses is first reported (rule 2.109).

The court will consider the merits of the application and if it thinks no sufficient cause is shown for a reduction dismiss it. The court will however give the applicant 5 business days notice of its' intention to do so. On receipt the applicant can request a 'without notice to any other party' hearing * at which the court's decision will be reviewed. As a result of that review the application will either be dismissed or listed for a full hearing.

At any full hearing the court may order that the remuneration be reduced, the basis changed, or expenses either disallowed or repaid.

[*Formerly known as an *ex-parte* hearing.]

5 B SIP 10 Proxy Forms

6 Any four of the following:

(a) Any expenses or costs which:

(i) Are properly chargeable or incurred by the provisional liquidator in carrying out the functions conferred on him by the court.

(ii) Are properly chargeable or incurred by the official receiver or the liquidator in preserving, realising or getting in any of the assets of the company or otherwise relating to the preparation and conduct of any legal proceedings which he has power to bring or defend whether in his own name or the name of the company

(iii) Relate to the employment of a shorthand writer, if appointed by an order of the court made at the instance of the official receiver in connection with an examination, or

(iv) Are incurred in holding an examination under r4.214 where the application for it was made by the official receiver

(b) Any other expenses incurred or disbursements made by the official receiver or under his authority, including those incurred or made in carrying on the business of the company

(c) The fees payable under any order made under s414 or s415(A), including those payable to the official receiver and any remuneration payable to him under general regulations

(d) (i) The fee payable under any order made under s414 for the performance by the official receiver of his general duties as official receiver

(ii) Any repayable deposit lodged under any such order as security for the fee mentioned in sub-paragraph (i).

(e) The cost of any security provided by a provisional liquidator, liquidator or special manager in accordance with the Act or Rules

(f) The remuneration of the provisional liquidator

(g) Any deposit lodged on an application for the appointment of a provisional liquidator

(h) The costs of the petitioner, and of any person appearing on the petition whose costs are allowed by the court

(i) The remuneration of the special manager

(j) Any amount payable to a person employed or authorised, under Chapter 6 to assist in the preparation of the Statement of Affairs or of accounts

(k) Any allowance made, by order of the court, towards costs on an application for release from the obligation to submit a statement of affairs, or for an extension of time for submitting such a statement

(l) The costs of employing a shorthand writer in any case other than one appointed by an order of the court at the instance of the official receiver in connection with an examination

(m) Any necessary disbursements by the liquidator in the course of his administration (including any expenses incurred by members of the liquidation committee or their representatives and allowed by the liquidator under r4.169

(n) The remuneration or emoluments of any person who has been employed by the liquidator to perform any services for the company, as required or authorised by or under the Act or the Rules.

7 (a) The complexity (or otherwise) of the case

Any respect in which in connection with the winding up there falls on the IP any responsibility of an exceptional kind or degree

The effectiveness with which the IP appears to be carrying out, or to have carried out, his duties as liquidator

The value and nature of the assets with which the IP has had to deal

(b) The requisite guidance notes to creditors

Sufficient supporting information to enable those responsible for approving his remuneration to form a judgment as to whether the proposed fee is reasonable having regard to the circumstances of the case

This will include:

(i) Up to date receipts and payments account

(ii) Details of the time spent and the charge out value of staff involved in the case

(iii) An explanation of what the office holder has achieved and how it was achieved

(iv) Where fees are charged on a % basis, the office holder should provide details of any work which has been or is intended to be sub-contracted out which would normally be carried out by the office holders themselves

8 B SIP 2

9 B R1.26A(4)/R5.31A(4): the supervisor must report annually within 2 months at the anniversary of commencement

10 D Reg 20 IP Regs 1990 (superseded by Reg 13 IP Regs 2005, which reduces the period to 6 years than the later of the date release or the date the specific bond expired)

11 A Schedule 6 scale

12 (a) Category 1 disbursement - specific expenditure relating to the administration of the insolvent's affairs and referable to payment to an independent third party. These expenses include postage, case advertising, external document storage. Category 1 disbursements do not require approval.

Category 2 disbursement - these expenses include elements of shared or allocated costs, for example internal room hire or document storage. Category 2 disbursements require approval by those responsible for approving remuneration.

(b) (i) Category 2 disbursement - approval required
(ii) Category 1 disbursement - no approval required
(iii) Category 2 disbursement - approval required
(iv) Not recoverable.
(v) Category 1 disbursement - no approval required
(vi) Category 1 disbursement - no approval required

13 D R2.47

14 B Paragraph 3(2)(e) Part 2 Schedule 2 Regulation 12 IP Regs 2005

15 Administrator should bond for the value of assets available for the unsecured creditors ('unsecured' includes preferential creditors in this regard)

	£
Fixed charge assets	80,000
less Fixed charge holder	(60,000)
Surplus available to unsecured creditors	20,000
Floating charge assets	30,000
	50,000

Administrator should bond for £50,000.

[Note that this answer assumes that the fixed and floating charge holders are different and that the surplus on the fixed charge is not caught by the floating charge. It also assumes that the floating charge was created pre 15 September 2003 and therefore that no prescribed part calculation is necessary. If you make assumptions when answering a question be sure to note the assumptions that you make.]

16 A Schedule 2 Insolvency Proceedings (Fees) Order 2004

17 E R2.110(2) lists the other four as being required

18 (a) SIP 9 – liquidator can recover disbursements, without authorisation, if they are classed as Category 1 disbursements. These comprise external supplies of incidental services which are specifically identifiable to the case.

The liquidator should be prepared to disclose information about these disbursements where reasonably requested.

These will include:

(ii) Case advertising
(v) Reimbursement of air fares

Category 2 disbursements are costs which include an element of shared or allocated costs. These should be subject to approval as if they were remuneration.

These will include:

(i) Specialist copying
(iv) Room hire
(vi) Document storage

The liquidator will be unable to recover iii) office and equipment costs.

(b) Costs recovered should have been directly incurred in respect of the liquidation. There should be a reasonable method of calculation of the cost and the resultant charge should be in line with the cost of external provision.

19 C £250,000 – Known as the 'general penalty sum'

20 D CPR part 6

21 C S246

22 D

23 A Rule 8.6(1)

24 C Regulation 12(1)(b) and schedule 2, part 2 4 (6)

25 A SI 1990 IP Regulations 1990 Sch 2 Part II(b) The bond should be based on the value of the assets to which the AR is appointed which at the date of the appointment would be available for the unsecured creditors of the company

26 (a) Entitled to % value of assets realised and distributed based on OR's scale (now called Schedule 6 scale)

Band		*Realisation scale*	*Distribution scale*
First	£5,000	20%	10%
Next	£5,000	15%	7.5%
Next	£90,000	10%	5%
All further sums		5%	2.5%

Realisations total £113,000

		£
£5,000	@ 20%	1,000
£5,000	@ 15%	750
£90,000	@ 10%	9,000
£13,000	@ 5%	650
		£11,400

Distributions total £65,000

£5,000	@ 10%	500
£5,000	@ 7.5%	375
£55,000	@ 5%	2,750
		£3,625

Total fees total £11,400 + £3,625 = **£15,025**

(b) SIP 9 Remuneration of Insolvency Office Holders

27 B

28 C

29

	Band	*Realisation* %	*Distribution* %
First	£5,000	20	10.0
Next	£5,000	15	7.5
Next	£90,000	10	5.0
All further sums		5	2.5

Realisation:

£5,000 x 20% = £1,000

£5,000 x 15% = £750

Distribution

£2,000 x 10% = £200

Total = £1,950

2 Key ethical issues

1 (a) An insolvency practitioner must comply with the following 5 fundamental principles:

Integrity

This requires an IP to be straightforward and honest in all professional and business relationships.

Objectivity

Consequently an IP should not allow bias, conflicts of interest or the undue influence of others to override professional and business judgments.

Professional competence and due care

An IP should not accept or perform work which he or she is not competent to undertake. An IP has a continuing duty to maintain professional knowledge and skill at the required level necessary to ensure that a client or employer receives professional and competent service based on current practice, legislation and techniques.

Confidentiality

This requires an IP to respect the confidentiality of information acquired as a result of professional and business relationships.

Professional behaviour

An IP should comply with relevant laws and regulation and avoid any action that may discredit the profession.

(b) There is no absolute prohibition on a supervisor taking an appointment as trustee but he must ensure that it would be correct for him to take up the appointment having given careful consideration to matters set out in the code of ethics.

Of particular importance will be the fundamental principle of objectivity which can be impaired by conflicts of interest (both real and perceived).

In this situation an IP may, as trustee, be required to review his actions as supervisor. It might also be that the IP's familiarity, either with the individuals or subject-matter connected with the appointment, is too great for him to remain objective. In such circumstances a significant threat to the fundamental principles exists.

It will always be for an IP to justify why he thought it appropriate to take up an appointment.

It may however be the case that the introduction of safeguards will negate any threat that he faces. For example he might consult with another IP in the practice to review the work done.

(c) The trustee will have to make decisions about how to deal with the disputed claim and the two parties may become involved in legal proceedings. As a consequence careful consideration will have to be given to whether or not he can accept the appointment.

There is no absolute prohibition on taking up an appointment in these circumstances. However the relationship between the firm and the parties involved in the dispute may give rise to conflict of interest (actual or perceived) which will be a threat to the fundamental principle of objectivity. Additionally this may be a threat to confidentiality.

It may be possible to act if appropriate safeguards are in place, for example taking independent advice and putting in place information barriers to protect confidentiality.

These matters must be given careful consideration before the IP proceeds further.

2 (a) Both potentially self-interest and familiarity threats arising out of the wife's connection to the debtor. She has a large financial claim which he may have to evaluate. IP's objectivity in dealing with disputed claim may be impaired.

(b) Intimidation threat – IP may be deterred from making a proper and impartial investigation by the threat of complaint to his professional body.

3 (a) Principal must have regard to the professional conduct guidance of his authorising body. He should:

- Agree and record the identity of the instructing client. It must be clear whether the instructing party is the company, its board of directors or one or more directors individually
- Act in the interests of his client with objectivity, integrity and independence
- Ensure that his client is made aware of the matters of his statutory obligations re acquisition of company assets by connected parties, re-use of name of insolvent company, protecting interests of creditors
- Consider whether client has any conflicts of interest or duty and bring any such conflicts to attention of client
- Not accept instructions to assist a client in conduct which will undermine public confidence in the proper administration of insolvency procedures

Principal must cease to act if his advice to the directors that an act or omission would amount to misfeasance is disregarded.

[Answers to Q25 (2) & (3) below are based on new SIP 16 which takes effect from 1 November 2013]

(b) The following information should be disclosed:

- The source of the administrator's initial introduction
- The extent of the administrator's involvement pre-appointment
- The alternative courses of action that were considered by the administrator with an explanation of possible financial outcomes
- Whether efforts were made to consult with major creditors and the outcome of any consultations
- Why it was not appropriate to trade the business and offer it for sale as a going concern during the administration
- Details of requests made to potential funders to fund working capital requirements
- Details of registered charges with dates of creation
- If the business or assets have been acquired from an IP within the previous 24 months or longer if the administrator deems that relevant to creditors' understanding, disclose details of that transaction and whether the administrator, his firm or associates were involved
- Any marketing activities conducted by the company and/or administrator and the outcome of those activities, or an explanation of why no marketing was undertaken
- The names and professional qualifications of the valuers/advisors and confirmation that they have confirmed their independence
- The valuations obtained of the business or assets
- Summary of the basis of the valuation adopted by the administrator or his valuers/advisors
- Rationale for the basis of the valuations obtained and an explanation of the sale of the assets compared to those valuations
- If no valuation has been obtained, the reason for not having done so and how the administrator was satisfied as to the value of the assets
- The date of the transaction
- The identity of the purchaser

- Any connection between the purchaser and the directors, shareholders or secured creditors of the company or their associates
- The names of any directors, or former directors, of the company who are involved in the management or ownership of the purchaser, or of any other entity into which any of the assets are transferred
- In transactions impacting on more than one related company the administrator should ensure that the disclosure is sufficient to enable a transparent explanation (ie allocation of consideration paid)
- Whether any directors had given guarantees for amounts due from the company to a prior financier and whether that financier is financing the new business
- Details of the assets involved and the nature of the transaction
- The consideration for the transaction, terms of payment and any condition of the contract that could materially affect the consideration
- Sale consideration disclosed under broad asset valuation categories and split between fixed and floating charge realisations
- Any options, buy back agreements, deferred consideration or other conditions attached to the contract of sale
- If the sale is part of a wider transaction, a description of the other aspects of the transaction

(c) The information should be provided in every case unless there are exceptional circumstances in which case the reason why the information is not being provided should be stated. If the sale is to a connected party, it is unlikely that confidentiality will outweigh the creditors' right to the information.

The information should be provided with the first notification to creditors, and in any event within 7 calendar days of the transaction. If the administrator has been unable to meet this requirement they should provide a reasonable explanation for the delay.

3 Insolvency computations

1 (a) Calculate the Ad Valorem Fee charged to the estate by the Secretary of State. Show your full workings. **(5 marks)**

Realisations	£
Matrimonial home	30,400
Car	7,000
Insurance policy	8,520
	45,920

Secretary of State fee	£
First £2,000 @ 0%	0
Next £1,750 @ 100%	1,750
Next £1,500 @ 75%	1,125
Next £396,000 @ 15% (here, 15% on £45,920 less £2,000, £1,750 and £1,500)	6,101
1% on remainder (up to fees of £80,000 maximum)	0
	8,976

Workings

1. Proceeds from the realisation of the matrimonial home

		£
Sale proceed		187,000
Less	Cost of sale	(5,600)
	Outstanding mortagage	(105,000)
		76,400
50% equity owned by Mr Smith		38,200
Less	Charge against Mr Smith's	(7,800)
		30,400

(b) Dividend to non-preferential creditors

		£
Total claims received		94,020
Less	Preferential creditors Holiday pay – 2 weeks of 40 hours each at £7.50 per hour	(600)
Total unsecured creditor claims received		93,420

(c) Prepare an Estimated Outcome Statement for presentation to the final meeting of creditors. **(6 marks)**

Estimated Outcome Statement for
the Bankruptcy Estate of Mr John Smith

		£
Realisations		45,920
Less	Secretary of State fee	(8,976)
		36,945
Less	Expenses of the bankruptcy	
	Official Receiver's costs	(1,715)
	Bond	(180)
	Petitioning creditor's costs	(1,850)
	Statutory advertising	(150)
	Agent's charges	(1,200)
	Legal fees	(8,400)
		(12,495)
		23,450
Less	Trustee's remuneration (£12,000 +VAT @ 20%)	(14,400)
		9,050
Less	Preferential creditors	(600)
		8,450
Less	Unsecured creditors	(93,420)
Shortfall to unsecured creditors		(84,971)
Outcome for preferential creditors		100 p in the £
Outcome for unsecured creditors		9 p in the £

2

ASHTON CONTROLS (1995) LIMITED
Estimated Statement of Affairs as at 30 June 2012
Summary of Assets

	NOTES	BOOK VALUE £	ESTIMATED TO REALISE £
Fixed charge assets			
Goodwill		150,000	100,000
Less due to ABL Lenders		(24,600)	(24,600)
		125,400	75,400
Less due to Midwest		(362,000)	(362,000)
Shortfall to Midwest		(236,600)	(286,600)
Computer System		50,000	17,000
Less due to Control Designs		(32,000)	(32,000)
Shortfall to Control		18,000	(15,000)
Floating charge assets			
Fixtures and fittings		55,450	35,000
Book debts		275,000	178,500
		330,450	213,500

Summary of Liabilities

	NOTES	BOOK VALUE £	ESTIMATED TO REALISE £
Available to preferential creditors			213,500
Less preferential creditors	2		(19,825)
NET PROPERTY			193,675
Less prescribed part	4		(41,735)
Available to Midwest Bank			151,940
Less due to Midwest Bank			(286,600)
Shortfall to Midwest			(134,660)
Add prescribed part			41,735
Less unsecured creditors	3		(659,100)
Shortfall to unsecureds			(617,365)
Shortfall to unsecureds			(617,365)
Shortfall to Midwest			(134,660)
Shortfall to Control Designs			(15,000)
			(767,025)
Less share capital			(25,000)
Deficiency to members			(792,025)

Notes

1. Book debts

	£
Book value	275,000
Bad debts	(65,000)
	210,000
Bad debts provision (15%)	(31,500)
	178,500

2. Preferential creditors

	Pref	Unsecured
Holiday	19825	
	19825	

3. Unsecured creditors

	£		£
HMRC PAYE	228,300	Plus Shortfall to Control	15,000
VAT	35,200		
Trade	263,500		
Loans	95,350		
Subcontractors	36,750		
	659,100		

4. Prescibed part

Net property	193,675
50% of £10,000	5,000
20% of £183,675	36,735
	41,735

ASHTON CONTROLS (1995) LIMITED
Deficiency Account (31 July 2011 – 30 June 2012)

	NOTES	£	£
Balance profit and loss account			(167,300)
Asset write downs			
Goodwill		(50,000)	
Computer System		(33,000)	
F + f		(20,450)	
Book debts		(96,500)	(199,950)
Less items arising on insolvency		–	–
			(367,250)
Balancing figure (assumed trading loss)			(424,775)
Deficiency to member as per SPA			(792,025)

3 (a)

Summer Ltd (In Administration)

Estimated Outcome Statement as at x/x/xx

	£	£
Assets subject to fixed charge		
Freehold property		175,000
Goodwill		25,000
		200,000
less: costs		
Agents fees (w3)	1,250	
Legal fees	3,500	
Insurance	500	
Remuneration (w7)	10,000	
		(15,250)
Available to fixed charge holder		184,750
Due to Best Bank plc.		(400,000)
Shortfall to fixed charge holder		(215,250)
Assets Subject to floating charge	£	£
Book Debts (w1)		128,000
Stock		10,000
Goodwill		20,000
Motor Vehicles		10,000
		168,000
less: costs		
Statutory disbursements	1,000	
Book Debt collection fee (w2)	12,800	
Agents fees (w3)	3,750	
Legal fees	10,000	
Insurance (w4)	1,000	
Remuneration (w7)	25,200	
		(53,750)
Available to preferential creditors		114,250
less: preferential creditors		
Employee wages (w5)	3,200	
Employee holiday pay	8,200	
		(11,400)
Net property available for prescribed part		102,850
less: prescribed part (w8) c/f		(23,570)
Available for floating charge holder		79,280

	£	£
Floating charge holder		(215,250)
Shortfall to floating charge holder		(135,970)
Prescribed part for unsecured creditors b/f (w8)		23,570
less costs of distributing		(3,500)
Available for unsecured creditors		20,070
less: unsecured creditors		
Employee wages (w5)	3,600	
Notice pay	12,500	
Redundancy	16,250	
HM Revenue & Customs - VAT	12,500	
- PAYE/NIC	30,000	
Trade creditors (w6)	420,000	
Total unsecured creditors		(494,850)
Shortfall to unsecured creditors		(474,780)
Shortfall to floating charge holder		(135,970)
Shortfall to creditors		(610,750)

Workings

(w1) Book Debts

	£
Book value @ appointment	200,000
less: contra (w6)	(30,000)
bad debts	(10,000)
	160,000
less: 20% general provision (20% x 160,000)	(32,000)
	128,000

(w2) Book Debt Collection Fee

Realisable Book debts	128,000
Fee	× 10%
	12,800

(w3) Agent's fee

5,000 × 25% = 1,250 fixed

5,000 × 75% = 3,750 floatings

(w4) Insurance

1,500 – 500 = 1,000 floating.

(w5) Employee wages

Owed	1,700 × 4 =	6,800
Pref	800 × 4 =	(3,200)
Unsecured		3,600

(w6) Trade creditors

Book Value	450,000
Less contra (w1)	(30,000)
	420,000

(w7) Administrator's Remuneration

Fixed chg	= 5% x (175,000 + 25,000)
	= 10,000.
Floating chg	= 15% x (128,000 + 10,000 + 20,000 + 10,000)
	= 15% x 168,000
	= 25,200.

(w8) Prescribed part

10,000 x 50%	=	5,000
92,850 x 20%	=	18,570
102,850	=	23,570

(b) Distribution to creditors (IA'86 SchB1 Para 65).

- Move from administration to creditors voluntary liquidation
- Apply to court for permission to distribute the prescribed part in the administration to unsecured creditors.

(c) Dividend for unsecureds

$$\frac{\text{Assets available less costs of distributing}}{\text{Total unsecured creditors(excl. Shortfall to floating charge holder)}}$$

$$= \frac{20{,}070}{494{,}850}$$

= 4p in £

4 **Holiday pay**

All of employees' accrued holiday is preferential.

Days due (36/12 x 2 = 5 days)

Holiday pay due £600 (one week's wages)

Of the £600 the RPO will pay £430 per week.

Conclusion: RPO preferential for £430, employee preferential for the balance of £170.

Salary

Up to 4 months salary is preferential but capped at £800 per employee. Employee can claim against RPO for up to 8 weeks pay capped at £430.

RPO pay a total of £1,720 (£430 x 4) of which £800 preferential £920 unsecured.

Employee will have an unsecured claim for the balance of wages due.

5 Part (a)

Est. Statement of Affairs of Be Tools Ltd as at XX.XX.XX

	Notes	Book value	Est. Realisable value
ASSETS SPECIFICALLY PLEDGED		£	£
Assets subject to fixed charge			
Freehold factory		180,000	275,000
Less: Amounts to charge holder	N1		**(291,000)**
Shortfall to charge holder			**(16,000)**
ASSETS NOT SPECIFICALLY PLEDGED			
Assets subject to floating charge			
Finished goods		60,000	30,000
Raw materials	W1	42,000	8,400
Book debt surplus	W2	43,000	2,800
Motor vehicles		27,000	14,000
Financed motor vehicles	W3	–	–
Fixtures and Fittings		42,000	8,000
Plant and machinery		33,000	24,000
Available for preferential creditors			87,200
SUMMARY OF LIABILITIES			
PREFERENTIAL CREDITORS	W5		**(58,000)**
Surplus for preferential creditors			29,200
PRESCRIBED PART	W6		(8,840)
Available for floating charge holder			20,360
FLOATING CHARGE HOLDER	N1		**(16,000)**
Surplus/deficiency			4,360
Prescribed part carried down			**8,840**
Available for unsecured creditors			13,200
UNSECURED CREDITORS	W7		**(538,800)**
Deficiency as regards creditors			**(525,600)**
ISSUED AND CALLED UP S/C			**(1,000)**
Est. Deficiency as regards members			**(526,600)**

N1 Fixed and floating charge

Amount of 291,000 made up of loan and overdraft

Shortfall on fixed charge assets paid out of floating charge realisations (assume fixed and floating charge on property).

Workings

W1 Raw materials

BV = 42,000

ERV = 42,000 x 20% = 8,400

W2 Book debts

BV = 78,000 – 35,000 = 43,000

BV	78,000
Bad debt	(15,000)
	63,000
W/O 40%	(25,200)
Realisable	37,800
Due to factor	(35,000)
	2,800

W3 Financed vehicles

BV	10,000
Due to finance	(10,000)
Realisable	nil
Value = 2 x 4,000	8,000
Due to finance	(10,000)
Shortfall	(2,000)

W5 Preferential creditors

Employee wages:

90,000/15 = 6,000 per employee

800 each preferential = 12,000 [Balance unsecured = 78,000]

Holiday pay = 46,000

Total preferential (12,000 + 46,000 = 58,000)

W6 Prescribed part

10,000 × 50% =	5,000
19,200 × 20% =	3,840
	8,840

W7 Unsecured creditors

Trade creditors	230,000
Directors loan	50,000
HMRC – VAT	7,200
HMRC PAYE/NIC	14,600
Redundancy	87,000
PILON	70,000
Shortfall on finance vehicles	2,000
Employee wages (non-pref)	78,000
	538,800

Part (b)

Be Tools Ltd in Liquidation - Deficiency account for the period xx.xx.xx to xx.xx.xx

	Notes	£
Balance on profit and loss account at 1/1/09		(110,000)
Add: Asset gains: Freehold (275–180)		95,000
Less: Assets written down in statement of affairs	W1	(161,800)
Less: Items arising on insolvency	W2	(157,000)
Less: Loss on disposal of P&M (25–10)		(15,000)
Balancing figure attributable to loss in period		(177,800)
Deficit to members as per statement of affairs		**(526,600)**

W1 Asset write downs

Finished goods (60 – 30)	30,000
Raw materials (42 – 8.4)	33,600
Book debts (43 – 2.8)	40,200
Motor vehicles (27 – 14)	13,000
Financed vehicles	2,000
Fixtures and Fittings (42 – 8)	34,000
Plant and machinery (33 – 24)	9,000
	161,800

W2 Items arising on insolvency

Redundancy	87,000
PILON	70,000
	157,000

6 D

7 (a)

Statement of Affairs
Bear Limited
As at 18 March 20X8

	Workings	*Book value*	*Estimated To realise*
		£	£
Assets subject to fixed charge:			
Intellectual property (website)		300,000	125,000
Printing presses	1	1,400,000	800,000
Less: Stearn plc			(1,400,000)
Shortfall under fixed charge			(475,000)
Assets subject to floating charge:			
Debtors – customers	2	675,000	407,550
– others	2	20,000	1,000
Office furniture		50,000	7,500
Motor vehicle	3	10,000	Nil
Computer equipment	4	220,000	85,000
			501,050
Less Preferential creditors:			
Holiday pay	5		(90,000)
Wage arrears	6		(32,000)
			(122,000)
Net property			379,050
Less Prescribed Part	7		(78,810)
Assets available to floating chargeholder			300,240
Less: Stearn plc			(475,000)
Shortfall as regards floating			(174,760)
Prescribed part brought forward			78,810
Less Unsecured creditors:			
Motor vehicle shortfall			(3,000)
Wage arrears			(28,000)
Redundancy			(45,000)
HM Revenue and Customs			(25,000)
Landlord	8		(15,000)
Creditors ledger	10		(2,655,000)
			(2,692,190)
Stearn plc	9		(174,760)
Shortfall as regards unsecured creditors			(2,866,950)
Share capital			(75,000)
Shortfall as regards members			(2,941,950)

Workings

			£
1	Printing presses		
	Cost		2,000,000
	Less: depreciation (2 years @ £100,000 × 3 presses)		(600,000)
			1,400,000

2 Book debts

		£
(i)	Customers – Outstanding	675,000
	Less: set-off	(45,000)
	SIV plc	(12,500)
		617,500
	Less: provision of 34%	(209,950)
	Realisable value	407,550
(ii)	Others	
	Book value	20,000
	Realisable 5%	1,000

		£	£
3	Motor vehicles		
	Written down value	25,000	
	Expected to realise		12,000
	Less HP arrears	(15,000)	(15,000)
		10,000	(3,000)
4	Computer equipment		
	Written down value	270,000	
	Estimated to realise @ 50%		135,000
	Less outstanding charges	(50,000)	(50,000)
		220,000	85,000

5 Holiday pay

All claimed preferentially without limit

40 staff @ six weeks × £15,000 = £90,000

6 Wage arrears

Up to four months wage arrears may be claimed preferentially up to a maximum preferential claim per employee of £800.

40 staff × £800 = £32,000 preferential claim

four weeks @ £15,000 = £60,000

7 Prescribed part

(Assumes floating charge was created after 15.09.03 and therefore prescribed part rules apply.)

Note: This information was not given in the exam question. You should clearly state any assumptions made such as this.

	£
£10,000 @ 50%	5,000
£369,050 @ 20%	73,810
£379,050	78,810

8 Landlord

One quarter's rent is outstanding @ £15,000.

The landlord may claim for this and also for rent due for the year remaining on the lease. The landlord will have a duty to mitigate the claim by, for example, re-letting the property. The landlord may also have a claim for dilapidations. In the absence of other information allow claim for £15,000.

9 Stearn plc and prescribed part:

Permacell Finesse Limited (in liquidation) – the holder of a floating charge cannot participate in a distribution to unsecured creditors from the prescribed part in respect of any shortfall under their floating charge

10 Unsecured creditors

Per creditors ledger £2,700,000 less set-off £45,000 = £2,655,000

(b) Creditors should be provided with sufficient information to have a full appreciation of the nature of the transaction. This would normally include the following information:

(i) The date of the transaction

(ii) Details of the assets involved and the nature of the transaction

(iii) The consideration for the transaction and when it was paid

(iv) The name of the counterparty

(v) The nature of the counterparty's connected party relationship with the vendor

(vi) If the transaction took place before the appointment of the member as office holder, the name of any adviser to the vendor

(vii) Whether the purchaser and (if the transaction took place before the appointment of the member as office holder) the vendor were independently advised

(viii) Where the transaction took place before the commencement of liquidation or administration, the scope of the office holder's investigation and the conclusion reached

(ix) Where the disclosure is to a liquidation committee and the committee has not been consulted prior to contract, the reason why such consultation did not take place

(x) Where, in a liquidation, the disclosure is to creditors, whether the liquidation committee (if there is one) has been consulted and the outcome of such consultation

8 (a) Statement of Affairs for Kili Limited as at 30 June 20X9

	Workings	*Book value* £	*Estimated to realise* £
Assets subject to fixed charge			
Internet domain name		NIL	30,000
Less: Blanc Bank plc			(65,000)
Shortfall to Blanc Bank plc			(35,000)
Assets subject to floating charge			
Book debts	1	85,000	55,200
Laser printing press		15,000	11,000
Machinery and equipment	2	42,000	15,000
Stock		65,000	15,000
Vehicle		15,000	10,000
Office furniture and equipment		12,000	2,000
			108,200

	Workings	Book value £	Estimated to realise £
Less preferential creditors:			
Wage arrears	3		(12,000)
Holiday pay	3		(12,000)
			(24,000)
Less Prescribed part	4		(19,840)
Assets available for floating charge Holder			64,360
Less Blanc Bank plc			(35,000)
			29,360
Prescribed part b/fwd			19,840
Assets available for unsecured creditors			49,200
Less Unsecured creditors:			
Redundancy	3		30,000
Pay in lieu	3		26,000
Wage arrears	3		11,000
HM Revenue and Customs			62,000
Landlord	5		7,500
Trade and expense creditors			165,000
			(301,500)
Shortfall as regards creditors			(252,300)
Share capital			(20,000)
Shortfall as regards members			(272,300)

Note: The statement does not take into account the costs of liquidation.

Workings/assumptions

1 **Book debts**

	£
Outstanding	85,000
Less specific bad debt	(16,000)
	69,000
Less general bad debts @ 20%	(13,800)
	55,200

2 **Machinery and equipment**

	Book value £	Estimated to realise £
Value	52,000	25,000
Less Jura Finance Ltd	(10,000)	(10,000)
	42,000	15,000

3 **Employees**

Up to four months wages arrears may be claimed preferentially subject to a maximum preferential claim per employee of £800.

	£
15 employees @ £800 (preferential claim)	12,000
Unsecured claim	11,000
	23,000

Holiday pay – all preferential without limit

Redundancy pay and Pay in lieu of notice are all unsecured claims.

4 **Prescribed part**

Where a floating charge is created on or after 15.09.03 (we are not told the date of creation here so assume that it is created after 15.09.03): **(when making such an assumption in the exam it is important to state clearly what assumptions you have made)** the liquidator must make a prescribed part of the company's net property available for the unsecured creditors. Net property is the amount that would have been available for the floating charge holders.

The prescribed part is calculated as follows:

£	£
10,000 x 50%	5,000
74,200 x 20%	14,840
84,200	19,840

5 **Landlord**

	£
Two quarters rent @ £30,000 per annum	15,000
Less: rent deposit	(7,500)
Unsecured claim	7,500

(b)

Kili Limited
Deficiency account for the period
31.03.X8 to 30.06.X9

	£	£
Balance per accounts 31.03.X8		12,000
Items written down on the Statement of Affairs:		
Internet domain name	30,000	
Book debts	(29,800)	
Machinery and equipment	(27,000)	
Stock	(50,000)	
Vehicles	(5,000)	
Office furniture	(10,000)	
Laser printing press	(4,000)	
		(95,800)
Items due to insolvency:		
Redundancy	(30,000)	
Pay in lieu of notice	(26,000)	
		(56,000)
Profit/loss on sale of assets:		
Sale of vehicle	3,000	
Disposal of machinery	(8,000)	
		(5,000)
Loss for period 31.03.X8 to 30.06.X9 (balancing figure)		(127,500)
Shortfall per statement of affairs		(272,300)

Note: The internet domain name is a positive figure since it is valued at zero in the accounts and has therefore increased in value.

9 (a)

Tacul Limited in Administration
Statement of Affairs as at X.X.09

	Workings/ notes	*Book value* £	*Estimated to realise* £
Assets subject to fixed charge			
Freehold property		450,000	600,000
Less: Pina Bank plc		(750,000)	(750,000)
			(150,000)
Assets subject to floating charge			
Debtors – Factored	1	200,000	–
– Non-factored	2	140,000	70,000
Motor vehicles	3	28,000	14,000
Machinery	4	90,000	30,000
Stocks		120,000	45,000
Furniture and equipment		15,000	2,000
Assets available for preferential creditors			161,000
Less: preferential creditors			
Employee wages claims	5		16,400
Holiday pay	6		15,000
			(31,400)
			129,600
Prescribed part	7		(28,920)
Assets available for floating charge holder			100,680
Less: Pina Bank plc			(150,000)
Shortfall to Pina Bank plc			(49,320)
Prescribed part available to unsecured creditors			28,920
Less: unsecured creditors	8		(425,600)
Shortfall after prescribed part			(396,680)
Shortfall to floating charge holder			(49,320)
Shortfall as regards creditors			(446,000)
Share capital			1,000
Shortfall as regards members			(447,000)

Workings/notes

(1) **Factored debts**

Book value	200,000
Less: bad debts	(80,000)
Less: 10% general provision	(12,000)
Collectible debts	108,000

X Factors have already advanced 70% ie 140,000 therefore they will have an unsecured claim of £32,000

(2) **Non factored debts**

Book value	140,000
Less: provision	(70,000)
	70,000

Assume that invoices relating to maintenance contracts which expire on 30/4/09 will not be renewed.

(3) **Motor vehicles**

Four × £3,500 = £14,000

(4) **Drilling machine**

	£
Book value	30,000
Less: Loxley Finance Ltd	(15,000)
	15,000
Other machines	15,000
Estimated to realise	30,000

(5) Wages may be claimed preferentially for a period of four months arrears up to a maximum claim of £800 per employee.

25 staff are owed less than £800, therefore all arrears will be claimed preferentially.

Directors - PAYE employees so will have a preferential claim re arrears

800 × 3 = 2,400 preferential claim
1,200 × 3 = 3,600 unsecured claim

(6) **Prescribed part**

	£
50% × 10,000	5,000
20% × 119,600	23,920
	28,920

(7) **Unsecured creditors**

	£
X Factors Limited	32,000
Redundancy	32,000
Pay in Lieu of Notice	20,000
HM Revenue and Customs – PAYE/NIC	43,000
– VAT	65,000
Wages	3,600
Trade and expense creditors	230,000
	425,600

(8) Floating charge holder cannot rank as an unsecured creditor in respect of the prescribed part.

(b) (i) If selling immediately upon appointment, administrator may face challenge from creditors that such a quick sale was not in the creditors best interests.

Administrator must ensure that he obtains valuations for the business to ensure that the best possible price is obtained.

Should also obtain agents advise that such a sale is in the best interests of creditors as a whole.

Should identify charged assets and seek approval of fixed charge holders to a sale of their assets.

Administrator must send proposals to creditors within eight weeks of his appointment, he need not wait until creditors have agreed the proposals, he can sell the business and then send proposals to creditors advising them of the sale.

(ii) First obtain agents' valuations on a going concern and forced sale business. This will determine strategy.

If a greater value would be achieved by selling as a going concern then the administrator should continue trading. If not, the business should be closed and a sale of assets at public auction sought.

Advertise the business for sale using specialist press.

Agree on mode of sale.

Identify possible interested parties - talk to directors, possible MBO, firms database etc.

Identify assets subject to fixed charges - obtain agreement of charge holders to a sale of the assets.

10 D SIP 11

11 B S176A

12

	£
Net property	440,000
Less preferential creditors	(20,000)
	420,000
Prescribed part	
50% @ 10,000 =	5,000
20% @ 410,000 =	82,000
	87,000
Floating charge realisations	440,000
Less preferential creditors	(20,000)
Less prescribed part	(87,000)
Available to floating charge holders	333,000
1st floating chargeholder	310,000
2nd floating chargeholder	23,000
Unsecured creditors totalling	400,000
– 21.75p in £	87,000

Unsecured creditors
£400,000. The 2nd floating chargeholder will not receive a dividend from the prescribed part in respect of its shortfall (s176A).

13 (a) (i) Request copies of all documentation ie order, invoice, ROT clause

(ii) Seek legal advice about validity

(iii) Supplier has already identified goods on site

(iv) In order to be valid, the supplier must show that the clause was incorporated into the contract:

- By notice prior to the contract
- In the terms of the contract itself
- Established through a regular course of dealings

(v) It would appear from the facts of the question that the clause was included on the reverse of the invoice which was submitted after delivery of the goods

(vi) First supply, therefore no regular course of dealings established

(vii) Unless supplier can prove that Peg Limited agreed to the terms of the ROT clause prior to delivery, the claim should be rejected

(viii) Jack would be an ordinary unsecured creditor in respect of his claim

(b) Interest may only be proved for a period up to the date the company entered liquidation. Therefore a claim for interest for the period after 31 May 20X8 will be rejected.

For periods prior to the date of liquidation interest will only be provable:

(i) Debt is due by virtue of a written instrument, payable at a certain time ie a bill of exchange

(ii) The contract itself provides for payment of interest

(iii) The creditor has served written demand for payment of interest stating that interest will be payable from date of service of the demand to the date of payment

The rate of interest charged will be the lower of that in the Judgments Act (currently 8%) or the demanded rate of interest.

Here, written demand for payment was made on 31 August 20X7. Interest may be claimed from 31 August 2007 to 31 May 20X8, being the date of liquidation. The rate of interest allowable would be 8%.

(c) If a company has partly paid shares the liquidator may make calls in order to pay the expenses and debts of the liquidation.

Liquidator must first settle a list of contributories:

(i) Two lists are drawn up:

1 Persons who were members at the date of liquidation. These are primarily liable for calls and will include Josie.

2 Those who ceased to be members within the preceding 12 months. They will only be liable up to the amount, if any, which the preceding holder is unable to pay.

R4.198 – Liquidator must give notice to Josie and other contributories that he has settled the list of contributories.

If compulsory liquidation:

(i) Sanction of the court or liquidation committee must be obtained

(ii) 5 business days notice of intended meeting to be sent to each committee member showing the proposed amount of the call and the purpose for which it is intended R4.203

If CVL:

(i) Liquidator may make a call on his own authority, s165 by sending a notice and request for payment to the contributory

(ii) A contributory who is also a creditor cannot set off a call against amounts owing by the company to him as a creditor.

(iii) Josie would not be allowed to offset the debt owed to her by the company (£5,000) against the call by the liquidator. This is because set-off is only allowed where there have been mutual dealings between the parties which does not apply here.

(d) Facts to be taken into consideration in determining whether an individual is an employee:

(i) Express contract of employment as opposed to a contract for services
(ii) Remuneration paid by way of salary or wages on a regular basis
(iii) Remuneration fixed in advance
(iv) The individual pays PAYE income tax and Class 1 National Insurance contributions
(v) Entitlement to sick pay and holiday pay
(vi) Working every day from 8.30 to 5.30
(vii) Continual employment

(e) Para 11 includes as a preferential debt 'so much of any sum owed in respect of money advanced for the purpose as has been applied for a payment of a debt which, if it had not been paid, would have been a preferential debt'.

Wages may be claimed preferentially for a period of up to four months prior to the company entering liquidation, to a maximum claim per employee of £800.

Payments made in respect of wages payments in the four months pre-liquidation are as follows.

		£
Gina	15/3	350
	15/4	350
	15/5	350
		1,050

Max pref claim = £800

		£
Katy	13/5	150
	15/4	150
	15/3	150
	15/2	150
		600

Pref claim = £600

Ricky	13/5	150
	15/4	150
	15/3	150
	15/2	150
		600

Pref claim = £600

Total bank's preferential claim = 800 + 600 + 600 = £2,000

14 C Paragraph 10 Schedule 6 IA86

15 D Paragraph 3 Insolvency Act 1986 (Prescribed Part) Order 2003

16 C S176A(6) ie floating charge realisations less costs and preferential debts

17 D

18 A It will not necessarily apply in receivership either unless the receiver is appointed under a floating charge (see s176A)

19 (a)

Tuckers Food Supplies Limited in liquidation
Estimated Statement of Affairs
as at 4 June 20X9

	Workings	*Book Value* £	*Estimated to realise* £
Assets specifically pledged			
Freehold property		150,000	230,000
Less Best Bank plc			(75,000)
			155,000
Factored book debts	1	65,000	52,000
Less Two Way Factors PLC			(42,250)
			9,750
Vans	2	18,000	8,000
Less Finance UK Limited			(7,500)
			500
Other assets			
Non factored book debts	3	15,650	5,985
Stock	4	18,640	3,728
Office furniture and equipment		7,500	3,600
Total assets available for creditors			178,563
Preferential creditors			
Wage arrears	5	7,800	

	Workings	Book Value £	Estimated to realise £
Holiday pay	5	12,000	
			(19,800)
Assets available for unsecured creditors			158,763
Unsecured creditors			
HMRC (VAT)		48,800	
HMRC (PAYE)		80,600	
Trade and expense creditors		195,000	
Redundancy		78,000	
Pay in lieu of notice		31,200	
Director's loan accounts		25,000	
			(458,600)
Deficit as regards creditors			(299,837)
Share capital			(999)
Deficit as regards members			(300,836)

Note: The statement does not take into account the costs and expenses of liquidation.

WORKINGS

(1) **Factored book debts**

	£
Outstanding	65,000
Factors are owed 65%	(42,250)
Bad debts @ 20%	(13,000)
Outstanding debts	9,750

(2) **Delivery vans**

	£
Two vans estimated to realise	8,000
Less outstanding finance	(7,500)
	500

One van – rented only, assumed returned to rental company

(3) **Non factored book debts**

	£
Outstanding	15,650
Less bad debt	(9,665)
	5,985

(4) **Stock**

	£
Book value	18,640
Estimated to realise 20%	3,728

(5) **Employees**

Up to four months wage arrears may be claimed preferentially to a maximum claim per employee of £800.

30 employees are owed one week's wages, all less than £800, therefore preferential claim of £7,800.

Holiday pay is preferential without limit.

Redundancy pay and pay in lieu of notice are unsecured claims.

(b) **Remuneration**

The following information should be provided to creditors.

1 Up to date receipts and payments account.

2 Details of the time spent and charge out value to date and any material changes in the rates charged for the various grades since the resolution was passed.

3 The amount of the remuneration drawn in accordance with the resolution taken at the s98 meeting.

4 Details of any remuneration received from a secured creditor for realising assets subject to a fixed charge.

5 Any additional information as may be required.

- An explanation of what has been achieved and how it was achieved to enable the value of the exercise to be assessed and to establish that the time has been properly spent on the case.
- An analysis of the time spent on the case by type of activity and grade of staff, ie
  - Administration and planning
  - Investigations
  - Realisation of assets
  - Trading
  - Creditors
  - Any other specific matters
- Any significant aspects of the case should be explained, particularly those which affected the amount of time spent.
- Agents and solicitors' fees.

There is no requirement to obtain approval for agents and solicitors' costs. They should be disclosed in the receipts and payments account. The liquidator may wish however to give details of how they were chosen, how they were contracted to be paid and what steps have been taken to review their fees.

20 B SIP 7 Presentation of financial information in insolvency proceedings

21 The amount of the bond is the amount which would be available for unsecured creditors if the company went into liquidation. 'Unsecured' includes preferential creditors in this respect.

	£
RECEIPTS	
Fixed charge assets	
Goodwill	100,000
Intellectual property	95,000
Freehold property	600,000
	795,000
Less: costs (50% x £130,000)	(65,000)
Bank	(475,000)
Assets available to unsecured creditors	255,000
Floating charge assets	
Book debts	50,000
Computer equipment	10,000
Office furniture	5,000
	65,000
Less: costs (50% x £130,000)	(65,000)
Assets available for creditors	NIL
Total assets available for unsecured creditors	255,000

Bond for the sum of £255,000

22

	£
Funds available	350,000
Less; remuneration	(25,000)
Expenses	(685)
Agent's costs	(4,500)
Solicitor's fees	(6,250)
	(36,435)
Assets available to creditors	313,565
Less Preferential creditors	(8,250)
Assets available to unsecured creditors	305,315
Unsecured creditors	
Trade creditors	(252,000)
Local authority	(1,000)
Unsecured bank loan	(12,000)
Credit card debts	(5,000)
	(270,000)
Interest payable on creditor claims	
10/12 x £278,250 @ 8%	(18,550)
Monies available to bankrupt's spouse (deferred debt)	16,765

23 E

24 **Cromwells Limited**

(a) **Statement of Affairs as at 31 May 20X0**

	Notes	Book value	Estimated to realise
		£	£
Assets specifically pledged			
Freehold property		500,000	625,000
Less: Due to Better Bank			(450,000)
Surplus			175,000
Factored book debts	1	117,250	55,350
Financed plant and machinery	2	85,000	–
			230,350
Assets not specifically pledged			
Unfactored book debts	1	201,000	180,900
Unfinanced plant and machinery	2	190,000	75,000
Stock	3	350,000	70,000
Directors loan		45,000	45,000
Assets available for preferential creditors			601,250
Preferential creditors			
Employees Holiday Pay			(23,000)
Assets available for unsecured creditors			578,250
Unsecured creditors			
Shortfall to finance company		75,000	
Redundancy		110,000	
Notice pay		65,000	
PAYE//NIC	4	160,000	
Corporation tax		25,000	
VAT	5	110,000	
Trade creditors		750,000	
			(1,295,000)
Shortfall to creditors			(716,750)
Share capital			(15,000)
Total deficiency to members			(731,750)

NOTES

1 **Book debts**

	£
Total book debts = £670,000	
Of which 70% is factored (70% @ 670,000)	469,000
Less 10% provision for bad debts	(46,900)
Realisable factored debt	422,100
Less: Debts advanced (75% @ £469,000) Termination charges	(351,750)
	(15,000)
Available to the company	55,350
Unfactored book debts (30% @ £670,000)	201,000
Less 10% provision for bad debts	(20,100)
Available to the company	180,900

2 **Plant and machinery**

Subject to finance:

	Book value	*Estimated to realise*
	£	£
60% @ £475,000	285,000	125,000
Less o/s finance	(200,000)	(200,000)
Unsecured claim	85,000	(75,000)
Not subject to finance:		
40% @ £475,000	190,000	75,000

3 **Stocks and WIP**

Current value	350,000	
Estimated to realise 20%		70,000

4 **PAYE/NIC**

All unsecured liability as proceedings commence on or after 15 September 2003.

5 **VAT**

All unsecured liability as proceedings commence on or after 15 September 2003.

(b) Cromwells Limited

Deficiency account for period 1/1/X8 to 31/5/X0

	£	£
Balance on profit and loss account as at 1/1/X8		125,000
Less: Asset write downs		
Book debts	67,000	
Plant and machinery	115,000	
Stock	280,000	
		(462,000)
Add: Gain on freehold property		125,000
Less: Items arising on insolvency		
Termination charge	15,000	
Redundancy	110,000	
Notice pay	65,000	
		(190,000)
Balancing figure: Trading loss in period		(329,750)
Deficiency as regards members		(731,750)

(c) In the light of the Brumark and Spectrum cases the purported fixed charge will be treated by the court as being in reality a floating charge. Legal advice should be sought.

25 (a) **To:** Principal
From: A N Assistant
Re: Stewards Equestrian Limited - proposed Company Voluntary Arrangement

Where there has been a significant professional, or personal relationship with a company, no principal or employee of the practice should accept appointment as a Supervisor of a Company Voluntary Arrangement.

A significant professional relationship arises where material professional work has been carried out in the last three years. The work being carried out by a partner or employee of the firm.

Such work includes:

(i) Audit work for a company or individual

(ii) One or more assignments (whether or not of a continuing nature) of such overall significance or in such circumstances that a members objectivity in carrying out an appointment could reasonably be seen to be prejudiced.

Here, a tax partner has provided tax advice to the company in return for a fee, within the last three years.

This does not appear to constitute a significant professional relationship with the company, however, it should be investigated further in terms of the fee received and its significance.

It would appear that instructions to act as nominee could be accepted.

(b) **Stewards Equestrian Limited**

Contributions from trading profits

	Year 1	*Year 2*	*Year 3*	*Year 4*	*Year 5*
	£	£	£	£	£
Sales	480,000	518,400	559,872	604,662	653,035
Gross margin @ 30%	144,000	155,520	167,962	181,399	195,910
Less overheads	102,000	105,570	109,265	113,089	117,047
Net profit	42,000	49,950	58,697	68,310	78,863
Tax @ 25%	–			17,077	19,715
Net profit after tax	42,000	49,950	58,697	51,233	59,148
Less 40%	16,800	19,980	23,479	20,493	23,659
Contribution	25,200	29,970	35,218	30,740	35,489

WORKINGS

1 **Sales**

Year 1	480,000 = 480,000
Year 2	480,000 × 108% = 518,400
Year 3	518,400 × 108% = 559,872
Year 4	559,872 × 108% = 604,662
Year 5	604,662 × 108% = 653,035

2 **Overheads**

Year 1	102,000 = 102,000
Year 2	102,000 × 103.5% = 105,570
Year 3	105,570 × 103.5% = 109,265
Year 4	109,265 × 103.5% = 113,089
Year 5	113,089 × 103.5% = 117,047

(c) **Stewards Equestrian Limited**

Estimated Outcome Statement Company Voluntary Arrangement

	Workings	£
Contributions from trading		156,617
Less Supervisor's fees (5 x 3,000)		(15,000)
Assets available for unsecured creditors		141,617
Unsecured creditors		
VAT	2	20,700
PAYE/NIC	1	45,000
Trade and expense creditors		158,898
Directors loan account		75,000
		(299,598)
Shortfall as regards unsecured creditors		(157,981)

Summary

Unsecured creditors

Creditors totalling £299,598 receive a dividend of 47.26p in £

WORKINGS

1 **PAYE/ NIC**
All unsecured

2 **VAT**
All unsecured

3 **Employee claims**

All employees are retained by the company so no claims arise.

(d) The director could assist in improving the dividend to creditors by writing off the balance on his directors' loan account. If this were done, unsecured creditors would receive a dividend of 63.05p in the pound. This represents an increased dividend of 15.79p in the pound.

(e) Rules for requisite majority in obtaining approval for a Company Voluntary Arrangement:

R1.19(1) Subject as follows, at the creditors' meeting for any resolution to pass approving any proposal or modification there must be a majority of three-quarters in value of the creditors present in person or by proxy and voting on the resolution. (Majority reduced 6.4.2010 by deletion in the rule of the words 'in excess of'.)

R1.19(4) Any resolution is invalid if those voting against it include more than half in value of the creditors, counting in the latter only those:

(i) To whom notice of the meeting was sent;

(ii) Whose votes are not to be left out of account under paragraph (3); and

(iii) Who are not, to the best of the chairman's belief, persons connected with the company.

26 (a) **Estimated Outcome Statement**

Peter Gerrard

	Workings	*Bankruptcy*	*Voluntary Arrangement*
		£	£
Assets available			
Peter's father	1	–	60,000
Payment for loss of office		20,000	20,000
Share capital holding co.		10,000	10,000
Greenways partnership		56,000	56,000
Freehold property	2	27,000	–
Leasehold property	3	–	–
Fixtures and fittings	4	2,500	–
Stock in trade	5	3,750	–
Matrimonial home	6	16,700	16,700
Stocks and shares		22,750	22,750
		158,700	185,450
Less: costs		(29,000)	(12,000)
Available for unsecured creditors		129,700	173,450
Unsecured creditors			
PAYE/NIC	7	79,000	79,000
VAT	9	42,000	42,000
Income tax	8	13,650	13,650
Trade creditors		23,235	23,235
Vehicle finance		3,918	3,918
Loan – Peter's father		15,000	-
Income tax		40,950	40,950
Capital gains tax		33,400	33,400
		(251,153)	(236,153)
Shortfall as regards creditors		(121,453)	(62,703)
Dividend to unsecured creditors		51.6p	73.4p

WORKINGS

1 This is only available in an IVA

2 Assume the freehold property is realisable in a bankruptcy, but required for continued trading in an IVA

3 This has a nil value in bankruptcy. In an IVA this has been retained for business use.

4 This will be excluded in an IVA as it is necessary for continued trade

5 Estimated to realise 50% of value in a bankruptcy. Excluded from IVA since necessary for trading.

6 **Matrimonial home**

	£
Value	225,000
Less: mortgage	(137,600)
Equity	87,400

	Mrs Gerrard	*Mr Gerrard*
	£	£
Assume 50:50 split	43,700	43,700
Less: Western Bank Ltd – loan	–	(22,000)
O/draft	–	(5,000)
Equity available		16,700

– Assume 50:50 split. This will have to be confirmed

– Assume whole of indebtedness to Western Bank Ltd is that of the business and charged against the home

7 **PAYE/ NIC** – All unsecured

8 **Income tax** – All unsecured

Capital gains tax – Unsecured claim

9 **HMRC (VAT)** – All unsecured

10 **Motor vehicles**

	£
Current value	23,750
O/s finance	(27,668)
Unsecured claim	(3,918)

(b) Increased dividend to unsecured creditors, 73.4p in £ as opposed to 51.6p in a bankruptcy.

Debtor appears to have a business plan to continue trading profitably, would need to see sales forecasts etc however.

IVA is not reliant on future income, if voluntary contributions could be made then the dividend to unsecured creditors would increase.

Main creditor, Western Bank Limited, is paid in full from the matrimonial home, therefore will not have a vote in IVA. HM Revenue and Customs will receive an unsecured dividend of 73.4p in the pound. May be enough for them to support the VA. Would have to discuss with HM Revenue and Customs whether they will support the VA.

(c) No certainty of monies being recovered from dissolved partnership or outstanding monies from sale of Yelloways and Blueways.

Creditors may wish to see action taken against debtor in respect of pension contributions made. Supervisor of IVA would have no powers to take action in this regard.

No information given re trade, past insolvencies etc.

In view of lack of taxes paid over last four years, HMRC may not support debtor continuing to trade.

No contributions from trading envisaged. Creditors may not support continued trading in view of past trading history.

27 B 54p/£

	Unsecured Creditors
	£
HMRC	7,000
Trade creditors	15,000
	22,000
Realisations	20,000
Less costs:	
Secretary of State administration fee	(3,060)
OR's costs	(700)
Trustee's fees	(4,000)
Disbursement	(300)
Available for creditors	11,940

$$\text{Dividend} = \frac{11,940}{22,000} = 54\text{p}$$

28 Lost Hope Limited

Estimated Statement of Affairs as at 30/4/X0

	Notes	Book Value £	Estimated to Realise £
Assets subject to fixed charge			
Freehold Property		350,000	385,000
Less: Slow Bank plc			(215,000)
			170,000
Assets subject to floating charge			
Book Debts	1	138,000	105,570
Machinery – Unfinanced		6,000	2,500
Machinery – Low Cost Finance plc	2	26,000	4,000
– Quick Finance plc	2	40,000	–
Stock	3	30,000	16,000
			298,070
Less: Preferential Creditors	4		(13,100)
Estimated surplus as regards preferential creditors			284,970
Estimated prescribed part of net property c/f	9		(59,994)
Estimated total assets available for floating charge holder			224,976
Floating charge holder			(62,000)
Estimated surplus of assets after floating charge			162,976
Estimated prescribed part of net property b/f			59,994
Estimated total assets available for unsecured creditors			222,970
Unsecured creditors	4		(456,400)
Estimated deficiency as regards creditors			(233,430)
Share Capital			(25,000)
Estimated total deficiency as regards members			(258,430)

Notes to Statement of Affairs

1 **Machinery**

Low Cost Finance plc

	m/c 1 £	m/c 2 £	m/c 3 £	Total £
Realisable value	7,500	500	9,500	
Less o/s finance	(5,000)	(3,500)	(8,000)	
Est. to realise	2,500	(3,000)	1,500	4,000
Book value	10,000	5,000	11,000	26,000

Quick Finance plc

	m/c 1 £	m/c 2 £	Total £	£
Realisable Value	20,000	6,000		
Less o/s finance	(15,000)	(12,000)		
Est. to realise	5,000	(6,000)	(1,000)	
Book value	25,000	15,000	40,000	

2 **Stock**

	£
Realisable value	20,000
Less: ROT	(4,000)
	16,000

3

	Notes	*Preferential*	*Unsecured*
		£	£
Quick finance PLC			1,000
Low Cost Finance PLC			3,000
Unsecured trade creditors			335,000
Adjust re ROT			(4,000)
Director's loan			6,000
VAT			35,000
PAYE			40,000
Redundancy	5		25,000
Pay in lieu	6		15,000
Holiday pay	7	6,000	
Wages	8	7,100	400
		13,100	456,400

4 **Redundancy** – All unsecured

5 **Pay in lieu** – All unsecured

6 **Holiday pay** - all preferential without limit

7 **Wage arrears** – Up to four months arrears may be claimed preferentially up to a maximum £800 per employee.

	Preferential	*Unsecured*
	£	£
Two Employees owed £1,000	1,600	400
Remainder	5,500	-
	7,100	400

8 **Prescribed Part**

£		£
10,000	× 50%	5,000
274,970	× 20%	54,994
284,970		59,994

29 D Insolvency Regulations 1994 and (since this exam was drafted) The Insolvency Practitioners and Insolvency Services Account (Fees) Order 2003, which came into force on 01.04.04.

30 **Floating charge monies**

From floating charge realisations the administrative receiver must pay the preferential creditors in priority to the debt secured by the floating charge.

	£
Floating charge realisations	18,000
Preferential creditors total	23,600

Receive 76.27p in the pound

Summary

	Total Preferential	*Unsecured*	*Dividend to Preferential (76.27p in £)*
Wage arrears:			
Six employees	4,800	1,200	3,661
(Maximum preferential claim £800 per employee)			
Holiday pay:			
Ten employees	15,000	-	11,441
(All preferential without limit)			
Andrew Evans	3,800	29,200	2,898
	23,600	30,400	18,000

Fixed charge surplus

Fixed charge surplus is not available for preferential creditors or the floating charge holder.

The administrative receiver has no power to pay the unsecured creditor claims. The administrative receiver should either:

(a) Pay the money to the company (the directors) if the company is to continue, or
(b) Pass the money to the liquidator (if appointed) for distribution to the unsecured creditors

31 **Start again Ltd (in admin receivership)**

(a) **Estimated outcome statement**

	Notes	£	£
Assets subject to fixed charge			
Freehold Property			200,000
Goodwill			35,000
Plant & Machinery			60,000
			295,000
Less: costs			
Solicitor/Agent Fees	2	3,718	
Remuneration	5	13,125	
			(16,843)
Available to chargeholder			278,157
Due to chargeholder			(800,000)
Shortfall to chargeholder			(521,843)
Assets subject to floating charge			
Plant & Machinery	1		140,000
Stock & WIP			160,000
Trading Results	3		12,250
Book debts	4		240,000
			552,250
Less: costs			
Solicitor/Agent Fees	2	3,782	
Remuneration	5	22,500	
Sundry Costs		1,000	
Legal Costs		500	
ROT Payment		2,500	
			(30,282)
Available to Preferential Creditors			521,968
Preferential creditors			
			–
Available to Floating Chargeholder			521,968
Floating chargeholder			
Due to chargeholder			(521,843)
Surplus available for unsecured creditors			125

WORKINGS

1 **Plant and machinery**

		£
Fixed Charge	200,000 × 30%	60,000
Floating Charge	200,000 × 70%	140,000

2 **Solicitor/agent fees**

Solicitor's Fees		5,000
Agent's Fees		2,500
Total		7,500
Fixed proceeds		295,000
Floating proceeds		300,000
Total		595,000
Fixed Charge	7,500 × 295/595	3,718
Floating Charge	7,500 × 300/595	3,782

3 **Trading results**

		£
Sales	(3 × 25,000)	75,000
Purchases	(3 × 24,000)	(21,000)
Wages	(3 × 8,000)	(24,000)
Supervision charge	(3 × 4,000)	(12,000)
Utilities	(3 × 750)	(2,250)
Insurance		(3,500)
Trading Profit		12,250

4 **Book debts**

		£
Book Value		300,000
Realised to date		(190,000)
		110,000
Write Off (50%)		(55,000)
Balance to Collect		55,000
Total Book Debts	190,000 + 55,000	245,000
Solicitor's Fees		(5,000)
Estimated to Realise		240,000

Following the decision in Spectrum case, charges over book debts, whenever created, will be treated as floating.

5 **Remuneration**

Fixed Charge	(50 × 150) + (75 × 75)	13,125
Floating Charge	(50 × 150) + (200 × 75)	22,500

6 **Preferential creditors**

Since the charge was created prior to 15.09.03 no prescribed part calculation is required.

(b) Transfer of Undertakings (Protection of Employment) Regulations will apply.

... where an undertaking is transferred from one person to another, individuals employed by X, immediately before the transfer, automatically become the employees of Y from the time of the transfer, on the same terms as before.

... the buyer inherits all the liabilities under the employee contracts ie arrears of wages and holiday pay.

The employees do not have a claim in the administrative receivership as any outstanding monies will be claimed against the new employer

32 Mr Ronald Jones

Estimated Outcome Statement – Bankruptcy v IVA

	Notes	Bankruptcy £	IVA £
Assets			
Fixtures and fittings	1	5,000	–
Matrimonial home	2	20,000	30,000
Endowment policy	3	5,000	5,000
Contributions from trading	4	–	36,000
Total assets available		30,000	71,000
Less: costs			
OR costs		(1,000)	–
Trustee's fees		(5,000)	–
Nominee's fees		–	(1,500)
Supervisor's fees		–	(4,500)
Secretary of State Administration fee	5	(4,760)	-
Petitioning solicitors costs		(1,000)	-
Agent's costs		(1,500)	(750)
Accountant's fees		–	(500)
Solicitor's fees		(3,000)	(1,000)
Assets available for preferential creditors		13,740	62,750
Preferential creditors	6		
Employee wages		(600)	–
Surplus as regards preferential creditors		13,140	62,750
Unsecured creditors			
Landlord		(20,000)	–
HMRC – Schedule D		(10,000)	(10,000)
PAYE		(10,000)	(10,000)
HMRC – VAT		(20,000)	(20,000)
Business rates		(10,000)	(10,000)
Sundry creditors		(40,000)	(40,000)
Redundancy pay		(6,000)	–
Petitioning solicitors costs		–	(1,000)
Shortfall as regards creditors		(102,860)	(28,250)
Estimated dividend			
Preferential creditors		100p in £	100p in £
Unsecured creditors		11.32 in £	68.96p in £

WORKINGS

(i) Assumed retained in a voluntary arrangement to facilitate trading

(ii) **Bankruptcy**

		Mr Jones	*Mrs Jones*
	£	£	£
Property	100,000		
Less 1st mortgage	(20,000)		
	80,000		
Assume 50:50 split		40,000	40,000
Less 2nd mortgage		(20,000)	–
		20,000	40,000

Voluntary arrangement

		Mr Jones	*Mrs Jones*
	£	£	£
Property	100,000		
Less 1st mortgage	(20,000)		
Less 2nd mortgage	(20,000)		
	60,000		
Assume 50: 50 split		30,000	30,000

(iii) **Endowment policy**

Assume that in joint names.

Therefore, can only claim 50% of surrender value = £5,000

(iv) **Contributions from trading**

36 months @ £1,000 per month = £36,000

Not available in bankruptcy, assumed business will cease trading.

(v) **Secretary of State Administration fee**

17% on realisations over £2,000. (New scale from 06.04.2010)

£28,000 @17% = £4,760

Not applicable in a voluntary arrangement

(vi) **Preferential creditors**

Employees - up to four months wage arrears may be claimed preferentially to a maximum of £800 per employee

Three employees @ £200 = £600

(vii) **Landlord**

Bankruptcy

Landlord can claim rent for full period of lease ie 10 remaining years: but has a duty to mitigate claim.

Assumption that landlord secures new tenant after one year, therefore claim is limited to one year's rent @ £20,000 per year.

Assume bond of £5,000 offset against rent arrears of £5,000.

Unsecured claim £20,000

Voluntary agreement

Property required for ongoing trading.

Assume £5,000 arrears paid to secure property for this purpose.

Future rent paid as and when due under terms of the arrangement.

33

(a)

	£
Realisations	84,570
Less:	
Costs	16,390
Remuneration	11,250
Preferential creditors	10,700
	46,230
Prescribed part	
10,000 x 50%	5,000
36,230 x 20%	7,246
46,230	
Total prescribed part	12,246

(b)

	£
Net realisations	46,230
Less prescribed part	12,246
Balance for bank	33,984

Dividend 33,984/113,280 = 30p in £

(c)

Divided to unsecured creditors 12,246/244,920 = 5p in £

(d)

Final outcome statement

	£
Realisations	
Plant & machinery	485
Motor vehicles	7,250
Stock	400
Trade debtors	76,435
	84,570
Less: Costs	
Expenses	16,390
Remuneration	11,250
Preferential creditors	10,700
Prescribed part	12,246
Available for floating chargeholder	33,984

Unsecured creditors receive 5p in £

Bank receives 30p in £

34

(A)

Payment in full calculation

	Notes	£	£
Realisations			
Home		500,000	
Less mortgage		220,000	
Less agents fee		9,000	
Less solicitors fee		2,400	
		268,600	
Equity split (50:50)		134,300	
Expenses			
Sec of State fee			10,300
OR costs			1,715
Trustee remuneration (inc VAT)			9,000
Property valuation			120
Advertising			120
Insurance			200
Bond (inc VAT)			252
Petitioning creditor costs			2,000
ISA Fees			132
			23,839
Available for creditors			110,461
Creditors paid in full			

NOTE 1

Both items are subject to VAT

(B)

Secretary of State fee scale

	Band	Fee %
First	£2,000	0
Next	£1,700	100
Next	£1,500	75
Next	£396,000	15
Charge on balance until total of £80,000 taken		1

(C)

- By r6.207, not less than 21 days before the date of the hearing, the trustee must file a report at court dealing with all the matters set out in that rule
- A copy of the report must be sent to applicant at the same time that it is filed in court

4 Position of directors in insolvency situations

1 B SIP 4 - paragraph 16

2 C SIP13 Para 6.3

3 C S7(3) CDDA 1986 and paragraph 4(1) Insolvent Companies (Report or Conduct of Directors) Rules 1996

4 B S214

5 (a) The Disqualification Unit attaches particular importance to the following:

(i) Attempted concealment of assets or cases where assets have disappeared or a deficiency is unexplained

(ii) Appropriation of assets to other companies for no consideration, at an undervalue or on the basis of unreasonable charges for services

(iii) Preferences

(iv) Personal benefits obtained by directors

(v) Overvaluing assets in accounts for the purpose of obtaining loans or other financial accommodation, or to mislead creditors

(vi) Loans to directors in making share purchases

(vii) Dishonoured cheques

(viii) Use of delaying tactics

(ix) Non-payment of Crown debts to finance trading

(x) Phoenix operations

(xi) Misconduct in relation to operation of a factoring account

(xii) Taking of deposits for goods or services ultimately not supplied

(xiii) Cases where criminal convictions have resulted

(b) The following items should be appended to every report, where the information is available:

(i) A copy of the statement of affairs: where none has been submitted the report should include an estimate of the financial position of the company by listing known assets and liabilities

(ii) Notes issued for purposes of the creditors' meeting (liquidations only), any original notes signed by the directors from which the final issued note was prepared and any record of the proceedings at the meeting

(iii) Section 48 report to creditors (receivership)

(iv) Copy accounts as available – last statutory accounts and any other draft, management or interim accounts

(v) A summary of asset realisations, unrealised assets yet to be dealt with and claims notified

(vi) Dividend prospects

(vii) Aged creditor analysis – if readily available from the company's records

(c) A shadow director is defined as 'a person in accordance with whose directions or instructions the directors of a company are accustomed to act' (s251 CA 06)

A person isn't to be taken as a shadow director if they are giving advice in a professional capacity.

M C Bacon - to have been a shadow director the bank would have had to exert a degree of influence beyond that which is normal in bank/customer relations.

The following matters are relevant when assessing whether someone is a shadow director:

(i) Did they attend board meetings?
(ii) Did they sign company documentation eg contracts, letters etc?
(iii) Did they negotiate contracts?
(iv) Did they sign company cheques?
(v) Were they authorised signatories on any other company documentation?
(vi) What powers did they have?
(vii) Did the board follow their decisions?

If a person is found to be a shadow director they may be liable for the following actions:

(i) Wrongful trading
(ii) Misfeasance

A 'D' report can also be submitted which may lead to their disqualification for between two and 15 years.

6	D	SIP 13
7	E	S4 Insolvent Companies (Reports on Conduct of Directors) Rules 1986
8	B	SIP 4 Disqualification of Director's Statutory Reports
9	A	S212
10	D	Para 75(2) of Schedule B1 lists those who can apply to make an administrator liable for misfeasance
11	C	SIP 13 – Acquisition of assets of insolvent companies by directors
12	C	SIP 4 Disqualification of Director's statutory reports

5 Voluntary liquidation

1 (a) Directors meeting – where the directors of the company hold a board meeting and decide that due to the financial situation of the company (that it is unable to pay its debts as and when they fall due) that meetings of the company and creditors should be called to propose a voluntary liquidation. Also decide on which director to be responsible for chairing the necessary meetings and who is to prepare the company's Statement of Affairs

Company meeting – meeting of the company shareholders. Resolutions to be passed at the meeting include:

- Special Resolution to wind the company up
- Ordinary Resolution to appoint relevant liquidators (although the resolution passed at the creditors meeting will take precedence over this)

(b) s98(1A)

- Creditors meeting to be summoned for a day not later than the 14th days after the day on which there is to be held the company meeting at which the resolution for voluntary winding up is to be proposed;
- The notices of the creditors meeting shall be sent to the creditors not less than 7 days before the day on which that meeting is to be held:
- Notice of the creditors meeting to be advertised once in the Gazette; and
- Notice of the meeting to be advertised in such other manner as the directors think fit

s84(2A)

- Before a company passes a resolution for voluntary winding up it must give written notice of the resolution to the holder of any qualifying floating charge to which s72A applies

s84(2B)

- Where notice is given under subsection 2A a resolution for voluntary winding-up may be passed only:
  (a) After the end of the period of five business days beginning with the day on which the notice was given, or
  (b) If the person to whom the notice was given has consented in writing to the passing of the resolution

(c) s98(2)

- Name and address of a person qualified to act as an insolvency practitioner in relation to the company who, during the period before the day on which that meeting is to be held, will furnish creditors free of charge with such information concerning the company's affairs as they may reasonably require; or
- A place in the relevant locality where, on the 2 business days falling next before the day on which that meeting is to be held, a list of the names and addresses of the company's creditors will be available for inspection free of charge.

R4.51

- Name of the company
- Registered number of the company
- Venue for the meeting
- Time (not earlier than 12:00 hours on the business day before the day fixed for the meeting) by which, and the place at which, creditors must lodge any proofs and proxies necessary to entitle them to vote at the meeting

(d) s99(1)

- A statement of the affairs of the company in the prescribed form s99(2A)(a)

- Statement to be verified by some or all of the directors by a statement of truth

(e) s99(2)

- Particulars of the company's assets, debts and liabilities;
- Names and addresses of the company's creditors;
- The securities held by them respectively;
- The dates when the securities were respectively given; and
- Such further or other information as may be prescribed

2 C Schedule 4 Part I paragraph 3A

3 Pursuant to section 98 (2) the notice shall:

(i) State the name and address of a person qualified to act as IP in relation to the company who during the period before the day on which the meeting is to be held, will furnish the creditors free of charge with such information about the company's affairs as they may reasonably require, and

(ii) State a place in the relevant locality where on the 2 business days before the day on which the meeting is to be held, a list of the names and addresses of the company's creditors will be available for inspection free of charge.

Pursuant to section 98 (1):

(i) The meeting shall be summonsed for a day not later than the 14th day after the date of the company meeting at which a resolution for voluntary winding up is to be proposed

(ii) Notice to creditors should be sent not less than 7 days before the day on which the meeting is to be held (but see SIP 8 below)

(iii) The meeting should be advertised once in the Gazette and in such other manner as the director(s) thinks fit.

Pursuant to SIP 8 the notice:

(i) Should be sent to all classes of known creditors simultaneously and no later than the date that notice is sent to company members

(ii) Notice in the Gazette should appear as soon as possible

(iii) As appropriate notice should be sent to solicitors and other agents known to be acting for creditors

(iv) Provide creditors with explanatory notes setting out the manner in which remuneration is to be fixed.

4 (a) Steps to close case:

- Ensure all assets have been realised and that all costs have been paid or provided for.
- Ensure all ERA matters finalised.
- Ensure D returns submitted and all matters disposed of.
- Check all undertakings have been withdrawn no matters outstanding in the hands of agents, solicitors, professional advisers.
- Take money out of interest bearing accounts.
- Obtain clearance from agents, solicitors, that all matters are completed.
- Obtain price for future storage costs and pay.
- Prepare draft estimated distribution to include all future receipts and payments.
- Raise final fee/disbursement invoice.

- Ensure VAT refunds/payments dealt with.
- Submit final corporation tax return has been submitted and request clearance.
- Obtain clearance re VAT and PAYE/NIC.
- Transfer any unclaimed dividends to Central Accounting Unit, Birmingham (Insolvency Service Account).
- Send notice that no dividend or further dividend will be declared (R11.7).
- Prepare draft final report, notice of final meeting and proxy form (R4.490 and R4.126).
- Circulate the final report to creditors at least 8 weeks before final meeting date (R4.490) and circulate notice at least 28 days before the final meeting (R4.126).
- Advertise final meeting in the London Gazette at least one month before the final meeting (S106).
- If there is an outstanding challenge to liquidators fees or expenses final meeting can't be held (R4.49E).
- Prepare documentation for meetings of members and creditors:
  - Consent to chair final meeting (if not going to be the liquidator chairing meeting)
  - attendance register
  - schedule of proxies received
  - draft minutes of the final meetings. (R4.56).
- Hold meetings – ensure all attendees sign attendance register and present liquidator's report on the administration and summary receipts and payments account. (S106).
- After meeting finalise the minutes of the meeting signed by chairman together with proxy schedule and attendance record.
- Finalise 'draft' report after meeting:
  - redate at date of meeting
  - update R and P to the date of meeting
  - update SIP 9 information
  - update report if required.
- Send Form 4.72 to Companies House within 7 days of meeting stating whether creditors/shareholders granted liquidator their release. (Deemed to have happened unless voted against).
- Advise government departments of release if appropriate.
- Cancel bordereau.
- Ensure Regulation 13 forms are on file (Reg 13 IP Regs). Must be kept for 6 years
- Books and records to be destroyed 12 months after dissolution (15 months from filing final return (R4.72) at Companies House).
- Case file to be retained for 6 yrs from vacation of office.

(b) R4.126 (a):

- Total of all receipts with separate specification thereunder of:-
  - Receipts from trading carried on by liquidator
  - Payments made in the course of trading carried on by liquidator
  - Source of all other receipts
  - Payments to redeem securities
  - Costs of execution, and
  - Net realisations
- Costs of employing a solicitor

- Other legal costs
- Liquidator's remuneration
- Costs of employing an auctioneer
- Costs of employing a valuer
- Costs of taking possession of and maintaining the company's property
- Costs of advertising in the Gazette and other newspapers
- Incidental outlays
- Statement of the total of costs and charges incurred
- Amount paid to holders of debentures of each class of debenture, setting out the amount paid per debenture, the nominal value of each debenture in each class and the total amount paid in respect of each class
- The aggregate numbers of preferential and unsecured creditors and the aggregate amounts paidout to them, the aggregates for preferential and unsecured creditors set out separately unless all creditors have been paid in full
- Statements of the aggregate dividend paid on each pound of preferential and of unsecured debt and of the estimate of the value of company's net property which had been made under R4.49(2)(a)(ii)
- Amount of interest paid under s189
- Amount paid to contributories in respect of each class of share, setting out the amount per share and the nominal value of each share in each class
- Statement of the total amount paid to holders of debentures, preferential and unsecured creditors and contributories
- Statement of assets which have proved to be unrealisable, including the value of those assets which had been made for the purpose of R4.49(2)(a)(ii)
- Amounts paid into the Insolvency Services Account, set out separately in respect of:-
  - Unclaimed dividends payable to creditors in the winding up.
  - Other unclaimed dividends in the winding up
  - Monies held by the company trust in respect of dividends or other sums due before the commencement of the winding up to any person as a member of the company.

[Note can exclude items where the amount is zero.]

5 A Rule 4.34(2) (3) [from 6.4.2010 5 business days]

6 D S.84(2A)

7 (a) All the directors unless there are more than 2 directors, in which case a majority of them (s.89).

(b) 12 months from the commencement of the winding up (s.89).

(c) Making the declaration without reasonable grounds is an offence and a culpable director will be liable to a fine, imprisonment or both. If a company becomes insolvent after the resolution to put the company into MVL has been passed it will be presumed that the statutory declaration was not made on reasonable grounds s89(5). The company will then be placed into insolvent liquidation.

8 Particulars of the company's assets, debts and liabilities
Names and addresses of the company's creditors
Securities held by them respectively
Dates when the securities were respectively given
Such further or other information as may be prescribed

9 (a) At the initial creditors' meeting and in the subsequent report to creditors the liquidator should invite creditors to bring to his notice any particular matters which they consider require investigation.

The liquidator should also invite members of the liquidation committee to bring to his attention any matters requiring investigation. The liquidation committee should be advised of any decision to bring or defend any action or other legal proceedings in the name of and on behalf of the company which may be appropriate following the outcome of his investigation work.

Enquiries should be made of the officers of the company and other senior officials as to the company's affairs, including the reasons for failure and the location of its property and records.

The statutory books of the company, including the minute book, should be examined and compared with a search obtained from Companies House.

Details of all security held by banks and other parties should be obtained and the liquidator should check registration and consider the possible invalidity of any charge.

The liquidator should ascertain the location and safeguard and list the books, records and other accounting information belonging to the company.

The records of the company covering the period since the last date of the last audited accounts, or if none, since the incorporation of the company, should be examined to ensure that changes in the financial position of the company can be accounted for.

The books and records of the company should be examined to ensure that any transactions with associated companies or connected persons were carried out at arm's length and material transactions should be examined in detail.

The liquidator should aim to identify any rights of action which the company or the liquidator may have against third parties.

(b) Any three of the following:

The liquidator should examine:

Statutory books of the company – minute books (company and director meetings)

(i) Register of directors
(ii) Register of members
(iii) Register of charges

Accounting books and records of the company:

(i) Charges
(ii) Bank statements
(iii) Audited accounts
(iv) Management accounts
(v) Fixed asset register
(vi) Debtor's ledger
(vii) Cash books

(c) (i) Category 1
(ii) Category 2
(iii) Category 2
(iv) Category 1
(v) Category 1
(vi) Category 1

(d) The liquidator must give notice of his intention to declare and distribute a dividend to all creditors whose addresses are known to him and who have not proved their debts (rule11.2).

The notice must state a last date for proving (not less than 21 days from that of the notice) and that the liquidator shall declare a dividend within two months from the last date for proving.

Unless the liquidator has previously, by notice, invited creditors to prove their debts, the notice shall be gazetted and the liquidator may also advertise the notice in such other manner as he thinks fit.

Within 5 business days from the last date for proving the liquidator must deal with every creditor's proof.

(e) A proof may be admitted for dividend either for the whole amount claimed by the creditor or for part of that amount.

If the liquidator rejects a proof in whole or in part, he shall prepare a written statement of his reasons for doing so and send it, as soon as reasonably practicable, to the creditor.

If a creditor is dissatisfied with the liquidator's decision with respect to his proof he may apply to the court for the decision to be reversed or varied. The application must be made within 21 days of his receiving the statement.

The court shall fix a venue for the application to be heard, notice of which shall be sent by the applicant to the creditor who lodged the proof in question (if not himself) and the liquidator.

The liquidator shall, on receipt of the notice, file in court the relevant proof, together with a copy of the statement.

10 A R4.153(1) – the committee comes into being when the liquidator issues a certificate of due constitution

11 B R4.34(2)

12 (a) Letter of engagement

(b) Board resolutions – recommending MVL, authorising calling GM, authorising swearing declaration of solvency

(c) Written notice to QFC of intention to pass resolution to wind up

(d) Declaration of solvency – Form 4.70

(e) Statement of company's assets and liabilities – Form 4.18

(f) Notice of GM – to include date, time, place of meeting, resolution to wind up and proxy form – Form 8.5

(g) Notice of resolution to wind up

(h) Notice of liquidator's appointment

(i) Certificate of appointment

13 D S105 [From 6 April 2010 (except Scotland) no creditors' meeting is required instead the liquidator must send out a progress report to the company and creditors – s.104A]

14 A R4.158

15 A S85

16 C S110

17 **SIP 8**

(a) Name and address of liquidator

(b) Name and address of creditors forming a liquidation committee

(c) Details of resolutions passed at the meeting

(d) There is no need to supply a detailed report on all that transpired at the meeting, but matters of particular reference should be mentioned

(e) Creditors should be asked to bring to the liquidator's attention any matter of which they consider he should be aware

18 C S84 (2A)

19 C S89

20 A Power to bring legal proceedings under S213, 214, 238, 239, 242 or 423 of IA 86

D Power to pay any class of creditor in full

F Power to make any compromise or arrangement with creditors or persons claiming to be creditors, or having or alleging themselves to have any claim against the company or whereby the company may be rendered liable

21 C R4.139(4) – 28 days from the appointment of the liquidator

22 B R4.158 – two creditor members present or represented

23 E From 6 April 2010 there is no longer a requirement for a general meeting at each year's end in England and Wales

24 (a)

Dalwood (2002) Limited
Statement of Affairs as at 31 May 20X9

	Workings/ Notes	*Book Value*	*Estimated to Realise*
		£	£
Assets specifically pledged			
Book debts	1	420,000	290,700
Less: due to Full-on-Factors	2	(354,500)	(354,500)
Surplus/Deficit) to Full-on-Factors		65,500	(63,800)
Leasehold		222,000	40,000
Goodwill		1,000	50,000
Intellectual Property	3	18,000	–
		241,000	90,000
Less: due to Full-on-Factors	2	–	(63,800)
Assets available to Bank		241,000	26,200
Less: due to Bank of Oxford	2	(85,000)	(85,000)
Surplus/(Deficit) to Bank of Oxford		156,000	(58,800)
Assets not specifically pledged			
Refrigeration Units		184,000	90,000
Stock		85,000	21,250
Assets Available for Preferential Creditors		269,000	111,250
Preferential creditors			
Wages arrears		700	
Holiday Pay		12,000	
			(12,700)
Estimated surplus as regards preferential creditors			98,550
Estimated prescribed part of net property to C/F	4		(22,710)
Estimated total assets available for floating chargeholder			75,840

	Workings/ Notes	Book Value	Estimated to Realise
		£	£
Floating charge			
Bank of Oxford			(58,800)
Assets available for unsecured creditors			17,040
Prescribed Part B/D			22,710
			39,750
Unsecured creditors			
Trade Creditors		342,000	
Hire Purchase		112,000	
PAYE/NIC	5	8,000	
VAT	5	30,000	
Notice Pay		7,500	
Redundancy		14,000	
Directors Loan		32,000	
Corporation Tax		5,000	
			(550,500)
Deficiency to creditors			(510,750)
Share Capital			(10,000)
Deficiency to members			(520,750)

WORKINGS/NOTES

(1) **Book debts**

	£
Book Value	420,000
Less: bad debt	(78,000)
	342,000
Less: 15% provision	(51,300)
Estimated to Realise	290,700

(2) **Deed of Priority**

- **Fixed Charges**
  - Full-on-Factors
  - Bank of Oxford
- **Floating Charges**
  - Bank of Oxford
  - Full-on-Factors

(3) **Intellectual Property**

Assume value less as the directors offer allocates no consideration to R and D <u>or</u> candidates should use the book value (which will result in an overall deficit lower by £18,000).

(4) **Prescribed Part**

	£
50% of first £10,000	5,000
20% of balance of £88,550	17,710
	22,710

(5) **VAT and PAYE/NIC**

All unsecured

Note: Since the Brumark case, charges over book debts, whenever created, will be treated as floating charge.

(b) S166 limits the director's powers to:

(i) Take control and custody of the company's property
(ii) Dispose of goods of a wasting nature
(iii) Do all things necessary to protect the company's assets

If the liquidator wishes to do anything else he must apply to the court for leave

The liquidator must attend the creditor's meeting and report to it on the exercise by him of his powers under the act and with sanction of the court

(c) Where the directors indicate to the liquidator prior to the s98 meeting that they intend to make an offer for some/ all of the business the liquidator should advise the directors that he will advise any committee of the director's offer, who will have an opportunity to comment.

The liquidator also has a duty to report any connected party transactions to the members and creditors when he first reports to them after the transaction has taken place.

At the s98 meeting, the director has a statutory duty to give notice of any disposals of company property to a person connected to the company.

Any such disclosure should provide creditors with sufficient information to have a full appreciation of the nature of the transaction.

The liquidator must ensure that any such sale is:

(i) At arms length
(ii) On the basis of a professional valuation of the assets concerned
(iii) In the best interests of the creditors and the company

The liquidator, in advising the directors in respect of the purchase of company assets, should consider his appointment as liquidator of the company, to ensure that no conflicts arise.

The liquidator should encourage the directors to make an offer, however such an offer should not be accepted until after the s98 meeting has been held, to enable creditors views to be obtained and a thorough marketing of the assets to be undertaken.

(d) Depending on the terms of the hire purchase agreement, if there is a consolidation clause on the agreements, the directors may have to pay the outstanding liability to the HP company in the sum of £112,000 in order to purchase the refrigeration units.

(e) The liquidator should submit a proof of debt form in the liquidation of the debtor company and any dividend then paid would be received for the benefit of the creditors of Dalwood (2002) Limited.

25 (a) (i)

Cash book

	£		£
Balance b/f	25,148.97		
		Returned Cheque	3,100.00
Bank Interest	33.24		
Bank Interest	36.99		
Bank Interest	27.55	Balance c/f	22,146.75
	25,246.75		25,246.75

Reconciliation Statement

	£	£
Balance per Bank Statement		121,347.82
Less: *Unpresented Cheques*		
Preferential Dividend – HMRC	62,587.99	
Preferential Dividend – DSS	23,487.99	
Unsecured Dividend – Paper Ltd	2,114.21	
Unsecured Dividend – Ink Ltd	311.10	
Unsecured Dividend – Colours Ltd	2,337.11	
Unsecured Dividend – F Paper Ltd	4,775.28	
Unsecured Dividend – HMRC	3,587.39	
		(99,201.07)
Balance per Adjusted Cash Book		22,146.75

Note: The bank statement receipt of £22,127.50 on 5.9.X8 represents the following cash book entries on that date:

	£
Receipt	
Freehold property	260,000.00
Less: payments	
Property agent's fees	(6,110.00)
Fixed charge holder	(230,000.00)
Solicitors' fees	(1,762.50)
	22,127.50

(ii) **Quarter to 30/08/X8**

	£	£
Output (Sales)	11,375.00	
	16,362.50	
	836.85	
		28,574.35
Input (Purchases)	4,588.02	
	875.00	
	140.00	
		(5,603.02)
Amount Payable		22,971.33

Quarter to 30/11/X8

	£	£
Output (Sales)	–	
Input (Purchases)	910.00	
	262.50	
		(1,172.50)
Amount Receivable		(1,172.50)
Final Return to 13/03/09		
Output (Sales)		–
Input (Purchases)	1,137.50	
		(1,137.50)
Amount Receivable		(1,137.50)

(b) Accounts may be maintained by a liquidator at any clearing bank of his choice

(i) Reg 24 requires the liquidator to make payments into the ISA within 14 days of the expiration of the period of six months from the date of his appointment and of every period of six months thereafter until he vacates office.

(ii) 'Payments' include:

- The balance of funds in his hands or in his control
- Unclaimed or undistributed assets or dividends

(iii) But excluding such part as the liquidator considers necessary to retain for the immediate purposes of the liquidation.

Balance at bank after six months (as at 1 Dec 20X8) – £191,925.48

Entitled to retain monies required immediately ie to pay preferential dividend totalling £144,267.89 and to retain unsecured dividend declared totalling £22,247.94. This leaves a sum of £25,409.55 to be invested at ISA. This hasn't happened to date.

Liquidator should also query why preferential dividends paid to HM Revenue and Customs and DWP (Department of Works and Pensions) on 15/12/X8 remain uncashed at 13/3/X9. Have the correct references/addresses been used?

Liquidator has a duty under r4.180 to pay a dividend whenever he has sufficient funds in hand. Query whether a dividend could have been paid earlier?

(c) s192 requires the liquidator to send a Statement of Receipts and Payments on Form 4.68 to Registrar of Companies not more than 30 days after the expiration of the first year and thereafter at six monthly intervals. (For liquidations commenced after 06.04.2010 see s.92A

The Secretary of State has the power to require the liquidator to send him an account of receipts and payments. He may require this account to be audited.

26 D Ordinary resolution

27 A A majority of the directors

28 E The ISA is no longer used in voluntary liquidations, in **compulsory** liquidations monies must be paid in at least once every 14 days or immediately if £5,000 or more is received

29 (a) **Powers requiring sanction**:

Any four of the following:

(i) Power to pay any class of creditors in full

(ii) Power to make any compromise or arrangement with creditors or persons claiming to be creditors, or having or alleging themselves to have any claim (present or future, certain or contingent, ascertained or sounding only in damages) against the company, or whereby the company may be rendered liable.

(iii) Power to compromise, on such terms as may be agreed:

- All calls and liabilities to calls, all debts and liabilities capable of resulting in debts, and all claims (present or future, certain or contingent, ascertained or sounding only in damages) subsisting or supposed to subsist between the company and a contributory or alleged contributory or other debtor or person apprehending liability to the company, and
- All questions in any way relating to or affecting the assets or the winding up of the company, and take any security for the discharge of any such call, debt, liability or claim and give a complete discharge in respect of it.

(iv) Powers requiring sanction: compulsory liquidation

- Dispensing with duty to settle a list of contributories
- Making a call
- Transaction with committee member

(v) Powers requiring sanction: voluntary liquidation

- Transaction with committee member
- Where the liquidator proposes to re-imburse himself after commencement of liquidation for assistance given to the directors in connection with the preparation of the statement of affairs

(b) **Powers requiring sanction in a winding up by the court but not in a voluntary winding up**:

(i) Power to bring or defend any action or other legal proceeding in the name and on behalf of the company.

(ii) Power to carry on the business of the company so far as may be necessary for its beneficial winding up

(c) **Powers exercisable without sanction**:

Any four of the following:

(i) Power to sell any of the company's property by public auction or private contract, with power to transfer the whole of it to any person or to sell the same in parcels.

(ii) Power to do all acts and execute, in the name and on behalf of the company, all deeds, receipts and other documents and for that purpose to use, when necessary, the company's seal.

(iii) Power to prove, rank and claim in the bankruptcy, insolvency or sequestration of any contributory for any balance against his estate, and to receive dividends in the bankruptcy, insolvency or sequestration in respect of that balance, as a separate debt due from the bankrupt or insolvent, and rateably with the other separate creditors.

(iv) Power to draw, accept, make and endorse any bill of exchange or promissory note in the name and on behalf of the company, with the same effect with respect to the company's liability as if the bill or note had been drawn, accepted, made or endorsed by or on behalf of the company in the course of its business.

(v) Power to raise on the security of the assets of the company any money requisite.

(vi) Power to take out in his official name letters of administration to any deceased contributory, and to do in his official name any other act necessary for obtaining payment of any money due from a contributory or his estate which cannot conveniently be done in the name of the company.

(vii) Power to appoint an agent to do any business which the liquidator is unable to do himself.

(viii) Power to do all such other things as may be necessary for winding up the company's affairs and distributing its assets.

30 C Rule 4.52

31 A s112(1)

32 B See rule 12A.21(2)(b)

33 (a) In fixing the venue for the meeting of creditors, the convenor shall have regard to the convenience of the persons (other than whoever is to be chairman) who are invited to attend. If the majority of attendees are coming from the North East of England, he should consider holding the meeting there instead of in Birmingham. Note from 6.4.2010 remote attendance at meetings possible.

(b) (c) Rule 4.60

(c) (i) Rule 4.56 – the liquidator, or a person nominated by him in writing to act, shall be chairman of the meeting.

A person nominated under this paragraph must be either:

- One who is qualified to act as an IP in relation to the company,
- An employee of the liquidator or his firm who is experienced in insolvency matters

Need not attend s98 meeting, but must, in writing, appoint another suitable person to act as chairman per R4.56.

(ii) If already appointed as liquidator, he must attend the meeting and report to the meeting on any exercise of his powers.

(d) (i) (b) s166(4)

(ii) (c) SIP 8 Conduct at meetings of creditors held pursuant to s98

34 (a) The committee does not come into being and cannot act until the liquidator has issued a certificate of due constitution in Form 4.47.

The certificate lists the members of the committee and who they are representing if acting on behalf of a company.

The liquidator cannot issue the certificate until all members have agreed to act.

The committee must have a minimum of three persons – R4.153(4)

To be eligible to be a member, he/she must be a creditor of the company and have lodged a proof which has not been wholly disallowed for voting purposes or distribution or dividend.

(b) R4.170 covers dealings by committee members.

The Rule applies to:

(i) Any member of the liquidation committee,

(ii) Any committee member's representative, any person who is an associate of a member of the committee or a committee member's representative, and

(iii) Any person who has been a member of the committee at any time in the last 12 months.

A person to whom this Rule applies shall not enter into any transaction whereby he:

(i) Receives out of the company's assets any payment for services given or goods supplied in connection with the administration, or

(ii) Obtains any profit from the administration, or

(iii) Acquires any asset forming part of the estate.

Such a transaction may be entered into by a person to whom this Rule applies:

(i) With the prior leave of the court, or

(ii) If he does so as a matter of urgency, or by way of performance of a contract in force before the date on which the company went into liquidation, and obtains the court's leave for the transaction, having applied for it without undue delay, or

(iii) With the prior sanction of the liquidation committee, where it is satisfied that the person will be giving full value in the transaction.

The committee member who is seeking to purchase the assets should not be allowed to participate in any committee discussions or voting on this issue.

The court may, on the application of any person interested:

(i) Set aside a transaction on the ground that it has been entered into in contravention of this Rule, and

(ii) Make with respect to it such order as it thinks fit, including an order requiring a person to whom this Rule applies to account for any profit obtained from the transaction and compensate for any resultant loss.

Since the committee is not yet established, must get sanction from the court under R4.170(3)

(c) The liquidator has a duty to report to the committee all such matters as appear to him to be of concern to them – R4.155(1)

R4.155(2) – In case of matters so indicated to him by the committee, the liquidator need not comply with any request for information where it appears to him that:

(i) The request is frivolous or unreasonable, or

(ii) The cost of complying would be excessive, having regard to the relative importance of the information, or

(iii) There are insufficient assets to enable him to comply.

R4.168 – The liquidator shall, as and when directed by the liquidation committee, send a written report to every member of the committee setting out the position generally as regards the progress of the winding up and matters arising in connection with it, (but not more often than once in any period of two months)

R4.155(3) – Where the committee has come into being more than 28 days after the appointment of the liquidator, he shall report to them, in summary form, what actions he has taken since his appointment, and shall answer all such questions as may be put to him regarding his conduct of the winding up.

R4.155(4) – A person who becomes a member of the committee at any time after its first establishment is not entitled to require a report to him by the liquidator, otherwise than in summary form, of any matters previously arising.

R4.155(5) – Nothing in this rule disentitles the committee, or any member of it from having access to the liquidator's records of the liquidation, or from seeking an explanation of any matter within the committee's responsibility.

(d) It is a function of the liquidation committee to decide on what basis the liquidator's fees shall be calculated (failing which a general meeting of creditors).

In determining the mode, the committee/general meeting should take into account the following factors:

(i) Complexity or otherwise of the case
(ii) Any responsibility of an exceptional kind or degree which falls on the office holder
(iii) Effectiveness with which duties carried out
(iv) Value and nature of assets

The liquidator should not be allowed to determine his own fees. The committee should vote on the basis of his remuneration.

(e) Powers which cannot be exercised by the liquidator unless he obtains sanction of the court or creditors are:

(i) Pay any class of creditor in full
(ii) Make compromises or arrangements with creditors
(iii) Compromise claims against contributories or debtors of the company

All other powers can be exercised without sanction, therefore the liquidator is incorrect. May be prudent to obtain sanction anyway.

35 D s95

36 B R4.34(2)

37 A (S89(2))

38 A

39

- Special resolution to wind up company as MVL
- Ordinary resolution to appoint liquidator
- Ordinary resolution to agree liquidator's remuneration
- Special resolution to agree a distribution in specie

6 Compulsory liquidation

1 C Paragraph 1, Schedule 4 Part 1, and s.165 and s.167

2 B Section 123

3 B R.4.54(3)

4 Any four of the following:

(a) Power to sell any of the company's property by public auction or private contract, with power to transfer the whole of it to any person or to sell the same in parcels.

(b) Power to do all acts and execute, in the name and on behalf of the company, all deeds, receipts and other documents and for that purpose to use, when necessary, the company's seal.

(c) Power to prove, rank and claim in the bankruptcy, insolvency or sequestration of any contributory for any balance against his estate, and to receive dividends in the bankruptcy, insolvency or sequestration in respect of that balance, as a separate debt due from the bankrupt or insolvent, and rateably with the other separate creditors.

(d) Power to draw, accept, make and indorse any bill of exchange or promissory note in the name and on behalf of the company, with the same effect with respect to the company's liability as if the bill or note had been drawn, accepted, made or indorsed by or on behalf of the company in the course of its business.

(e) Power to raise on the security of the assets of the company any money requisite.

(f) Power to take out in his official name letters of administration to any deceased contributory, and to do in his official name any other act necessary for obtaining payment of any money due from a contributory or his estate which cannot conveniently be done in the name of the company. In all such cases the money due is deemed, for the purpose of enabling the liquidator to take out the letters of administration or recover the money, to be due to the liquidator himself.

(g) Power to appoint any agent to do any business which the liquidator is unable to do himself.

(h) Power to do all such other things as may be necessary for winding up of the company's affairs and distributing its assets.

5 C s136(5)

6 D s137

7 C s122

8 C s123

9 B s267(4)

10 A s129(2)

11 B R4.54 – 14 days (from 6.4.2010 – previously 21 days)

12 (a) If the company was already in voluntary liquidation, the liquidation is deemed to commence from the date of the resolution to wind up voluntarily.

(b) **R4.102**

(i) State whether he proposes to summon meetings of creditors and contributories for the purpose of establishing a liquidation committee, or proposes to summon only a meeting of creditors for that purpose, and

(ii) If he does not propose to summon any such meeting, set out the powers of the creditors under the Act to require him to summon one.

(c) **s140**

(i) Where a winding up order is made immediately upon the ending of administration the administrator may be appointed liquidator

(ii) When a winding up order is made at a time when there is a supervisor of a company voluntary arrangement approved in relation to the company, the supervisor may be appointed liquidator

13 A R4.106A(2)(a)

14 C R4.125

15 A S267(4)

16 B S133(4)

17 (a) All money received by the trustee must be sent to the ISA at least once every 14 days

(b) If > £5,000 is received, it must be banked in the ISA immediately

18 C S122

19 B, D R4.125 – The report must now also state the amount, if any, paid under prescribed part rules.

20 A

21 By s143 the functions of a liquidator are to secure that the assets of the company are got in, realised and distributed to the company's creditors and, if there is a surplus, to the persons entitled to it.

22 By r4.71 and SIP 12 which sets out best practice to include:

- A record of every resolution passed at the meeting and in the event of a poll being taken, the value or number of votes for and against
- If a liquidation committee has been established include the names and addresses of those elected
- Title of proceedings
- Date, time and venue of meeting
- Name and description of chairman and any other person involved in conduct of proceedings
- A list of creditors attending or represented at meeting
- Name of any officer or former officer attending the meeting
- The exercise of any discretion by the chairman in relation to admissibility or value of any claim for voting purposes

Where a meeting has been asked to approve the liquidator's remuneration, the information provided to the meeting in support of that request should be included. The minutes must be authenticated by the chairman.

7 Liquidator's investigations and antecedent transactions

1 As a priority the office holder should ascertain the location and safeguard and list the company's books, records and other accounting information.

Other steps to be taken under the SIP to ascertain information and make an initial assessment as to how to proceed include:

Inviting the creditors' committee and creditors of the company to bring to his attention any matters of concern about the operation of the business in the run up to the insolvency and identify potential recoveries that the office holder might pursue. The committee should be provided with a copy of SIP 2.

The office holder is required to demonstrate that he has determined if any matters require further investigation. He will do this by considering the information acquired in the conduct of the case and by questioning directors/senior employees of the company as to the company's affairs, including the reasons for the company's failure and the location of the company's books and records.

2 First in any liquidation the liquidator needs sanction to bring legal proceedings under ss. 213, 214, 238, 239, 242, 243 or 423.

Second Special rules are in place with regard to litigation expenses (incurred for the purpose of either swelling the assets available for creditors or for protecting or realising the estate assets). No consent is needed to deduct litigation expenses of up to £5,000 but if the expense is in excess of that sum and deduction from the floating charge pool will reduce the sums available to a floating charge holder the prior consent of the affected charge holder(s) / preferential creditors will be required before the deduction can be made. Alternatively, approval must be sought from the court.

Rule 4.218C sets out the required content of any request:

- Statement describing the legal proceedings
- The power to bring these proceedings
- The amount of litigation expenses for which approval is being sought
- Notice that approval or authorisation or other reply must be made in writing within 28 days from date of receipt.
- A statement explaining the consequence of failure to reply.

3 Section 435 (6)

A company is an associate of another company:

(a) if the same person has control of both, or a person has control of one and persons who are his associates, or he and persons who are his associates, have control of the other, or

(b) if a group of two or more persons has control of each company, and the groups either consist of the same persons or could be regarded as consisting of the same persons by treating (in one or more cases) a member of either group as replaced by a person of whom he is an associate.

4
- Payments made before 1st July – may be investigated as potential preference payments per s239 IA86.
- Liquidator would need to prove a desire to put the creditor in a better position – 'desire to prefer is presumed where connected'.
- It would also be necessary to prove that the company was insolvent at the time of making the payments, or became insolvent as a result.
- The payments made in July and August will be void per s.127 as they are dispositions made after the commencement of the winding up (unless validation orders obtained from the court).
- Payments may also be pursued as transactions defrauding creditors s.423.

5 C

6 C

7 (a) **Letter format**

Statutory obligations to co-operate with the trustee and consequences of failing to do so:

The bankrupt is under a duty to (s333(1)):

(i) Give to the trustee such information as to his affairs
(ii) Attend on the trustee at all times
(iii) Do all such other things

As the trustee may, for the purposes of carrying out his functions, reasonably require.

The bankrupt must, within 21 days, give notice to the trustee of any property acquired by him after commencement or any increases in income (s333(2)).

Failure to comply constitutes contempt of court.

The bankrupt must deliver up to the trustee possession of any property, books, papers or other records of which he has possession or control and of which the trustee is required to take possession (s312(1)).

Failure to comply is a contempt of court.

(b) The official receiver may apply for the public examination of the bankrupt under s290. The trustee may attend and ask questions of the bankrupt who will be examined as to his affairs, dealings and property and the causes of failure.

The trustee or official receiver may apply for the private examination of the bankrupt under s366 and the following persons:

(i) Bankrupt's spouse or former spouse or civil partner or former civil partner

(ii) Any person known or believed to have property comprised in the bankrupt's estate in his possession

(iii) Bankrupt's debtors

(iv) Any person appearing to the court to be able to give information concerning the bankrupt or the bankrupt's affairs, dealings or property

The court has a general power to issue a warrant for the arrest of a bankrupt or the seizure of books, papers, records, money or goods of the bankrupt where he;

(i) Has absconded or is about to abscond

(ii) Is about to remove goods with a view to avoiding or delaying possession by official receiver or trustee

(iii) Has failed to attend any examination ordered by the court

(iv) Has removed any goods in his possession exceeding £1,000 in value

(v) Has concealed or destroyed any goods, papers or records which might be of use to creditors

The trustee or official receiver may apply to court to issue a warrant for the seizure of any property comprised in the bankrupt's estate or books, papers or records relating to the bankrupt's affairs or property.

The court may order the production of records by HM Revenue and Customs for the purposes of public or private examination.

(c) The trustee can apply to court for an order that excessive pension contributions previously made by the bankrupt into his pension, that have unfairly prejudiced creditors, be paid back to the estate (s342A).

The court will consider whether:

(i) Any of the contributions were made for the purpose of putting assets beyond the reach of creditors and

(ii) The total amount of any contributions made are excessive in view of the bankrupt's circumstances when those costs were made

The court may make such order as it thinks fit for restoring the position to what it would have been had the excessive contributions not been made. This might include:

(i) Requiring the person responsible for the pension arrangement to pay an amount

(ii) Adjusting the liabilities of the arrangement in respect of the bankrupt or any other beneficiary

(iii) Payment of the costs of the person responsible for complying with the court order

8 (a) Note format

To: Liquidation committee

Re: Fleece Limited in Liquidation

Date:

There are six possible remedies available which might result in the recovery of funds. These are detailed as follows:

(i) Reduction in bank overdraft:

Mr Sornoff has personally guaranteed the bank overdraft and therefore he is in a better position following the reduction in the bank overdraft from £80,000 to £3,000.

This is potentially a preference under s340. In order to take action the liquidator must show:

- The person preferred is a creditor, guarantor or surety (Mr Sornoff is a guarantor)
- The company must do anything or suffer anything to be done which puts that creditor, guarantor or surety in a better position in the event of insolvency than they would otherwise be in the event of insolvent liquidation (here the company actively reduced the overdraft by collecting new deposits and seeking payment from existing customers)
- The company must have been influenced by a desire to prefer. This is assumed in the case of an associate (Mr Sornoff is an associate since he is a director of the company)
- The company must have been insolvent at the time of the transaction (the accounts show that the company has been making trading losses over the last two years. The liquidator would have to show that the company was actually insolvent at the time of the reduction in the overdraft)
- The transaction must have taken place within two years of the onset of liquidation

If the preference is proven, then the court may order that the position of the company be restored to what it was prior to the preference taking place. Mr Sornoff could be asked to pay funds into the liquidation.

It could also be argued that the bank has been preferred since its debt has been significantly reduced over the period. As the bank is not connected to the company the relevant time period for a preference to be challenged is reduced to six months pre liquidation and the liquidator must show that the company desired to prefer the bank. This may be rebutted by evidence of the bank making demands for the overdraft to be repaid.

(ii) Settlement of debt due to Ice Axe Limited:

This may be challenged as a preference under s340 and the liquidator must show the same matters as discussed in i. above.

The company is owned by Mr Sornoff's brother so the parties are connected and the relevant time to challenge the transaction is two years prior to the onset of liquidation (here the transaction took place eight months prior to liquidation).

The desire to prefer is also assumed.

If shown, Ice Axe Limited could be ordered by the court to repay the moneys to the liquidator.

(iii) Taking of customer deposits:

This could be evidence of fraudulent trading under s214.

Fraudulent trading occurs where any person is knowingly a party to the carrying on of the business with the intention of defrauding creditors or for any fraudulent purpose.

This is also a criminal offence under CA 2006 s993 and the court may order Mr Sornoff to make a contribution to the company's assets as it thinks proper.

Fraudulent trading is difficult to prove.

(iv) Wrongful trading s214:

This is where a director of the company in insolvent liquidation knew, or ought to have known, that the company was unable to pay its debts and did not take steps to minimise losses to creditors.

Wrongful trading is a civil matter and if found guilty Mr Sornoff can be ordered to make a contribution to the company's assets as the court thinks proper. Such a contribution will be based on the losses incurred by creditors due to the wrongful trading.

Here the accounts for the last two years show a loss. Mr Sornoff should have been aware that the company couldn't avoid insolvent liquidation.

(v) Installation of conservatory at daughter's house:

This could be challenged as a transaction at an undervalue under s339.

In order to succeed the liquidator must show:

- There was a transaction with no consideration given (here the daughter has not paid for her conservatory)
- The company must have been insolvent at the time of the transaction (accounts show that the company was making losses). Insolvency is presumed if the transaction was with a connected party (here, Mr Sornoff is connected to his daughter so insolvency will be assumed)
- The transaction must have taken place at a relevant time which is two years prior to the onset of liquidation (transaction took place within that period)

There is a defence, that the transaction was entered into in good faith and there were reasonable grounds for believing it would benefit the company.

The court can order that the position of the company be restored to what it was prior to the transaction. The daughter can be ordered to pay for the conservatory.

(vi) Increase in salary:

This would appear to be a breach of the director's fiduciary duty to act in the best interests of the company, creditors and members.

The liquidator can take an action for misfeasance under s212 and the court may order Mr Sornoff to contribute to the company's assets as it thinks fit.

(vii) Cars not disclosed on statement of affairs:

This is a matter to be disclosed in the directors' report under CDDA.

The liquidator should seek the immediate return of the assets held by Mr Sornoff.

Under s234 the liquidator may apply to the court for an order requiring Mr Sornoff to deliver the property to him.

(b) The liquidator is required to submit a D1 report as soon as reasonably practicable to the Secretary of State where it appears that the conduct of a director makes him unfit to be concerned in the management of a company.

The report should be submitted within six months of the date of the winding up resolution (this is to allow the Secretary of State time to bring proceedings – must be done within two years of the company becoming insolvent).

If the liquidator is unable to submit a report within the six month period he should submit an interim return (indicating when a report or a final return will be submitted) or a final return (where no matters have arisen which require a report).

The liquidator should submit a return or a report in respect of all directors and shadow directors who were in office in the three years preceding the winding up resolution.

Reports should be based on information coming to light in the ordinary course of the liquidator's work, no specific investigations are required.

The basis of the liquidator's opinions in the report should be documented. Details of the conduct giving rise to the decision to submit a report should be included and the following matters should be dealt with in the body of the report:

- Position on any civil recovery action
- Adequacy of the accounting records
- Evidence available in support of insolvent trading
- Professional advice taken by the directors and specific correspondence which sheds light on the director's conduct ie with banks, solicitors, accountants or creditors

The following items should be attached to every report:

- Copy of the Statement of Affairs
- Notes issued for the purposes of the creditors' meeting
- Copy accounts where available, last statutory accounts and any other draft, management or interim accounts
- A summary of asset realisations, unrealised assets yet to be dealt with and claims notified
- Dividend prospects
- Aged creditor analysis

Directors' reports should be kept confidential.

9 (a)

Scam Limited in Liquidation
Deficiency account for the period
31/12/X6 to 30/04/X8

	£
Balance per reserves 31/12/X6	(10,000)
Amounts written down per Statement of Affairs	
Freehold property	(75,000)
Fixtures and fittings	10,000
Plant and machinery	125,000
Book debts	20,000
Inter co debt	40,000
Office furniture and equipment	15,000
Stock	90,000
Motor vehicles	25,000
	(250,000)
Movement on fixed assets between 31/12/X6 and 30/04/X8	
Loss on sale of lathe	(15,000)
Profit on sale of car	1,000
IT equipment	(5,000)
	(19,000)
Additional liabilities as a result of liquidation	
Redundancy pay	30,000
Pay in lieu of notice	25,000
	(55,000)
Trading losses 1/01/X7 to 30/06/X7	(220,000)
Estimated trading loss 1/07/X7 to 30/04/X8 (balancing figure)	(86,000)
Estimated deficiency per Statement of Affairs	(640,000)

(b) (i) Payment of £40,000 to Royal Limited would appear to be a preference s239

- The person preferred is a creditor, guarantor or surety

  (Applies to Mr Steel who guaranteed the debt)

- The company must do anything which puts that person in a better position, in the event of the insolvent liquidation of the company, than they would otherwise have been in

- The company must have been influenced by a desire to prefer (assumed in the case of a connected party)

- Company must have been insolvent at the time of the transaction

- Transaction must have taken place at a relevant time:

  - Within six months of onset of insolvency, or
  - Within two years where parties are connected

  (Here, transaction took place in January X8, within six month period)

- The court may make such order as it thinks fit for restoring the position to what it would have been if the company had not entered into the transaction.

(ii) Possible phoenix operation re Scam2 Limited:

- Applies to anyone who was a director or shadow director of a company in the 12 months ending with the day before it went into insolvent liquidation

- (Applies here to Mr Steele)

- s216 prohibits such a person, for a period of five years, from being:

  - A director of a company known by a prohibited name

        – In any way concerned, directly or indirectly, in the promotion, formation or management of such a company or in the carrying on of a business under a prohibited name

    – **'Prohibited name'**

        – Any name by which the liquidated company was known in the last 12 months

        – Or which is so similar a name that it suggests an association with the liquidated company

    Exceptions

    1 With sanction of the court

    2 When IP has arranged for the transfer of the whole or substantially the whole of the failed business to a 'successor' company, the successor notifying the creditors of the insolvent company

    3 When the company in question has been known by the name for the last 12 months consecutive to the failed company going into liquidation. Such a company must not have been dormant at any time during that period of 12 months

    None of the above appear to apply to Scam2 Limited.

    – **Penalties**

        – Criminal offence – Mr Steele could be liable to a fine and/ or imprisonment
        – May be held personally liable for the relevant debts of the new company

(iii) **Sale of lathe for £5,000 on 3/07/X8**:

- Possible sale at an undervalue s238
- Where a company has made a gift or the value received by the company is significantly less in money or moneys worth

Defence

That the transaction was entered into in good faith and there were reasonable grounds for believing that it would benefit the company.

Transaction must have taken place at a relevant time:

- Within two years of onset of insolvency, and
- Company must have been insolvent at the time of the transaction (Insolvency is presumed if parties are connected)

The court may make such order as it thinks fit for restoring the position to what it would have been if the company had not entered into that transaction.

10 C

11 D S240

12 B S216 – 12 months

13 A R4.218(3)(a)(i)

14 A S212 (the misfeasance provisions)

15 B SIP 2 – Investigations by officeholders in administrations and insolvent liquidations

16 (a) (ii) S238(1)

(b) (i) Yes

(ii) No, s214 only applies to insolvent liquidation

8 Asset protection regime

1 A S178(2)

2 B S184 – 14 days

3 (a) S176 – Where any person has distrained against the goods of the company in the three months prior to the winding up order....

...goods/effects/sale proceeds are charged for the benefit of the company with the preferential debts of the company....

....to the extent that the company's property is for the time being insufficient for meeting those preferential debts.

(i) Distraint took place on 31 December 20X9, within three months of the winding up order. The liquidator should therefore seek to recover the assets distrained upon if there are insufficient assets remaining with which to meet the preferential claims.

(ii) The liquidator is entitled to clawback the proceeds of sale if the goods have been sold.

(iii) The landlord would have a preferential claim in the liquidation to the extent of his surrender or payment to the liquidator. The landlord will form a separate class of preferential creditor, ranking below the general body of preferential claims but above the other unsecured creditors.

(b) A judgment creditor may seek to obtain payment of his judgment debt by execution against the company's property. A creditor cannot levy execution without a judgment and order of the court.

Distress is a self help remedy available to landlords where rent is in arrears. It does not require court involvement.

(c) (i) S128 – Distress put in force against the estate of a company after commencement is void.

Commencement is the date of the presentation of a petition to wind up the company.

Here, landlord distrained on 16 February 20Y0, after the date of the petition presented on 31 January 20Y0. The landlord should be advised that his distraint is not valid and cannot be continued with.

The landlord could apply for leave to distrain to the court.

(ii) S176 and s128 do not apply in a creditors' voluntary winding up. There is no restriction on distress, so the landlord's distraint would be valid and the liquidator would not be able to recover funds for the benefit of the preferential creditors.

The liquidator may be able to persuade the landlord to hold off, failing which application may be made to court under s112.

(d) (i) S183 – A creditor can only retain the benefit of an execution if he has completed it before commencement of the liquidation.

S183(3) – Execution against goods is completed by seizure and sale or by the making of a charging order:

- An attachment of a debt is completed by the receipt of that debt
- An execution against land is completed by seizure or the appointment of a receiver or the making of a charging order

The creditor would need to have completed execution by the date of the member's resolution to wind up the company or the date he received notice of the GM at which the resolution to wind up was to be passed, if earlier.

If execution is not completed the liquidator may require the creditor to hand assets over.

(ii) S184 – If, before the sale of goods seized in execution or receipt of the full amount of the levy, the sheriff receives notice that a resolution has been passed for voluntary winding up, he shall, on being required to do so, deliver goods or sale proceeds to the liquidator.

If judgment is for more than £500 the enforcement officer has to retain the proceeds for 14 days. If within those 14 days the enforcement officer is notified of a meeting having been called at which there is to be proposed a resolution to wind up, then, on the passing of the resolution, the enforcement officer must pay the proceeds of sale to the liquidator.

9 Proofs of debt in liquidation

1 C r.11.3(1) [the correct time period is actually 5 business days]

2 Rule 11.2/11.3

Before declaring a dividend the officeholder must give notice to all creditors (and member state liquidator if applicable) who are known to him and have not proved their debts of his intention to declare and distribute a dividend

Notice to be given by public advertisement (Gazette) [Unless creditors previously invited by Gazetted notice to prove debts]

Must specify a last date for proving (not less than 21 days from the date of the notice)

Office holder must deal within 5 business days from the last date for proving.

3 A R4.91

4 C R6.105/R4.83

5 R11.13 states that for the purpose of dividend only, the amount of the creditors proof should be reduced by a % calculated as follows:

$$\frac{x}{1.05^n}$$

where x = amount of the debt

n = decimalised amount of time from relevant date to date the debt is due

6 (a) Where there are surplus funds in the estate, these should be applied in paying interest on the creditors' claims in respect of periods during which they have been outstanding since the company went into liquidation (from the date of the winding up order to the date the debts were paid in full).

S189(4) – the rate of interest payable is the greater of:

(i) The rate specified in s17 Judgments Act 1838 on the day on which the company went into liquidation (currently 8%), and

(ii) The rate applicable to that debt apart from the winding up.

(b) S189 – All interest paid on any debt proved in the winding up in respect of post winding up order periods shall rank equally, whether or not the debts on which it is payable rank equally.

7 E

8 C R4.83 – Application must be made within 21 days of receiving the statement sent under r4.82(2)

9 E Rule 11.4

10 C R11.6

10 Vacation of office – liquidator

1	A	S106(3)
2	E	Regulation 16 Insolvency Regulations 1994
3	A	S106 – Within one week after the date of the meetings
4	D	S92(1)
5	A	See s106(3) and r4.142(5)

11 Company voluntary arrangements

1 D s.1(1) and s.1(3)(a) & (b)

2 C Paragraph 7(e), Schedule A1

3 The grounds for an appeal are unfair prejudice and/or material irregularity at the meeting.

On an unfair prejudice appeal if the court is satisfied that the ground is made out it may revoke or suspend approval and direct that a further meeting of creditors be held to consider revised proposals

On a material irregularity appeal if the court is satisfied the ground is made out it may revoke or suspend any decision made by the meeting and direct that a further company or creditors' meeting to consider the original proposal.

4 A Rule 1.24 (3)

5 SIP 3 paragraph 4.3(b)

- Where the value of an asset is material to the outcome of the arrangement, consideration should be given to obtaining corroborative evidence as to its value.
- The nominee should also ensure that a comprehensive schedule of non-trading assets in which the company has an interest be prepared, together with explanatory notes.
- If there is a business – consider (in conjunction with the directors) the manner in which it is to be dealt with. If the business is to be continued a business plan should be produced to justify any decision, stating the assumptions on which it is based, and in appropriate detail having regard to the circumstances and size of the undertaking.

6 (a) In *Greystoke v Hamilton-Smith and others*, the court set out three tests which the nominee should apply before concluding that a meeting of creditors should or should not be summoned. They are:

- That the debtor's true position as to assets and liabilities is not materially different from that which it is represented to the creditors to be.
- That the debtor's proposal has a real prospect of being implemented in the way it is represented to be.
- That there is no already manifest yet unavoidable prospective unfairness.

SIP 3 provides that where these conditions are not met and the nominee none the less recommends that meetings should be held to vote, the nominee should explain in his comments why the IVA is being recommended.

SIP 3 provides that an IP should comment, in his report to court, on the following matters:

- The directors' attitude and in particular any instances of failure to co-operate with the nominee
- The history of any previous failure in which the directors have been involved in so far as they are known to the nominee
- Basis of asset valuations
- The extent to which reliance can be placed on the director's estimate of the company's liabilities
- Information on the attitude of any major unsecured creditors
- The result of any discussion with secured creditors or other interested parties on whose co-operation the CVA depends
- An estimate of the result for creditors if the CVA is approved
- Why the CVA is more beneficial for creditors than alternative insolvency proceedings

- The likely effect of the proposals being rejected by creditors
- Details of claims better pursued in liquidation.

If not already dealt with in the proposal

- The source of any referral and any payments to be made
- Any payments to be made to the nominee or his firm by the company
- Estimate of fees

If there has been rejection of CVA in last 12 months why it is now considered appropriate for the creditor's to consider and vote on the new proposal.

(b) Pursuant to rule 1.17 any creditor who has notice of a creditors' meeting is entitled to vote at the meeting. However pursuant to rule 1.19 for a vote to be taken into account written notice must be given to the chair either at the meeting or before the start of the meeting.

Anna Bank plc

Pursuant to rule 1.17 any creditor who has notice of a creditors' meeting is entitled to vote at the meeting. However (pursuant to rule 1.19) votes will be left out of account if they are secured in whole or in part. Although Anna plc are owed £50,000 they have a floating charge in respect of that debt and have not valued their security. Consequently in the circumstances (and after discussions with the representatives of Anna Bank present at the meeting) the chair should value the unascertained unsecured element of any debt at £1 (rule 1.17.)

Admit the bank to vote for £1.

Yak Ltd

Pursuant to rule 1.17 any creditor who has notice of a creditors' meeting is entitled to vote at the meeting. Voting may be in person or by proxy. However pursuant to rule 8.7 where a proxy represents a company he must produce to the chairman of the meeting a copy of the resolution from which he derives his authority.

Mr Burnham should only be allowed to vote if the Chairman is satisfied that he has been validly appointed.

Under rule 1.19 for a vote to be taken into account written notice must be given to the chair either at the meeting or before the start of the meeting.

Mr Burnham gave written notice at the meeting and consequently his vote will count.

Provided Mr Burnham's proxy is valid admit Yak Ltd to vote for £38,000.

Mrs Lumley

Section 249 provides that a person is connected with a company if he is an 'associate' of a director or shadow director of the company. The term 'associate' is defined in section 435and includes a mother/son relationship.

As a connected party although Mrs Lumley is entitled to vote the resolution will only be passed if more than half in value of independent creditors vote in favour.

(c)

	Voting in favour on original proposal £	Voting against on original proposal £
Anna Bank plc	1	nil
Yak Ltd	38,000	nil
Mrs Lumley	nil	nil
HMRC	nil	40,000
Chair's proxies	75,000	nil

Total votes cast 153,001

% in favour 74% therefore proposal rejected

Voting in favour on modified proposal	£	Voting against on modified proposal £
Anna Bank plc	1	nil
Yak Ltd	nil	38,000
Mrs Lumley	200,000	nil
HMRC	nil	40,000
Chair's proxies	75,000	nil

Total votes cast 353,001

% in favour including connected party 78% therefore proposal accepted but need to do a second count excluding connected party.

Excludes Mrs Lumley's votes.

In favour 75,001

Against 78,000

∴ 49% of independent creditors in favour – proposal with modification rejected.

7 B S2(2)

8 S6(2) provides

(a) A person entitled, in accordance with the rules, to vote at either the meeting of creditors or the company

(b) A person who would have been entitled, in accordance with the rules, to vote at the creditors' meeting if he had had notice of it

(c) The nominee or any person who has replaced him under s2(4) or s4(2)

(d) If the company is being wound up or is in administration, the liquidator or administrator

9 B Paragraph 4 Schedule A1

10 (a)

Estimated Outcome Statement
Danco Limited as at X.X.00

	Working/ notes	*CVL* £	*CVA* £
Realisations			
Contributions from trading	1	–	240,000
Contributions from father	2	–	100,000
Sale of property	3	275,500	–
Debtors	4	90,000	–
Machinery, stock, vehicles	5	57,000	–
		422,500	340,000
Less: costs			
Liquidator's remuneration		25,000	–
Meetings fees		5,000	–
Nominee's fees		–	3,000
Supervisor's fees		–	12,000
		(30,000)	(15,000)

	Working/ notes	CVL	CVA
		£	£
Assets available to creditors		392,500	325,000
Less: creditors			
Pay in lieu of notice		30,000	–
Redundancy		35,000	–
Trade and expense creditors	6	600,000	450,000
		(665,000)	(450,000)
Shortfall/ surplus to unsecured creditors		(272,500)	(125,000)
Creditors will receive		59p in £	72.22p in £

Workings/notes

(1) **Contributions from trading**

- Only available in CVA
- 5,000 × 12 × four years = £240,000

(2) **Contribution from father**

Only available in CVA

(3) **Sale of property**

	£
Forced sale value	300,000
Less: estate agent fees @ 1.5%	(4,500)
Legal fees	(5,000)
Tax claim	(15,000)
	275,500

(4) **Debtors**

	CVL
	£
Realisations	100,000
Less: collection fees @ 10%	(10,000)
	90,000

Assumes all book debts are utilised if trading is continued under a CVA

(5) **Machinery, stock, vehicles**

	£
Machinery	40,000
Stock	15,000
Vehicles	5,000
Less: agents fees @ 5%	(3,000)
	57,000

(6) **Trade creditors**

CVA only, Boxter Limited will defer their claim

£600,000 – £150,000 = £450,000

(b) **Possible causes of action available**

(i) **Repayment of loan** = possible preference s239

In order to prove must show;

- Company was insolvent at the time of the transaction
- Transaction took place at a relevant time, within two years of onset of insolvency (parties are connected)

– Person preferred was put into a better position than they would otherwise have been

– Desire to prefer (assumed where parties are connected)

Here, Mr Becker has been put into a better position since his guarantee will not be called upon. Transaction took place within 12 months.

(ii) **Sale of property** = possible transaction at an undervalue s238

In order to prove must show;

– Transaction took place at a relevant time (within two years as parties are connected)

– Insolvency at time of the transaction is presumed (parties are connected)

– Transaction was for less consideration than the asset was worth - sold for £200,000, worth £300,000

Possible defence – that the transaction took place in good faith, believing it would benefit the company

(iii) **Loan repayment** – possible preference under s239

In order to prove must show – transaction took place at a relevant time (within six months of onset of insolvency as parties are unconnected)

Here, transaction took place in August 20X8, outside six month period, therefore transaction couldn't be attacked.

Investigate why loan was repaid – following demands for repayment/on due date?

(iv) **Floating charge** – possible to invalidate the charge under s245. This would mean that the bank would then rank as an unsecured creditor for the amount of its debt.

In order to prove must show:

– The company was insolvent at the time of creation of the charge
– The charge was created within 12 months of the onset of insolvency

Charge is only invalid to the extent that fresh consideration has not been provided. Since the original loan secured has been repaid in full, the bank's charge will be valid in respect of any overdraft outstanding at the date of liquidation.

The bank will therefore be fully secured and could not vote in respect of any CVA proposals

(v) **Transfer of property** – possible transaction at an undervalue s238

However, transaction took place three years ago which is outside the relevant time period for such a transaction to be pursued.

Could pursue under s423 as a transaction to defraud creditors.

Would have to take legal advice re terms of the divorce settlement.

Impact on creditors:

Supervisor of a CVA is unable to take action against directors under s238, s239 or s245, however transactions which could be challenged by a liquidator must be disclosed in the CVA proposals. This gives the creditors the opportunity to consider whether they would prefer the company to be placed into liquidation so such actions could be pursued. Alternatively the creditors would seek to be compensated for not pursuing such actions and agreeing to CVA proposals instead.

The existence of such transactions may also influence the creditors when forming an opinion as to the credibility of the directors.

11 E S2 IA 86

12 C S7A

13 E Para 32 Schedule A1

14 B Para 10(1)(a) Schedule A1 and rule 1.40(2)

Memo format

15 (a) A CVA would be beneficial to the company because:

(i) Directors remain in control of the company
(ii) Trading could continue
(iii) Returns from debtors could be maximised
(iv) Possible survival of the company
(v) Obtain moratorium under S1A and Schedule A1 of IA 86 introduced by the IA 2000

The moratorium would prevent creditors from taking action to wind up the company.

Only small companies can apply for a moratorium. In order to be 'small' two of the following conditions must be satisfied;

(i) Turnover less than £6.5m
(ii) Balance sheet total less than £3.26m, and
(iii) Having fewer than 50 employees.

Also, a company is excluded from being eligible for a moratorium if, on the date of filing –

(i) An administration order is in force in relation to the company
(ii) The company is being wound up
(iii) There is an administrative receiver of the company
(iv) A voluntary arrangement has effect in relation to the company
(v) There is a provisional liquidator of the company
(vi) A moratorium has been in force for the company at any time during the period of 12 months ending with the date of filing and –
   – No VA had effect at the time at which the moratorium came to an end, or
   – A VA which had effect at any time in that period has come to an end prematurely

(b) (i) Director's give the intended nominee written notice of their proposal accompanied by a copy of the proposal and statement of the company's affairs made up to a date not earlier than two weeks before the date of the notice to the nominee.

(ii) The intended nominee endorses a copy of the notice to the effect that it has been received by him on a specified date and returns it

(iii) Within 28 days of receiving the proposal from the directors, the nominee submits to court a statement in the prescribed form indicating whether or not in his opinion
   – The proposed VA has a reasonable prospect of being approved and implemented
   – The company is likely to have sufficient funds available to it during the proposed moratorium to enable it to carry on its business, and
   – Meetings of the company and its creditors should be summoned to consider the proposed VA

The statement should have annexed to it the nominee's comments on the proposal and a statement that he is willing to act.

(iv) The directors file in court
   – A document setting out the terms of the proposed VA
   – A statement of the company's affairs
   – A statement that the company is eligible for a moratorium
   – A statement from the nominee that he has given his consent to act, and
   – A statement from the nominee that, in his opinion

- The proposed VA has a reasonable prospect of being approved and implemented
- The company is likely to have sufficient funds available to it during the proposed moratorium to enable it to carry on its business, and
- Meetings of the company and its creditors should be summoned to consider the proposed VA

Filing must be within three working days of the date of submission of the nominee's statement. Four copies of a schedule listing the documents filed must also be submitted.

(v) The court endorses copies of the schedule with the date of filing and three copies of the schedule are returned to the directors.

(vi) The directors serve, forthwith, two sealed copies of the schedule on the nominee and the company.

(vii) The moratorium comes into force when the documents are filed in court.

During the period for which a moratorium is in force for a company:

- No petition may be presented for the winding up of a company
- No meeting of the company my be called except with the consent of the nominee or the court
- No resolution may be passed or order made for the winding up of the company
- No petition for an administration order in relation to the company may be presented
- No administrative receiver of the company may be appointed
- A landlord cannot exercise a right of forfeiture by peaceful re-entry except with leave of the court
- No other steps may be taken to enforce any security over the company's property except with leave of the court
- No other proceedings and no execution or other legal process may be commenced or continued and no distress levied except with leave of the court.

Every invoice, order or business letter shall state that the moratorium is in force for the company.

The company may not obtain credit to the extent of £250 or more from a person who has not been informed that a moratorium is in force.

The company can only dispose of any of its property or make a payment in respect of any debt or liability in existence before the moratorium if:

- There are reasonable grounds for believing that the disposal will benefit the company, and
- The disposal is approved by the nominee

Secured assets may be disposed of if the charge holder consents or the court grants leave – the net proceeds of sale must be applied towards discharging the sums owed to the secured charge holders.

(c) During the moratorium the nominee monitor the company's affairs for the purpose of forming an opinion as to whether:

(i) The proposed VA has a reasonable prospect of being approved and implemented, and

(ii) The company is likely to have sufficient funds available to it during the remainder of the moratorium to enable it to carry on its business.

16 C S6

17 (a) **Optimistic IT Limited**

Comparative Estimated Outcome Statement

	Working/ notes	*CVA* £	*CVL* £
Assets Subject to Floating Charge			
Debtors	3	–	120,000
Less: Costs	8	–	(24,000)
		–	96,000
Less: Due to Bank		(50,000)	(50,000)
(Shortfall)/Surplus to Bank		(50,000)	46,000
Office Furniture and Equipment	2	–	40,000
Motor Vehicles		–	30,000
Work in Progress	4	–	–
Contributions from Trading	7	250,000	–
		250,000	116,000
Less: Costs	8		
Supervisor's Remuneration		(25,000)	–
Nominee's Fee		(7,500)	–
Liquidator's Remuneration		–	(14,000)
Statements of Affairs		(5,000)	(5,000)
Available for floating charge holder		212,500	97,000
Floating charge holder			
Due to Bank		(50,000)	–
Available for unsecured creditors		162,500	97,000
Unsecured creditors			
HMRC – PAYE	5	(80,000)	(80,000)
HMRC – VAT	5	(72,000)	(72,000)
Trade and Expense		(200,000)	(200,000)
Landlord		(75,000)	(75,000)
Redundancy	6	(50,000)	(125,000)
Directors Loans		–	(200,000)
Shortfall to Unsecured Creditors		(314,500)	(655,000)
Directors Loans		(200,000)	
Shortfall to creditors		(514,500)	
Dividends			
Unsecured creditors		34.1p in £	12.9p in £

WORKINGS/NOTES

1 **Bank Security**

Fixed Charge – Goodwill
Floating Charge – All other Assets

Charges over book debts, whenever created, will be treated as floating charge: Re Brumark.

2 **Office Furniture**

CVL (Forced Sale) – 20% x Book Value = £40,000
CVA (Going Concern) – Needed for continued trading

3 **Debtors**

	£
Book value	150,000
Provision (20%)	(30,000)
Estimated to Realise	120,000

Needed for continued trading in CVA

4 **Work in Progress**

CVL – No realisable value
CVA – Utilised in CVA for continued trading

5 **HM Revenue and Customs – PAYE/NIC, VAT**

All unsecured

6 **Redundancy Costs**

CVL – £50,000 + £75,000 = £125,000
CVA – £50,000

7 **Contributions from Trading**

CVA only
Five years only @ £50,000 pa = £250,000

8 **Costs and Fees**

Supervisor's Fee = 10% × £250,000 = £25,000
Liquidator's Fee = 20% × £120,000 = £24,000
= 20% × £70,000 = £14,000

(b) The bank holds a fixed charge over book debts and a floating charge over all other assets.

CVA offers no statutory protection by way of an interim order (unless the company is eligible to apply for a 'small company' moratorium) therefore there is nothing to prevent the bank from appointing an administrative receiver under its floating charge.

The bank is entitled to 14 days notice of the creditors meeting to consider proposals for a CVA. The bank is entitled to vote in respect of any unsecured element of its claim - or can surrender its security and vote in respect of the whole debt (this is unlikely).

The proposal cannot affect the bank's rights as a secured creditor without the bank's agreement.

Once approved, the bank will be bound by the terms of the CVA and will be unable to enforce its security. The bank will however receive monies realised from the sale of charged assets.

75% majority is required to approve proposals for a CVA, the nominee will therefore contact the bank at an early stage to ascertain its views to the proposal and gain support both for the proposals and any funding required in respect of ongoing trading.

(c) The nominee should ensure that the following details are included in the proposal and in his report and comments on the proposal:

(i) Any payments made by the nominee prior to the approval of the VA, detailing the work done

(ii) Amounts paid and to whom

(iii) Any ethical considerations ie confirm that there is no link between the two firms

(d) Have to look firstly at the terms of the CVA to see what should happen in the event of the CVA failing. If the proposal is silent, then by *NT Gallagher and Sons* a trust is created by default. If the trust survives, then the CVA assets will remain for the benefit of the CVA creditors only. CVA creditors can prove in the liquidation for the balance of their claims.

18 (d) S5(2)

19 E Company voluntary arrangements

20 A R1.24

21 E S234(1)

22 (a) Rule 1.3(2) – The following matters shall be stated or otherwise dealt with in the director's proposal:

(i) An explanation why a voluntary arrangement is desirable

(ii) The company's assets, with an estimate of their respective values

(iii) The extent to which the assets are charged in favour of creditors

(iv) The extent to which particular assets are to be excluded from the voluntary arrangement

(v) Particulars of any property, other than assets of the company itself, which is to be included in the arrangement , the source of such property and the terms on which it is to be made available for inclusion

(vi) The nature and amount of the company's liabilities, the manner in which they are proposed to be met, modified, postponed or otherwise dealt with by means of the arrangement, and

(vii) How it is proposed to deal with preferential creditors and creditors who are, or claim to be, secured

(viii) How persons connected with the company are proposed to be treated under the arrangement and

(ix) Whether there are, to the director's knowledge, any circumstances giving rise to the possibility, in the event that the company should go into liquidation, of claims under:

- S238 (Transactions at an undervalue)
- S239 (Preferences)
- S244 (Extortionate credit transactions)
- S245 (Floating charges invalid)

And whether, and if so how, it is proposed under the voluntary arrangement to make provisions for wholly or partly indemnifying the company in respect of such claims

(x) Whether any, and if so what, guarantees have been given of the company's debts by other persons

(xi) Proposed duration of the voluntary arrangement

(xii) Proposed dates of distributions to creditors, with estimates of their amounts

(xiii) The amount proposed to be paid to the nominee by way of remuneration and expenses

(xiv) The manner in which it is proposed that the supervisor of the arrangement should be remunerated and his expenses defrayed

(xv) Whether, for the purposes of the arrangement, any guarantees are to be offered by the directors, or other persons, and whether any security is to be given or sought

(xvi) The manner in which funds held for the purposes of the arrangement are to be banked, invested or otherwise dealt with pending distribution to creditors

(xvii) The manner in which funds held for the purpose of payment to creditors, and not so paid on the termination of the arrangement are to be dealt with

(xviii) The manner in which the business of the company is proposed to be conducted during the course of the arrangement

- The role of the IP in relation to the business
- Supervisor to avoid personal liability
- Duties of company management to provide supervisor with regular information and accounts
- Restrictions on powers of directors (ie to dispose of assets outside the ordinary course of business without sanction of the supervisor)

(xix) Details of any further credit facilities which it is intended to arrange for the company and how the debts so arising are to be paid

(xx) The functions which are to be undertaken by the supervisor of the arrangement

(xxi) The name, address and qualification of the person proposed as supervisor of the voluntary arrangement and confirmation that he is qualified to act as an insolvency practitioner in relation to the company.

(xxii) Whether the EC Regulation will apply and, if so, whether the proceedings will be main proceedings, secondary proceedings or territorial proceedings.

(xxiii) An estimate of the value of the prescribed part should the company go into liquidation if the proposal is not accepted, and the value of the company's net property on the date that the estimate is made.

(b) R1.24(3) – A copy of the chairman's report shall, within four business days of the meeting being held (from 6.4.2010), be filed in court.

R1.24(2) – Contents of the report:

(i) State whether the proposal for a voluntary arrangement was approved or rejected and, if approved, with what (if any) modifications

(ii) Set out the resolutions which were taken at each meeting, and the decision on each one

(iii) List the creditors and members of the company (with their respective values) who were present or represented at the meetings, and how they voted on each resolution

(iv) Include such further information as the chairman thinks it appropriate to make known to the court

(c) R1.26A(4) – Copies of the abstract shall be sent out within the two months following the end of the period to which the abstract relates.

The supervisor shall, not less than once in every 12 months ending with the anniversary of commencement, prepare an abstract of receipts and payments and send copies of it, accompanied by his comments on the progress and efficiency of the arrangement to:

(i) The registrar of companies
(ii) The company
(iii) All those of the company's creditors who are bound by the arrangement and of whose address he is aware
(iv) The members of the company who are so bound
(v) If the company is not in liquidation, the company's auditors for the time being

(d) R1.29(1) – Not more than 28 days after the final completion of the voluntary arrangement, the supervisor shall send to all creditors and members of the company who are bound by it a notice that the voluntary arrangement has been fully implemented.

23 D R1.14

24 E R1.24(2) lists the contents required by the s3 report

25 A SIP 3 – Voluntary arrangements

26 B (S1)

27

(a)

- Is it a composition in full and final settlement of debts or a scheme of arrangement?
- Background to arrangement and how company got into financial difficulties
- What is the estimated value of the investment property?
- Is the investment property mortgaged?
- What other assets does the company have? Estimated value?
- Are any assets to be excluded from the arrangement?
- The nature and amount of the company's liabilities?
- Are there any secured creditors? If so, are there any arrears and how will they be dealt with?
- Are there any preferential claims? How will they be dealt with?
- How will non notified creditors be dealt with?
- How will overseas creditors be dealt with?
- Are there any 'connected' creditors? If so, will they consider withdrawing their claims?
- An estimate of the value of the prescribed part should the company go into liquidation
- Are there any unliquidated/unascertained debts or contingent liabilities?
- Any claims for breach of contract including claims for faulty and incomplete work?
- Any creditors who have commenced execution or any other legal process?
- Are directors aware of any potential antecedent transactions?
- Have any guarantees been given for company's debts?
- Are any guarantees to be offered by directors/other parties for purposes of arrangement?
- Proposed duration of the arrangement?
- Proposed dates of distribution to creditors
- Amount to be paid to nominee
- How supervisor will be remunerated
- How much is director proposing to pay into arrangement?
- How will funds in the arrangement be held pending distribution?
- How will business be conducted?
- What credit terms does company have with overseas suppliers and how will they be paid?
- What functions are to be undertaken by supervisor? In what circumstances can he present a petition for winding up?
- Name, address and qualification of proposed supervisor
- Whether EC Regulation will apply?

(b)

By r1.24 report must state:

- Whether the proposal for VA was approved by the creditors alone or by both the creditors and members of the company and whether such approval was with any modifications
- Wet out the resolutions which were taken at each meeting and the decision on each one
- List the creditors and members of the company (with their respective values) who were present or represented at the meetings and how they voted on each resolution
- State whether, in the opinion of the supervisor (i) the EC Regulation applies to the VA and (ii) if so, whether the proceedings are main, secondary or territorial proceedings and
- Include such further information as the chairman thinks it appropriate to make known to the court

12 Introduction to administrations

1 B Paragraph 3(1) Schedule B1

2 (a) (i) Commercial insolvency test – Proved to the satisfaction of the court that the company is unable to pay its debts as and when due. This is shown by an unsatisfied statutory demand or an unsatisfied judgment execution.

(ii) Balance sheet test – the value of the company's assets are less than the amount of its liabilities, taking into account its contingent and prospective liabilities. Court must be satisfied that the company has reached the point of 'no return'.

(b) Possible insolvency procedures available to Piton Limited are:

(i) Administration
(ii) Company voluntary arrangement
(iii) Creditors' voluntary liquidation
(iv) Compulsory liquidation

(c) An administrator can be appointed as follows:

(i) Out of court by Crampon Bank PLC (as holder of a qualifying floating charge) under Schedule B1 para 14.

The directors cannot make an out of court appointment because a winding up petition has been presented.

(ii) An application may be made to court for an administration order by:

- The company
- The directors
- One or more creditors of the company

(d) (i) The petition will be dismissed.

(ii) HM R&C's ability to enter into walking possession ceases except with the consent of the administrator or leave of the court.

(iii) The landlord will be prevented from exercising his right of forfeiture by peaceable re-entry except with the consent of the administrator or the leave of the court.

(iv) The directors can only exercise management powers with the consent of the administrator. They retain their duties such as filing of accounts etc.

(e) The most effective strategy for the company is to enter into administration, with the purpose of rescuing the company as a going concern.

Filing notice of appointment in court triggers an interim moratorium which will give immediate protection from:

(i) HM Revenue and Customs walking possession
(ii) ROT creditors seeking to recover stock
(iii) Landlord
(iv) Winding up petition by supplier.

The administrator would be able to continue to trade the company whilst marketing the business for sale as a going concern. The directors/administrator could also investigate sources of additional funding or investigate the possibility of a MBO.

The alternative would be a CVA, however this would not provide any protection from duress creditors unless the company was able to apply for a small company moratorium. In order to do this it must meet two out of the following three criteria:

(i) Turnover less than £6.5m
(ii) Balance sheet total less than £3.26m
(iii) Less than 50 employees.

There is insufficient information to determine whether this would apply in this case.

The directors should apply to court for an administration order. The court will need to be satisfied that the company is or is likely to become unable to pay its debts and that the administration order is reasonably likely to achieve the purpose of the administration (rescuing the company as a going concern).

Administrator's written statement must be prepared and a witness statement in support and submitted to court with the application for the administration order.

The above documents must be served on Crampon Bank PLC and the petitioning creditor.

Once an order is made the administrator should take steps to identify interested parties and market the business for sale.

3 D Para 3(1) Sch B1

4 (a)

MEMORANDUM

To: Partner
From: Administrator
Subject: Administration
Date: XX.XX.XX

(i) Purpose of administration (Para 3(1) Sch B1):

- Rescuing the company as a going concern
- Achieving a better result for the creditors as a whole than would be likely if the company were wound up
- Realising property in order to make a distribution to one or more secured or preferential creditors

(ii) Would an alternative insolvency procedure be more appropriate ie Liquidation or CVA?

(iii) Are creditors threatening to take enforcement action against the company - protection given by moratorium may be required

(iv) Consider making an application for an administration order out of court or in court. Para 25 Sch B1 – administrator cannot be appointed out of court by the directors where:

- A petition for winding up has been presented and has not yet been disposed
- An application to court for an administration order has been made and has not yet been disposed of
- An AR of the company is in office
- The company is in liquidation

(v) Identify any QFC holders – give them five days notice of the intention to appoint an administrator

(vi) Prepare relevant documentation:

- Form 2.8B, notice of intention to appoint
- Statutory declaration (company is unable to pay its debts, not in liquidation, appointment not prevented by para 23 to 25)
- Board Resolution authorising appointment
- Form 2.9B, notice of appointment

(vii) Confirm company is or is unlikely to become unable to pay its debts

(viii) Find IP who is qualified and willing to accept appointment

(ix) Hold Board meeting – resolve to place the company into administration

(x) Advise of advantages of administration:

- Moratorium which prevents creditors taking enforcement action against the company
- Seen as a rescue procedure so less damage to goodwill
- May lead to rescuing of the company as a going concern
- Directors retain office and employment

(xi) Advise of disadvantages of administration:

- Administrator owes a duty to all creditors and will be acting to achieve the statutory purpose (may be different to objectives of the directors)
- Administrator controls the company (directors powers cease unless authorised by the administrator)
- Administrator has to submit a 'D' return on the directors

(b) The administration may be terminated in the following ways:

(i) Hand company back to the directors:

- Where the administrator has achieved the statutory purpose set out in para 3(1)b and has rescued the company as a going concern, the company may be handed back to the control of the directors
- Notice should be filed with the court and registrar of companies
- The appointment of administrator will then cease to take effect

(ii) Petition the court for the compulsory winding up of the company:

- May be appropriate where the creditors want a thorough investigation into allegations of fraud against the directors
- Administrator may be appointed liquidator

(iii) Place the company into creditors voluntary liquidation:

- This is a simple procedure, requires filing of notice in court. No need to hold s98 meeting of creditors. The administrator may become liquidator
- May only be used where:
  - The total amount which each secured of the company is likely to receive has been paid or set aside
  - A distribution to unsecured creditors will be made

(iv) Distribute realisations and then file for dissolution of the company:

- File notice with registrar and court
- Administration ceases to have effect upon registration of the notice
- Three months later the company is deemed to be dissolved

(v) Obtain approval for a CVA and end the administration:

- This route is consistent with the statutory purpose of rescuing the company as a going concern
- Put proposals to creditors at the same time as the administrator's proposals
- Administrator may become supervisor

(vi) Obtain the creditors approval and sanction of the court to a s425 scheme and end the administration

(vii) Allow the administration to lapse through expiry of the 12 month fixed period

5 B Paragraph 12 Schedule B1

6 D Paragraph 22 Schedule B1

7 A Schedule 1 Powers of an administrator or administrative receiver

8 (a) (i) **CVA**

- This could ensure the survival of the company as a going concern
- Trade could continue leading to a better return for creditors
- But, here creditors are threatening enforcement action against the company. Could obtain a moratorium to prevent this – but only if the company is a 'small company'

(ii) **Administration** – Directors could obtain administration order without the need to go to court.

- Moratorium giving protection against creditors action
- One year time limit
- Clear exit routes
- Trade can continue

(iii) **Administrative receivership** – appointed by floating charge holder to realise assets subject to floating charge.

- Duty owed to floating charge holder not creditors generally
- Can trade the company
- May preserve company as a going concern
- But, the holder of a QFC created on or after 15/09/03 may not appoint a administrative receiver, therefore this is not appropriate here

(iv) **S895 CA 06 scheme of arrangement** – compromise between the company and its creditors and/or members.

- Flexible
- Requires two applications to court, costs and delays
- All classes of creditors and shareholders must approve

Administration is considered most appropriate to Thorney Construction Limited.

(b) No winding up petition has been presented so assume that directors appoint an administrator out of court.

Purposes of Administration – para 3(1) of Schedule B1 to the Act:

(i) Rescuing the company as a going concern

(ii) Achieving a better result for the company's creditors as a whole than would be likely if the company were wound up (without first being in administration)

(iii) Realising property in order to make a distribution to one or more secured or preferential creditors

Statutory requirements to be considered

The directors/company may not appoint an administrator where:

(i) Company has been in administration in previous 12 months

(ii) A Schedule 1A CVA small company moratorium was obtained in the previous 12 months and

- No CVA came into force, or
- The CVA ended prematurely

(iii) A petition for the winding up of the company has been presented and is not yet disposed of

(iv) The company is in liquidation

(v) The company is already in administration

Steps to be taken by the company/directors in placing the company into administration (no court application).

(i) The directors/company must give five business days' notice of their intention to appoint a named administrator to any person entitled to appoint an administrative receiver or an administrator. Under rule 2.20 notice must also be given to:

- Any court enforcement officer charged with execution or other legal process against the company
- Any person who has distrained against the company or its directors
- Any supervisor of a CVA
- The company.

(ii) The directors/company file a copy of the notice of intention to appoint together with any documents accompanying it in court. These will consist of a statutory declaration and:

- **Appointment by directors**: A valid board resolution authorising appointment
- **Appointment by company**: A resolution in GM authorising named shareholders to appoint administrator

(iii) The copy notice of intention to appoint must be accompanied by a statutory declaration made by the directors/company:

- Company is or is likely to become unable to pay its debts
- Company is not in liquidation
- Appointment is permitted ie no existing administrator in office etc.

(iv) The directors/company may not make the appointment:

- Until the five business days' notice to QFC holders has expired, and
- Not after 10 business days beginning with the day of filing of the notice of intention to appoint in court
- If there are no QFC holders entitled to appoint an AR or administrator, no notice of intention need be filed and the directors/company can go straight to the next stage

(v) Directors/company file three copies of a notice of appointment in court

- Notice must identify the administrator
- Notice includes a statutory declaration by the appointer stating that:
  - Appointer is entitled to make the appointment
  - Appointment is in accordance with Schedule B1
  - The statements made and information given in the statutory declaration filed with the notice of intention to appoint remain accurate
- Also filed with notice of appointment:
  - Statement from administrator that he consents to act and purpose of administration is likely to be achieved. Written consents of the QFC holders unless the five business day notice period has expired.
  - A statement re joint administrator appointments
  - Where no notice of intention to appoint filed, copy board resolution/GM resolution authorising the appointment of an administrator

(c) The directors/company may not appoint an administrator out of court where a petition for winding up has been presented and is not yet been disposed of. (para 25 Sch B1). They can however make an application to court for the appointment of an administrator.

A QFC holder may appoint an administrator, both in and out of court for the appointment (para 14 (1) and 36(1) Sch B1). The petition will be dismissed on the making of the order.

(d) Paras 37 and 38 empower the court, on the application of a floating chargeholder or the liquidator, to order that administration may be substituted for the winding up. No appointment may be made out of court.

9	E	Para 71
10	E	Para 12 (NB para 38 makes provision for a liquidator to apply for an administration order)
11	A	Para 3(1)

13 Procedure for administration

1 C r.2.33(5), r.2.37(1), and Paragraph 52 Schedule B1

2 The administrator must produce a progress report for the period of six months commencing on the date that the company entered administration and every subsequent period of six months or until he ceases to act. The final report must be sent together with a notice of the automatic end of the administration within not more than five business days of the end of the administration to all creditors and to the company, rule 2.111. Copies must also be sent to the Registrar of Companies and all other persons who received a copy of the administrator's proposals as soon as is reasonably practicable.

3 Rule 2.55 (4) provides

- Another member of the Committee;
- A person who is at the same time representing another committee member.
- A body corporate
- An undischarged bankrupt
- A disqualified Director
- A person subject to a bankruptcy restrictions order, a bankruptcy restrictions undertaking, a debt relief restrictions order or a debt relief restrictions undertaking. (R2.55(4) IR86)

4 (a)

- Meetings are to be held when and where determined by the administrator
- The first meeting shall take place within 6 weeks of the committees establishment
- After the first meeting, further meetings must be called if requested by a member of the committee/representative of member and then the meeting must be held within 21 days of the request being received and for a specified date if that was decided at the first meeting
- 5 business days written notice shall be given of the venue to every member
- The chairman shall be the administrator or a person appointed by the administrator in writing to act

(b)

- Send a copy of the proposed resolution to all members of the committee
- Resolution will allow member to record whether they vote for or against the resolution
- Give members the option of requesting a meeting of the committee to consider the proposed resolution (request to be made within 7 business days)
- Resolution passed when a majority have indicated to administrator in writing that they concur
- Copy of resolution to be kept with the records of the proceedings

(c)

- The date of the transaction
- Details of the assets sold
- Consideration paid for the assets
- Name of the buyer
- Details of the relationship of the buyer to the seller

- Names of the sellers advisors
- Whether the buyer and seller were independently advised
- The scope of the officeholders investigations and conclusions reached
- Whether the creditors committee has been consulted and if not, why not.
- The outcome of any consultation with the creditors committee.

(d)

- Vacancy need not be filled as still 4 members on the committee if administrator and majority of remaining members agree
- Administrator may appoint a new member if majority of remaining members agree and creditor consents
- A meeting of creditors can be called to resolve that a new creditor be appointed

5 C Schedule B1 paragraph 28(2)

6 Notice must comply with rule 12A.12 and:

- State that all relevant documents will be made available for viewing and downloading on a website
- Specify the address of the website
- Specify any password necessary to view and download a relevant document from the site
- Include a notice that any person to whom notice is given, delivered or sent may at any time request that hard copies of all, or specific, relevant documents are sent to that person
- Specify a telephone number, email address and postal address which may be used to make the request.

7 C Sch B1 Para 52

8

(a) There are provisions in the Act that prevent directors of a company from appointing an administrator via the out of court route, none of which apply here. The procedure is:

(i) Prepare notice of appointment (including statutory declaration) in form 2.8B

(ii) Directors must serve notice of intention to appoint on any qualifying floating charge holder 'QFCH' identifying proposed administrator with copies sent to any enforcement officer charged with execution; any distraining creditor; and the company.

[Note no need to serve supervisor of CVA as not relevant to the question.]

File in court with copy of the board resolution authorising the appointment of the administrator

(iii) Wait for 5 business days to give QFCH opportunity to appoint an administrator, or give consent to director's appointment.

(iv) Prepare and file notice of appointment of administrator in court Form 2.98B. The notice must identify the administrator and include a statutory declaration. The declaration must include statement that the appointor is entitled to appoint; the appointment is in accordance with schedule B1; statement that the statements made in the statutory declaration (filed with notice of intention to appoint) remain accurate. Will also file: administrator's consent to act and statement that the purpose of the administration is likely to be achieved and written consent of QFCH (unless 5 days expired).

(b) The following information should be disclosed to creditors in all cases where there is a prepackaged sale, as far as the administrator is aware after making appropriate enquiries:

- The source of the administrator's initial introduction

- The extent of the administrator's involvement prior to appointment
- Any marketing activities conducted by the company and/or the administrator
- Any valuations obtained of the business or the underlying assets
- The alternative courses of action that were considered by the administrator, with an explanation of possible financial outcomes
- Why it was not appropriate to trade the business, and offer it for sale as a going concern, during the administration
- Details of requests made to potential funders to fund working capital requirements
- Whether efforts were made to consult with major creditors
- The date of the transaction
- Details of the assets involved and the nature of the transaction
- The consideration for the transaction, terms of payment, and any condition of the contract that could materially affect the consideration
- If the sale is part of a wider transaction, a description of the other aspects of the transaction
- The identity of the purchaser
- Any connection between the purchaser and the directors, shareholders or secured creditors of the company
- The names of any directors, or former directors, of the company who are involved in the management or ownership of the purchaser, or of any other entity into which any of the assets are transferred
- Whether any directors had given guarantees for amounts due from the company to a prior financier, and whether that financier is financing the new business
- Any options, buy-back arrangements or similar conditions attached to the contract of sale.

Unless it is impracticable to do so, this information should be provided with the first notification to creditors. In any case where a pre-packaged sale has been undertaken, the administrator should hold the initial creditors' meeting as soon as possible after his appointment. Where no initial creditors' meeting is to be held and it is impracticable to provide the information in the first notification to creditors it should be provided in the statement of proposals of the administrator which should be sent as soon as practicable after his appointment.

(c) The administrator must call a creditor's meeting to consider his initial proposals (para 51 and rules 2.34 and 2.37). Pursuant to para 52 of schedule B1 no initial creditor's meeting is required where:

- Proposals state that the company has sufficient property to enable each creditor to be paid in full
- Proposals state that company has insufficient property to enable a distribution to be made to unsecured creditors (except under the prescribed part rules)
- Where neither of the objectives in para 3(1) (a) or (b) can be achieved

If 10% of creditor's (by value) requisition a meeting the administrator must hold one within 28 days.

9 As soon as reasonably practicable:

(a) Advertise his appointment in the London Gazette. The administrator may also advertise the appointment in such other manner as he thinks fit (r2.27(1)).

(b) Give notice of his appointment (in prescribed form) to:

(i) The company (paragraph 46(2)(a) Schedule B1)

(ii) The creditors of whose claim and address he is aware (paragraph 46(3)(b) Schedule B1)

(iii) Any receiver or administrative receiver who has been appointed (r2.27(2)(a))

(iv) Any petitioner for the winding up of the company and any provisional liquidator in office (r2.27(2)(b))

(v) Any court enforcement officer who to the administrator's knowledge is charged with execution or other legal process against the company (r2.27(2)(c))

(vi) Any person who to the administrator's knowledge has distrained against the company or its property (r2.27(2)(d))

(vii) Any supervisor of a CVA (r2.27(2)(e))

(c) Send notice of appointment to the Registrar of Companies within seven days of the date of the order as, if appointed order of court, the date of receiving the sealed copy of the notice of appointment from the appointer (paragraph 46(4) Schedule B1).

10 (a) **Mera Limited in administration Estimated Statement of Affairs**
As at 30 April 20X9

		Book Value	*Estimated To realise*
		£	£
Assets subject to fixed charge			
Freehold property		500,000	700,000
Less: Island Bank plc			(950,000)
			(250,000)
Assets subject to floating charge			
Factored book debts	1		44,500
Non-factored book debts	2	100,000	45,000
Stocks, raw materials, WIP		130,000	35,000
Plastic extrusion machine	3	95,000	15,000
Machinery and equipment		50,000	10,000
Office furniture and equipment		10,000	2,000
Vehicles		50,000	20,000
			171,500
Less: preferential creditors			
Wage arrears	4		(24,200)
Holiday pay	5		(20,000)
			(44,200)
Net property			127,300
Less: prescribed part	6		(28,460)
Assets available for floating chargeholder			98,840
Less: Island Bank plc			(250,000)
Shortfall			(151,160)
Prescribed part c/f			28,460
Less: unsecured creditors			
Director wage arrears	4		(10,800)
HM R&C – PAYE			(85,000)
– VAT			(75,000)
Trade and expense creditors			(450,000)
Redundancy			(55,000)
Pay in lieu			(30,000)
			(705,800)
Shortfall			(677,340)
Shortfall to Island Bank plc	7		(151,160)
Total shortfall as regards creditors			(828,500)

Share capital	(4,000)
Total shortfall as regards members	(832,500)

Workings

1 *Factored book debts*

	£
Balance	350,000
Less: known bad debts	(30,000)
Provision 15%	(48,000)
	272,000
Already advanced (65%)	(227,500)
Available	44,500

2 *Non factored book debts*

	£
Balance	100,000
Expiring contracts	(40,000)
Provision 25%	(15,000)
Available	45,000

3 *Plastic extrusion machine*

	£
Estimated to realise	25,000
Less: belay Finance Ltd	(10,000)
	15,000

4 *Wage arrears*

Up to four months arrears may be claimed preferentially up to a maximum preferential claim per employee of £800.

£21,000 all preferential.

Director's claims:

	Preferential	*Unsecured*
4 x £3,500	£3,200	£10,800

Total preferential claim £21,000 + £3,200 = £24,200.

5 *Holiday pay*

All preferential without limit.

6 *Prescribed part*

	£
10,000 x 50%	5,000
117,300 x 20%	23,460
127,300	28,460

7 Floating charge holder cannot participate in the prescribed part for any shortfall re the floating charge.

(b) ($^1/_2$ mark per point up to 5 marks)

(i) Details of the court where the proceedings are and the relevant court reference number

(ii) The full name, registered address, registered number and any other trading names of the company

(iii) Details relating to his appointment as administrator, including the date of appointment and the person making the application or appointment and, where there are joint administrators, details of the matters set out in para 100(2)

(iv) The names of the directors and secretary of the company and details of any shareholdings in the company they may have

(v) An account of the circumstances giving rise to the appointment of the administrator

(vi) If a statement of the company's affairs has been submitted, a copy or summary of it, with the administrator's comments, if any

(vii) If an order limiting the disclosure of the statement of affairs has been made, a statement of that fact, as well as:

- Details of who provided the statement of affairs
- The date of the order of limited disclosure
- The details or a summary of the details that are not subject to that order

(viii) If a full statement of affairs is not provided, the names, addresses and debts of the creditors including details of any security held

(ix) If no statement of affairs has been submitted, details of the financial position of the company at the latest practicable date, a list of the company's creditors including their names, addresses and details of their debts, including any security held and an explanation as to why there is no statement of affairs.

(x) The basis upon which it is proposed that the administrator's remuneration should be fixed under r2.106

(xi) To the best of the administrator's knowledge and belief an estimate of the value of the prescribed part and an estimate of the company's net property

(xii) How it is envisaged the purpose of the administration will be achieved and how it is proposed that the administration will end. If a CVL is proposed details of the proposed liquidator must be provided and a statement that creditors may nominate a different person as the proposed liquidator

(xiii) Where the administrator has decided not to call a meeting of creditors, his reason

(xiv) The manner in which the affairs and business of the company:

- Have, since the date of the administrator's appointment, been managed and financed, including, where any assets have been disposed of, the reasons for such disposals and the terms upon which such disposals were made

- Will, if the administrator's proposals are approved, continue to be managed and financed

(xv) Whether the EC Regulation applies and if so, whether the proceedings are main proceedings or territorial proceedings.

(xvi) Such other information as the administrator thinks necessary to enable creditors to decide whether or not to vote for the adoption of the proposals.

<u>From 6.4.2010</u>

- Disclose any pre-appointment costs charged or incurred by the administrator (or other IP). A full break-down must be provided.

11 B R4.153

12 B Paragraph 15(1) Schedule B1

13 A Paragraph 46(4) Schedule B1

14 D Para 51 schedule B1

15 C Para 48 schedule B1

16 A R2.57(1)

17 A Para 46 (4) Sch B1

18 C Para 28(2) Schedule B1

19 A Paragraph 49 Schedule B1

20	B	
21	D	R2.28(3)
22	A	Para 57(3) – The committee may on giving not less than seven days notice, require the administrator to attend before it
23	B	R2.46(a)
24	(a)	(i), (iii), (vi) per R2.4(2)
	(b)	(iii), (vi), (vii) per para 12(2), r2.6(3)
25	A	Rule 2.2
26	D	Para 12(2), r2.6 Require the petition to be served on all those listed except for the ROT creditor
27	E	Para 51
28	▸	The company is or is likely to become unable to pay its debts
	▸	The administration order is reasonably likely to achieve the purpose of the administration

Note: A director will apply to court for an administration only where he cannot appoint out of court eg undisposed winding up petition presented, undisposed application for administration order, administrative receiver in office or company in compulsory liquidation.

14 Implementation of administration

1 Occupation of premises for the purpose of seeking a sale of the business as a going concern would be considered to be occupation for the beneficial conduct of the administration. Consequently pursuant to rule 2.67(1) (f) rent and rates falling due within the period of occupation will constitute a 'necessary disbursement' and as such those payments falling due during this period will be payable as an expense of the administration.

This applies whether or not the administrator is in occupation for the whole period covered by the rent/rates. So for example if the quarter's rent becomes payable in the first week of the administration the whole quarter's rent will be an expense even though the administrator may occupy the premises for small proportion of the period only (2 weeks). Likewise even if only a small part of the premises is occupied the rent/rates for the whole premises will have to be paid.

Administration expenses are paid in the priority set out in rule 2.67(1) and will rank above other creditor claims.

'Rent' will include other sums such as service charge and insurance that may be due under the terms of the lease.

Any rent or rates due before the company entered administration or after the administrator ceased to occupy the premises will not rank as expense but as an ordinary unsecured debt.

2 Check that ROT clause valid and incorporated into the contract, request copies of all documentation: orders, invoices , ROT clause

To be incorporated ROT clause must have been agreed before completion of the contract. It must not amount to an unregistered charge.

Take legal advice as necessary.

Identify the stock subject to the ROT claims (with supplier as necessary).

Check what sums are still outstanding and reconcile with inventory of stock.

Ensure stock kept secure until ROT claims resolved.

3 Statutory purposes of administration are set out in para 3(1) Schedule B1

(a) Rescuing the company as a going concern, or

(b) Achieving a better result for the company's creditors as a whole than would be likely if the company were wound up (without first being in administration), or

(c) Realising property in order to make a distribution to one or more secured or preferential creditors

4 (a) The Partner must be clear about the nature and extent of his role and his relationship with the directors in the pre-appointment period.

He should make it clear that his role is to advise the company and not to advise the directors on their personal position. The directors should be advised to take independent advice.

The Partner should remember the duties and obligations which are owed to creditors in the pre-appointment period. He should ensure that the company does not incur liabilities which may not be repaid during the pre-appointment period as a result of his advice.

The Partner must perform his functions in the interests of the company's creditors as a whole.

The Partner should keep a detailed record of the reasoning behind the decision to undertake a pre-packaged sale and should be able to explain and justify why such a course of action was considered appropriate.

(b) (i) The source of the administrator's initial introduction

(ii) The extent of the administrator's involvement prior to appointment

(iii) Any marketing activities conducted by the company and/or the administrator

(iv) Any valuations obtained of the business or the underlying assets

(v) The alternative courses of action that were considered by the administrator, with an explanation of possible financial outcomes

(vi) Why it was not appropriate to trade the business and offer it for sale as a going concern, during the administration

(vii) Details of requests made to potential funders to fund working capital requirements

(viii) Whether efforts were made to consult with major creditors

(ix) The date of the transaction

(x) Details of the assets involved and the nature of the transaction

(xi) The consideration for the transaction, terms of payment, and any condition of the contract that could materially affect the consideration

(xii) If the sale is part of a wider transaction, a description of the other aspects of the transaction

(xiii) The identity of the purchaser

(xiv) Any connection between the purchaser and the directors, shareholders or secured creditors of the company

(xv) The names of any directors, or former directors, of the company who are involved in the management or ownership of the purchaser, or of any other equity into which any of the assets are transferred

(xvi) Whether any directors had given guarantees for amounts due from the company to a prior financier and whether that financier is financing the new business

(xvii) Any options, buy–back arrangements or similar conditions attached to the contract of sale

(c) S216 provides that a director of a company in insolvent liquidation is prohibited from being a director of a company known by a prohibited name for a period of five years.

A prohibited name is any name by which the liquidating company was known in the last 12 months or which is so similar that it suggests an association with the liquidating company.

Here, Sparse Scaffolding 2009 Limited is very similar to Sparse Scaffolding Limited and will therefore be covered by s216.

There are exceptions to the rule however which do not require an application to court:

(i) R4.228 This is where the IP has arranged for the transfer of the whole, or substantially the whole, of the business to a successor company. Notice must be given to creditors of the insolvent company by the successor company (Newco) within 28 days of the completion of the arrangement. The notice must give details of the prohibited name, name and registered number of the insolvent company and circumstances of the acquisition.

(ii) R4.230 This applies where the successor company has been known by the name for 12 consecutive months prior to the date the insolvent company (the Company) went into liquidation and that it wasn't dormant at any time in those 12 months. (This would not apply here as the Newco was only set up recently)

The directors should be advised to follow the requirements of r4.228.

5 A moratorium applies once the administration takes effect.

No steps may be taken to enforce security without the consent of the administrator or permission of the court.

The creditor therefore is unable to continue with the distraint unless they obtain leave to continue. It is unlikely that permission would be given as this would reduce funds available for the general body of creditors. They will have an unsecured claim for any arrears under the lease.

The court will carry out a balancing exercise and will apply the guidelines set out in *Re Atlantic Computers.*

The administrator is not able to continue using the equipment without the permission of the lease creditor or the court. He should:

(a) Obtain a copy of the lease agreement

(b) Establish the level of arrears under the agreement

(c) Obtain legal advice: does the lease contain a clause stating that it will terminate if an administrator is appointed?

(d) Establish whether equipment is necessary to achieve the purpose of the administration.

(e) If so, negotiate with the creditor to continue using the equipment

(f) Agree to pay ongoing rental costs whilst the equipment is in use as an expense of the administration

(g) Do not agree to pay arrears

If creditor will not allow ongoing use of the equipment, consider applying to court for leave to use the equipment.

6 (a) Administrator should first approach the HP Creditor for permission to include the assets in the going concern sale.

If no such permission is given, under Sch B1 para72 the administrator has the power to apply to court for an order giving him the power to dispose of the secured property as though it were not subject to the HP agreement.

The court must be satisfied that the disposal would be likely to promote the purpose of the administration order.

It will be a condition of the order that:

(i) The net proceeds of the disposal

(ii) Plus any additional money so as to produce the amount determined by the court as the net value of the property are passed to the HP creditor

Within 14 days of the making of the order, the administrator must send a copy of the order to the Registrar of Companies.

(b) (i) Administrator must obtain the permission of the court to make a distribution to unsecured creditors – Sch B1 para 65

(ii) Administrator must advertise for creditors to prove their debts. Notice must state;

- That it is the intention of the administrator to make a distribution to creditors within the period of two months from the last date for proving
- Whether the dividend is interim or final
- Date up to which proofs may be lodged being a date which:
  - Is the same for all creditors, and
  - Is not less than 21 days from that of the notice

(iii) The administrator must admit or reject all proofs submitted within 5 business days of the last date for proving

(iv) The dividend must be declared within two months of the advertisement for creditor claims

(v) R2.68 – The administrator must give 21 days notice to the creditors of his intention to declare and distribute a dividend in accordance with r2.95

The notice must state:

- Whether the distribution is to preferential creditors or preferential and unsecured creditors; and
- Where the distribution is to unsecured creditors, the amount of the prescribed part

(vi) Administrator must give a notice of declaration of dividend to all creditors who have proved their debts.

Notice shall include:

- Amounts raised from sale of assets indicating amounts raised by the sale of particular assets
- Payments made by the administrator when acting as such
- Where the distribution is to the unsecured creditors, the value of the prescribed part
- Provision (if any) made for unsettled claims and funds (if any) retained for particular purposes
- The total amount of dividend and the rate of dividend
- How he proposes to distribute the dividend
- Whether and if so when, any further dividend is expected to be declared

Payment of the dividend may be distributed simultaneously with the notice declaring it.

(c) (i) Creditors voluntary arrangement
(ii) Creditors voluntary liquidation
(iii) Compulsory liquidation
(iv) CA06 scheme of arrangement

7 (a) **R2.33**

(i) Details of the court where the proceedings are and the relevant court reference number

(ii) The full name, registered address, registered number and any other trading names of the company

(iii) Details relating to his appointment as administrator, including the date of appointment and the person making the application or appointment and, where there are joint administrators, details of the matters set out in para 100(2)

(iv) The names of the directors and secretary of the company and details of any shareholdings in the company they may have

(v) An account of the circumstances giving rise to the appointment of the administrator

(vi) If a statement of the company's affairs has been submitted, a copy or summary of it, with the administrator's comments, if any

(vii) If an order limiting the disclosure of the statement of affairs has been made, a statement of this fact, as well as:

- Details of who provided the statement of affairs
- The date of the order of limited disclosure

  - The details or a summary of the details that are not subject to that order

(viii) If a full statement of affairs is not provided, the names, addresses and debts of the creditors including details of any security held

(ix) If no statement of affairs has been submitted, details of the financial position of the company at the latest practicable date, a list of the company's creditors including their names, addresses and details of their debts, including any security held, and an explanation as to why there is no statement of affairs

(x) The basis upon which it is proposed that the administrator's remuneration should be fixed

(xi) To the best of the administrator's knowledge and belief:

  - An estimate of the value of the prescribed part and an estimate of the value of the company's net property
  - Whether, and if so why, the administrator proposes to make an application to court under s176A(5)

(xii) How it is envisaged the purpose of the administration will be achieved and how it is proposed that the administration will end.

(xiii) Where the administrator has decided not to call a meeting of creditors, his reasons

(xiv) The manner in which the affairs and business of the company:

  - Have, since the date of the administrator's appointment, been managed and financed, including, where any assets have been disposed of, the reasons for such disposals and the terms upon which such disposals were made, and
  - Will, if the administrator's proposals are approved, continue to be managed and financed

(xv) Whether the EC Regulation applies and if so, whether the proceedings are main proceedings or territorial proceedings

(xvi) Such other information as the administrator thinks necessary to enable creditors to decide whether or not to vote for the adoption of the proposals

(b)

MEMORANDUM

To: Principal
From: Administrator
Subject: Termination of administration
Date: XX.XX.XX

Options

(i) Creditors' voluntary liquidation
(ii) Compulsory liquidation
(iii) Dividend/ dissolution of company
(iv) Company voluntary arrangement

(i) **Creditors' voluntary liquidation**

  - Clear, simple procedure
  - Administrator files notice in court
  - No need for s98 meeting of creditors or board resolution
  - Administrator can become liquidator
  - Preferential creditors are clearly identified as at date the administration commences
  - Only available when secured creditors have been paid and monies are available to pay a dividend to unsecured creditors

(ii) **Compulsory liquidation**

- Administrator applies for discharge and petitions for winding up at the same time
- Administrator can become liquidator
- More expensive/ complex than CVL
- Could provide greater powers to investigate director's than CVL

(iii) **Dividend/ dissolution route**

- Administrator applies to court to pay a dividend to the unsecured creditors
- Then files notice to dissolve the company with the Registrar
- Company is deemed to be dissolved three months from the date of registration of the notice
- Quick, low cost exit route
- Avoids the need for a further insolvency procedure

(iv) **Company voluntary arrangement**

- Administrator puts proposals for CVA to creditors
- Once accepted, administrator can become supervisor
- Creditors claims are agreed under terms of the CVA

Any other relevant points

Style

8 D Rule 2.95(4)(a)

9 (a) In order to vote, the creditor must have:

(i) Given to the Administrator written details of the debt claimed
(ii) The debt must have been admitted by the chair
(iii) Any proxy must have been lodged with the Administrator

Votes are calculated according to the amount of the creditor's debt as at the date of the administration order.

(i) R2.40 – A secured creditor can only vote for the balance (if any) of his debt after deducting the value of his security as estimated by him

(ii) R2.40 – A retention of title creditor cannot vote for that part of his debt which is covered by a retention of title clause (**Note:** 'Secured' including ROT for these purposes)

(iii) R2.42 – A hire purchase creditor can only vote in respect of what they are owed at the date of the Administration order, not on the total amount owed under the terms of the agreement

(iv) R2.43(1) – Voting is by a simple majority in value of those creditors present and voting, but:

R2.43(2) – Any resolution is invalid if those voting against it include more than half in value of the creditors to whom notice of the meeting was sent and who are not, to the best of the chairman's belief, persons connected with the company

S249 A person is 'connected with' a company if:

- He is a director or shadow director of the company or an associate of such a director or shadow director, or
- He is an associate of the company

S435(7) A person is an 'associate' of a company if:

That person has control of the company or that person and persons who are his associates have control of it

S435(10) A person is to be taken as having control of a company if:

He is entitled to exercise or control the exercise of, one third or more of the voting power at any general meeting of the company.

Here, a 30% share holding is not a controlling stake,

- Not an associate of the company
- Not connected to the company

The votes are not to be taken into account when determining the validity of resolutions. The creditor votes as a creditor only, based on the value of his debt. His share holding is of no consequence.

(b) (i) Para 71 – The administrator has the power to apply to court for an order sanctioning the disposal of assets subject to a fixed charge.

The court must be satisfied that the disposal (with or without other assets) would be likely to promote the purpose of the administration.

The bank can appear at the court hearing.

The court sends two copy orders sanctioning the disposal to the administrator, who serves one on the chargee and copies to the Registrar.

(ii) Pay the net proceeds of sale to the bank in discharge of the secured debt (and make up any deficit if the court determines that the sale has taken place at less than market value) (Para 71).

(iii) The administrator has the power to dispose of floating charge assets without recourse to the court.

The charge holder retains priority in regard to the proceeds of sale, or derivative property (Para 70).

(c) Any 10 of the following:

(i) Power to take possession of, collect, and get in the property of the company and, for that purpose, to take such proceedings as may seem to him expedient.

(ii) Power to sell or otherwise dispose of the property of the company by public auction or private auction or private contract or, in Scotland, to sell, feu, hire out or otherwise dispose of the property of the company by public roup or private bargain.

(iii) Power to raise or borrow money and grant security therefore over the property of the company.

(iv) Power to appoint a solicitor or accountant or other professionally qualified person to assist him in the performance of his functions.

(v) Power to bring or defend any action or other legal proceedings in the name and on behalf of the company.

(vi) Power to refer to arbitration any question affecting the company.

(vii) Power to effect and maintain insurances in respect of the business and property of the company.

(viii) Power to use the company's seal.

(ix) Power to do all acts and to execute in the name and on behalf of the company any deed, receipt or other document.

(x) Power to draw, accept, make and endorse any bill of exchange or promissory note in the name and on behalf of the company.

(xi) Power to appoint any agent to do any business which he is unable to do himself or which can more conveniently be done by an agent and power to employ and dismiss employees.

(xii) Power to do all such things (including the carrying out of works) as may be necessary for the realisation of the property of the company.

(xiii) Power to make any payment which is necessary or incidental to the performance of his functions.

(xiv) Power to carry on the business of the company.

(xv) Power to establish subsidiaries of the company.

(xvi) Power to transfer to subsidiaries of the company the whole or any part of the business and property of the company.

(xvii) Power to grant or accept a surrender of a lease or tenancy of any of the property of the company and to take a lease or tenancy of any property required or convenient for the business of the company.

(xviii) Power to make any arrangement or compromise on behalf of the company.

(xix) Power to call up any uncalled capital of the company.

(xx) Power to rank and claim in the bankruptcy, insolvency, sequestration or liquidation of any person indebted to the company and to receive dividends, and to accede to trust deeds for the creditors of such a person.

(xxi) Power to present or defend a petition for the winding up of the company.

(xxii) Power to change the situation of the company's registered office.

(xxiii) Power to do all other things incidental to the exercise of the forgoing powers.

15 Introduction to receivership

1 The notice must contain the information specified in rule 3.2(2) including:

- The registered name of the company as at the date of the appointment, and its registered number
- Any name by which the company has been registered or has traded under in the 12 months before appointment
- The name and address of the AR and the date of his appointment
- The name of the appointer
- Nature of the business of the company
- The date of the instrument conferring the power under which the appointment was made, together with a brief description of the instrument
- A brief description of the assets of the company (if any) in respect of which the person appointed is **not** made receiver.

2 A S44(1)(a)

3 C S29

16 Effect of administrative receivership and duties of receiver

1	A	
2	D	R3.32
3	A	S47(4)
4	A	R3.32
5	D	S48
6	B	R3.32 – Within two months after the end of 12 months from the date of his appointment and of every subsequent period of 12 months
7	B	S47(3)
8	C	s48(4)(a)
9	E	SIP 14 – A Receiver's responsibility to preferential creditors
10	A	R3.32

17 Administrative receivership: practical aspects and closure

1 A

2 A SIP 17 An administrative receiver's responsibility for the company's records

3 (a) The landlord could exercise his right to levy distress (can distrain on goods on the rented premises regardless of whether they are charged in favour of someone else).

As the company is in arrears with the rent the landlord is entitled to end the lease (but not merely because the tenant is in receivership)

The lease may provide for forfeiture on appointment of an administrative receiver

The problems this may cause for the receiver are:

(i) The receiver may not be able to remain in occupation of the building and therefore continue trading

(ii) The landlord may distrain over stock and other assets which would otherwise be realised for the benefit of the chargeholder. Any stock distrained on may also be required for ongoing trading.

The receiver should:

(i) Contact the landlord as soon as possible

(ii) Seek to pay ongoing rentals for the period of occupation, but not arrears

(iii) Point out to the landlord that should a sale as a going concern be achieved, then any purchaser may also wish to take over the lease

(iv) The landlord cannot use force to enter premises in order to levy distress, therefore the premises should be kept secure, with all doors and windows being locked and access restricted to authorised persons.

(b) S44(1)(b) – Administrative receiver is personally liable for adopted contracts of employment to the extent of qualifying liabilities.

Qualifying liabilities:

(i) Wages/salaries
(ii) Contributions to an occupational pension scheme
(iii) Holiday pay
(iv) Sickness pay

for post adoption period of employment.

S44(2) – The receiver is not taken to have adopted a contract of employment by reason of anything done/not done within 14 days after his appointment.

The administrative receiver is entitled to an indemnity out of the company's assets and has the benefit of any indemnity negotiated with his appointer

The employees can claim against the company for any arrears of wages or holiday pay

The employee contracts remain with the company

The administrative receiver may have to provide funds to pay wage arrears in order to keep the employees working.

(c) S233 – If, after taking office, a receiver requests that supplies from an electricity supplier be continued, such supply cannot be made conditional upon the payment of charges owing in respect of supplies made before the receiver took office, though the supplier may agree to continue supplies only on the guarantee of the receiver personally.

So, arrears should not be paid.

Administrative receiver should agree to pay the deposit. The arrears will be an unsecured claim against the company.

(d) Invite both suppliers to submit full details of their claims and copies of documentation showing that the ROT claim has been validly incorporated into their contract with the company.

Obtain legal advice on the validity of each claim.

The all monies clause seeks to retain title to goods until all monies owing have been paid. The creditor ledger should be checked therefore to see if the balance has been reduced to zero at any time. If it has, title to goods supplied before that date will have passed.

Assuming the ROT claims are found to be valid:

(i) Bargain Fabrics Limited - this supplier should be allowed to recover the stock identified to outstanding invoices in the sum of £1,500. They will have an unsecured claim against the company in the sum of £4,500.

Should the stock be required for ongoing trading, some agreement should be reached with the supplier regarding payment for the stock subject to the valid ROT claim.

(ii) Taffatta Limited - the stock supplied by this company has been used by the company in the manufacture of dresses. The company will therefore not be able to recover any stock under its ROT claim.

Any claim by the supplier to the goods in which his stock has been incorporated will fail as a charge which is unregistered.

The supplier will have an unsecured claim against the company in the sum of £9,000.

(e) The presentation of a petition to wind up the company will have no effect on the receiver's ability to achieve a sale of the business.

However, should a winding up order be made, this will affect the receiver in a number of ways:

(i) s44(1)(b) - The administrative receiver's agency relationship with the company will be terminated by the winding up order.

- The administrative receiver will now enter post winding up order contracts as principal
- The administrative receiver will not have any indemnity out of the company's assets in respect of his or her personal liability in relation to such contracts

(ii) Contracts of employment will be automatically terminated by a compulsory winding up order.

- If employees are required to continue trading the administrative receiver will have to re employ them and will be personally liable on their contracts of employment
- Any liability will not be limited to qualifying liabilities

(iii) S245 will be triggered by a winding up order, so that a floating charge created within 12 months of the petition, at a time when the company is insolvent, will be invalid to the extent that fresh consideration is provided.

(iv) The administrative receiver retains custody and control of the charged assets and retains the power to realise and sell company property subject to the charges and may continue to carry on the company's business.

The above will have the practical effect of making it more difficult to continue trading in view of the potential liabilities.

The bank may review its decision to continue trading to achieve a sale as a going concern.

(f) SIP 14 A Receiver's responsibility to preferential creditors

4 D R3.33

18 Bankruptcy

1 What insolvency options are available for a creditor to pursue who has an unpaid debt due from a partnership business (not an LLP)?

- Wind-up the partnership as an unregistered company.
- Apply for a Partnership Administration Order.
- Sue one or more of the individual partners and enforce judgement in the usual way.
- Sue one of more of the individual partners and obtain bankruptcy orders against those individual partners personally.
- Sue all the partners and the company and obtain bankruptcy orders over all partners and the company.

2 In order to be eligible for a DRO the applicant must meet the following criteria:

- Must be unable to pay his debts
- Have unsecured debts of less than £15,000
- Have assets of less than £300. When assessing the value of assets motor vehicles with a maximum value of £1,000 are excluded. Also excluded are approved personal pensions.
- Have surplus income of less than £50 per month.
- **No DRO in previous 6 years.**
- Must not entered into a transaction with any person at an undervalue during the period between the start of the period of 2 years ending with the application date and the determination date.
- Not have given a preference in the period between the start of period of 2 years ending with the application date and the determination date.

3 Advice to Rachel on her options

- There are various forms of debt solutions, which can be categorised into two categories:
  - Non-statutory solutions
  - Statutory solutions.
- Non-statutory solutions are also classed as pre-insolvency options and would be the preferred option if any would be feasible in your circumstances.
- Since there is no equity in your home, the non-statutory options of re-mortgaging, or consolidating the debts into one secured loan, would not be options that are open to you.
- Further, since you currently have no income, it would not be possible for you to negotiate an informal agreement with any of your creditors yourself.
- The only possible non-statutory solution would potentially therefore be a Debt Management Plan (DMP) arranged through a Debt Management Company.
- To agree a DMP with your creditors, you would need to meet with a DMC who would assess your current financial resources – since you currently have no income, you would need to have other financial resources, such as savings, before a DMP could be arranged.
- The DMP would also asses your current expenditure, excluding the debt repayment to establish how much you can realistically afford to pay your creditors per month.
- If a DMP appeared feasible, the DMC would then negotiate with your creditors on your behalf to arrange an informal agreement.
- You would then pay the DMC one amount per month which the DMC would pay to creditors, in pro-rata amounts, after deducting an agreed fee.

- However, since you appears to have no other resources, a DMP would not appear to be a feasible option.
- You are therefore left with only the statutory solutions.
- The first of the statutory options is a Debt Relief Order (DRO).
- However, the maximum debt an individual has that would entitle them to apply for a DRO would be £15,000.
- Since your debts are much higher than this, a DRO would not appear to be an option for you either.
- The next option would be an IVA.
- An IVA is a formal agreement with your creditors, where you offer up assets and income in full and final settlement of the debts, and the creditors forgive you for the element you are unable to pay.
- However, since you appear to have no assets to offer, and no income, it does not appear that you have any resources to offer creditors in an IVA.
- The next possible option for you would be bankruptcy.
- Bankruptcy is a formal process, whereby your assets are taken by a trustee to pay your debts, and in return the creditors forgive you for the debts.
- The bankruptcy order would be made by the court, and your bankruptcy would last 12 months after which time you would no longer be liable for the bankruptcy debts.
- However, there are consequence, in that you would not be able to apply for any credit over £500 without disclosing to the lender that you are bankrupt.
- Further, the bankruptcy would stay on your credit record for six years after the making of the bankruptcy order.
- Bankruptcy may also affect the type of job you apply for in the future, particularly since you work in the legal industry.
- However, based on your current circumstance, there appears to be no other option at this time.
- If you do find a job in the future, you may be able to apply for an IVA at that stage, which could result in the annulment of your bankruptcy.
- Until such time, it would appear that your best option is to apply for your own bankruptcy, which will mean your creditors will stop pursuing you for the debts you owe.

4 C R6.7(1)

5 D

6 C

7 (a) Where the debtor has applied for an interim order under s252.

The court has a general power to dismiss a bankruptcy petition where there has been a contravention of the rules or for any other reason (s266(3)).

Where a criminal bankruptcy order is made in respect of an individual any bankruptcy petition presented by a creditor under s264(1) may be dismissed upon the application of the OR (S266(4)).

(b) (i) A 'stay of proceedings' is an order of the court to stop the insolvency from proceeding further. The OR is prevented from taking any further steps in the bankruptcy.

(ii) Where the debtor has applied for an interim order under s252 (intends to make a proposal for an IVA).

Where an application for annulment has been made.

8 (a) Income and expenditure account

Mr Boyle

	£
INCOME	
Salary	3,000
Annual bonus	950
Commission	250
	4,200
EXPENDITURE	
Credit cards – minimum repayment	425
Mortgage	1,400
Gas and electricity	150
Water	120
Council tax	125
Phone/internet	40
Life assurance	90
Gym membership	60
Local church covenant	100
Son	200
Payment to joint account	1,000
	(3,710)
Excess income	490

Note: An annual bonus of £950 was received this month giving rise to a surplus of £490 for this month only. Normally a monthly shortfall of £460 would be received.

(b) Given that Mark cannot currently afford the repayments on his debts his first priority will be to reduce the amount that he pays each month. He has many options both statutory and non-statutory. He should try to reduce his monthly expenditure by cancelling his gym membership and the covenant to the church and possibly the payments made to his son. This would save £400 per month which could be used to repay his debts.

(i) **Do nothing**

Mark could do nothing and just carry on as he is, however this does not actually deal with his debts and is likely to lead to a bankruptcy petition being presented by one of the credit card companies. This is not recommended.

(ii) **Re-mortgage**

Mark could seek to realise some of the equity in the property by re-mortgaging and using the capital raised to clear his debts. This would convert the debt from an unsecured debt to a secured debt and whilst the interest rate charged is likely to be lower the loan is over a much longer term and therefore repayments made over the term of the loan is likely to be higher. It is unlikely that Mark could remortgage without the knowledge of his wife as the property is held in joint names. Given Mark's uncertainty about his job and his poor credit rating (from missing repayments due) he may be unable to obtain a higher mortgage.

(iii) **Debt – management plan**

This is an agreement with his creditors where they agree to accept lower repayments over a longer term. This will enable Mark to meet the monthly repayments and would not require the involvement of his wife. However, this is not a formal agreement and provides no protection against creditors taking enforcement action at a later date. All creditors would have to agree to it. It could take a long time to clear the debts and additional interest charges would be incurred over this period. If Mark loses his job and is unable to meet the reduced payments it is likely that he would be made bankrupt by one of the credit card companies. This option is not really suitable if debts exceed £15,000.

(iv) **Bankruptcy**

This is a statutory option where Mark presents a petition for his own bankruptcy (however, equity in property may mean that Mark isn't actually insolvent). The trustee would realise Mark's assets for the benefit of his creditors, this would include Mark's share of the family home. His wife would have to be involved.

This procedure does give certainty however and would lead to Mark's debts being settled. If he retained his job he would be required to make contributions from income to his estate. The trustee would be likely to require him to reduce his expenditure as outlined above to give £400 per month which could be used to repay his creditors. He would be subject to the stigma, obligations and disabilities of bankruptcy. Bankruptcy would be likely to last for 12 months.

(v) **IVA**

This is a legally binding agreement with his creditors (requires more than 75% of creditors to agree) whereby the creditors agree to accept a certain sum in full and final settlement of the debts. Mark's wife would have to be involved given that it is most likely that any sums would come from a sale/ remortgage of the property. Mark could make contributions from income during the term of the arrangement which is likely to be three to five years to enable contributions to be made. If he were unable to meet the terms of the arrangement ie he lost his job, it is likely that bankruptcy would be the result.

9 (a) I would explain to John that the purpose of the initial meeting is to:

(i) Obtain information about John's current financial position (history, full details of assets and liabilities)

(ii) Explain to John the options available to him (bankruptcy and individual voluntary arrangement) and the advantages and disadvantages of each

(iii) Identify if any creditors are threatening enforcement action – is protection required?

(iv) Ascertain the most appropriate method of dealing with his financial affairs.

I would give John a copy of the booklet 'Is a voluntary arrangement right for me?'

I would not be able to make John bankrupt following the meeting. I would explain that a bankruptcy petition may be presented by:

(i) A creditor (owed at least £750)
(ii) John himself (on the grounds of inability to pay debts)
(iii) The supervisor of a voluntary arrangement (not relevant here).

Since none of the above apply to me, I would not be able to make him bankrupt following the meeting.

(b) There are two formal insolvency options available to John, bankruptcy and individual voluntary arrangement.

Bankruptcy

Bankruptcy commences on the making of a bankruptcy order, following the presentation of a petition. A petition can be presented by the debtor or a creditor.

Advantages of bankruptcy

(i) Automatic discharge after 12 months
(ii) Vast majority of debts will not survive bankruptcy
(iii) Bankrupt has no further contact with creditors which should lead to less stress

Disadvantages of bankruptcy

(i) Assets vest in trustee, debtor loses control of assets

(ii) Disabilities of bankruptcy eg restrictions on obtaining credit

(iii) Obligations to OR ie attend on OR, provide information, deliver up assets, provide Statement of Affairs and so forth

(iv) Stigma

(v) Potential liability for bankruptcy offences

(vi) Trustee can challenge transactions at undervalue (s339) or preferences (s340)

(vii) Affect credit rating even after discharge

(viii) Partnerships will terminate

(ix) Cannot be director or IP

(x) Some restrictions on acting in certain professions ie solicitor

(xi) Secretary of State fees lead to greater costs and lower returns for creditors

(xii) Debtor will have to pay court fee and deposit.

Individual voluntary arrangement

This is an agreement between the debtor and his creditors whereby the creditors agree to receive a sum in full settlement of their debts. All creditors notified of the arrangement will be bound by it. An interim order can be applied for which prevents creditors taking enforcement action against the debtor.

Advantages of voluntary arrangement

(i) Avoids the disabilities, obligations and stigma of bankruptcy

(ii) Binds all creditors

(iii) Realisations for creditors should be higher as costs are lower than bankruptcy

(iv) More chance that the debtor will retain employment allowing voluntary contributions from income to be made

(v) Assets do not vest in the supervisor. Debtor retains control over assets, flexibility over which assets to include in the arrangement and which to exclude

(vi) Supervisor has no power to challenge transactions under s339, 340 (though these must be disclosed in the proposal)

(vii) Interim order protects debtor from creditor action

Disadvantages of voluntary arrangement

(i) Duration - if arrangement based on contributions from income creditors are likely to seek a duration of three-five years to maximise returns

(ii) Debtor may have to pay nominee's fees up front and court fees

(iii) Requires support of 75% (in value) of creditors

(iv) If VA is not approved, bankruptcy is likely to result

(v) Stressful as have to maintain regular contact with creditors

(vi) Obligations to comply with terms of the arrangement

(c) Given that John wishes to have a political career in the future and he has a placement at a law firm, he would be best advised to seek the agreement of his creditors to a voluntary arrangement. If he were to be made bankrupt he would face a professional restriction from practising as a lawyer, this does not apply to an IVA.

Given that he has no assets, any proposal would be based on contributions from income. He should be advised to take up the law placement immediately (or if not possible, to obtain immediate employment rather than taking a break to go abroad). This would enable contributions from income of between £500 and £1,000 per month to be made depending on the level of contributions towards the household costs from his girlfriend. He should be advised to retain the paying tenants for the duration of the arrangement to increase income.

The arrangement could be completed in two years (or four if the lower contributions were made). This compares favourably with the bankruptcy duration of one year.

John would seek to exclude the property from the IVA which wouldn't be possible in a bankruptcy.

Given that the arrangement is based on contributions only, supervisor's fees should not be excessive and should compare favourably with costs in a bankruptcy (secretary of state fees are not incurred in a voluntary arrangement).

Student loans are not a provable debt in bankruptcy and would therefore survive. These would be unlikely to be included in a voluntary arrangement for the same reasons and must therefore still be paid by John in any event.

John's unsecured creditors total £20,000. A 75% majority is required to approve a voluntary arrangement. Given that the majority of debts are with credit card companies they are likely to seek a high return on their debt. An IVA is likely to give creditors a greater return than in bankruptcy so creditor support is likely to be forthcoming.

10 (a) His name, place of residence and occupation (if any)

(b) The name, or names, in which he carries on business, if other than his true name, and whether, in the case of any business of a specified nature, he carries it on alone or with others

(c) The nature of his business, and the address or addresses at which he carries it on

(d) Any name or names, other than his true name, in which he has carried on business in the period in which any of his bankruptcy debts were incurred and, in the case of any such business, whether he has carried it on alone or with others

(e) Any address or addresses at which he has resided or carried on business during that period and the nature of that business

11 D 21 days s268(1)(a)

12 A S278 – Bankruptcy of an individual commences with the day on which the order is made

13 A R6.73(1)

14 D S296(4)

15 E S286 – The functions of an interim receiver are similar to those of a provisional liquidator in compulsory winding-up.

16 (a) An order from the court can be avoided on the following grounds:

(i) That the debt due to the HP company has been paid

(ii) That Mr Careless has come to a satisfactory agreement with the HP company re payment of the outstanding debt

(iii) If Mr Careless applies for an interim order under s252 and makes a proposal for a voluntary arrangement. Although Mr Careless can propose an IVA without applying for an interim order, the existence of a petition here means that an interim order should be applied for

(iv) If Mr Careless can show that he is able to pay all his debts

(b) Grounds for an annulment (s282(1)):

(i) On any grounds existing at the time the order was made, the order ought not to have been made, or

(ii) That all bankruptcy debts and expenses have been paid or secured to the satisfaction of the court, or

(iii) Where an individual voluntary arrangement is approved to an undischarged bankrupt (s261)

(c) S364(1) – The court may cause a warrant to be issued to a constable or prescribed officer of the court:

(i) For the arrest of a debtor to whom a bankruptcy petition relates or of an undischarged bankrupt whose estate is still being administered under Chapter IV of this Part, and

(ii) For the seizure of any books, papers, records, money or goods in the possession of a person arrested under the warrant

S365(1) – The court may, on the application of the official receiver or the trustee of the bankrupt's estate, issue a warrant authorising the person to whom it is directed to seize any property comprised in the bankrupt's estate, or any books, papers or records relating to the bankrupt's estate or affairs which are, in the possession or under the control of the bankrupt or any other person who is required to deliver the property, books, papers or records to the official receiver or trustee.

S366(3) – Following a private examination under s366 the court may issue a warrant or the seizure of any books, papers, records, money or goods.

S365(2) – Any person executing a warrant under this section may, for the purpose of seizing any property comprised in the bankrupt's estate or any books, papers or records relating to the bankrupt's estate or affairs, break open any premises where the bankrupt or anything that may be seized under the warrant is or is believed to be and any receptacle of the bankrupt which contains or is believed to contain anything that may be so seized.

S365(3) – If, after a bankruptcy order has been made, the court is satisfied that any property comprised in the bankrupt's estate is, or any books, papers or records relating to the bankrupt's estate or affairs are, concealed in any premises not belonging to him, it may issue a warrant authorising any constable or prescribed officer of the court to search those premises for the property, books, papers or records.

(d) Where the bankrupt, any of his creditors or any other person, is dissatisfied by any act, omission or decision of the trustee, they may apply to court.

The court may confirm, reverse or modify any act or decision of the trustee and may give directions or make any such order as the court thinks fit.

The official receiver, the Secretary of State or a creditor may apply to the court on the grounds that:

(i) The trustee has misapplied or retained or become accountable for any money or other property comprised in the bankrupt's estate; or

(ii) The bankrupt's estate has suffered any loss in consequence of any misfeasance or breach of fiduciary duty by the trustee.

The court may order the trustee, for the benefit of the estate to repay, restore or account for money or other property or, as the case may require, to pay such sums by way of compensation as the court considers just.

The trustee requires court sanction in order to do the following:

(i) Carry on the business of the bankrupt so far as may be necessary for winding it up beneficially

(ii) Bring, institute or defend any action or legal proceedings relating to any property comprised in the bankrupt's estate, and bring legal proceedings under ss339, 340 and 423

(iii) Accept as consideration for the sale of any property comprised in the bankrupt's estate a sum of money payable at some future time

(iv) Mortgage or pledge any part of the property comprised in the bankrupt's estate for the purpose of raising money for the payment of his debts

(v) Where any right, option or other power forms part of the bankrupt's estate, to make any payments or incur liabilities with a view to obtaining, for the benefit of the creditors, any property which is the subject of the right, option or power

(vi) Make such compromise or other arrangements as may be thought expedient with creditors, or persons claiming to be creditors, in respect of the bankruptcy debts

(vii) Make such compromise or other arrangements as may be thought expedient with respect to any claims arising out of or incidental to the bankrupt's estate or made or capable of being made on the trustee by any person.

The court has the power to remove the trustee.

17 A

18

(a)

- Negotiated agreement with creditors appears to be out of the question as none of the creditors are supportive
- Re-organise/consolidate debts: Sally and James obtain a loan to reorganise or clear and therefore swap all existing debt for just one. However, the joint and sole debts are quite substantial so they would need to borrow a large sum to repay all debts for which the lender will require security. As they do not own their own property, this is not a viable option
- Debt management plan: a debt management company will deal with the creditors. Is suitable where the debtor has surplus income to make payments. Might be acceptable to creditors as neither Sally nor James have any realisable assets from which debts can be paid. However no protection for debtors either before or after agreement is put in place
- Debt relief order: formal order whereby both debtors get protection and relief from debts. However debtors must satisfy financial conditions for DRO (debts must not exceed £15,000 and must not have more than £50 surplus monthly income). Neither Sally nor James meet those conditions
- IVA: legally binding agreement between debtor and his creditors. Is suitable where debtors have surplus income so probably a better option for Sally as she has a higher surplus income. However high threshold of creditor approval required
- County court administration order: not possible as debts must be less than £5,000
- Deed of arrangement: simple and cheap procedure but dissenting creditors not bound
- Bankruptcy: debtors become subject to obligations, disabilities and stigma that arise in bankruptcy. Poor credit rating after discharge. Automatic discharge within a year. Most debts will not survive bankruptcy

(b)

Bankruptcy

For:

- Sally and James will have no further contact with creditors so less stress
- Creditors cannot take further action as bound by bankruptcy process
- Short timeframe – Sally and James will be free of debts (unless excluded debts) and restrictions within a year (unless wrongdoing)
- Costs are high but mostly borne by creditors

Against

- Adverse effect on James' employment. His practising certificate will be suspended which will affect his income. Even after discharge he may find it difficult to obtain work as a solicitor
- Student loans are not provable so Sally will still be liable for this loan after discharge

Debt Management Plan

For:

- Flexible as debtors can ask to reduce payments if necessary
- Debtors can make one affordable payment to creditors
- All negotiations and agreement carried out by debt management company
- Creditors can be persuaded to waive interest

Against

- There's no obligation on creditors to accept proposals (and so far they have been unsupportive)
- Debtors remain liable for full extent of debts unless creditors agree to waive part
- Creditors can take legal/enforcement action against debtors
- Can take years to clear debt

IVA

For

- Legally binding agreement which binds all creditors even dissenting creditors
- It avoids the stigma, disabilities and obligations of bankruptcy so James should be able to keep his job
- Opportunity to apply for interim order and therefore all proceedings are stayed and creditors are prevented from enforcing any debts

Against

- The IVA requires the support of 75% or more of creditors
- It will continue beyond the automatic discharge period for bankruptcy. IVAs usually last for 5 years
- IVA is a matter of public record. Therefore it may harm James' prospects of partnership

(c) Bankruptcy will adversely impact on James' employment and his future career prospects. Also Sally's student loan will survive bankruptcy. Accordingly, bankruptcy doesn't appear to be the right option. A debt management plan is also unlikely to succeed as the debts are quite large and it is very likely that the creditors may start legal proceeding soon. The most viable option would be an IVA with an interim order. This will protect Sally and James from legal action whilst the proposals are being prepared. If approved the IVA binds all creditors.

19 Post bankruptcy order procedure

1 **Memo format**

Formalities and documentation

- Obtain office copy of document of appointment and office copy of Bankruptcy Order.
- Advertise appointment as soon as reasonably practicable after receiving certificate of appointment:
  - In the *London Gazette*
  - Trustee may also advertise appointment in such other manner as he thinks fit
- Deal with OR's debit balance.
- Open file. Organise documentation – formal, case papers, working notes, correspondence, documents relating to assets and liabilities etc.

Professional

- Inform insurers in respect of bordereau – general penalty bond of £250,000 and specific penalty bond sum of not less than the estimated value of the bankrupt's assets (minimum value £5,000 and maximum value £5,000,000).
- Seek to recover premium out of first realisations.
- Complete IP record.

Assets – protection of estate

- Check that significant assets in the estate are insured, that the policies have not lapsed and cover is adequate and index linked.
- Notify any mortgagees (building society etc) of the trustee's interest.

  Obtain professional valuation of jointly owned property.

  Establish in what shares the property is held.

  Ensure that mortgage payments are continued with to avoid repossession proceedings by the mortgagee.
- If any property forming part of the estate is vacant check physical security, instruct agents with a view to sale etc.
- Notify any parties holding assets of the bankrupt of the trustee's interest (eg banks, pension providers).
- Consider disclaiming any onerous assets.

  Obtain an income and expenditure form from the debtor to see if there is surplus income which may be claimed by an income payments order.

  Obtain details of employment – is it affected by the bankruptcy of Mr Woods ie solicitor, IP etc?

Legal

- Notify solicitors.
- Carry out a Land Registry search.
- Register restrictions over land where appropriate.

Bankrupt

- Arrange for bankrupt to attend at office asap
- If no statement of affairs has been obtained from the bankrupt – call for one.

- Write to those owing money to the bankrupt requesting them to forward monies to the trustee direct.

  Advise bankrupt of appointment of the trustee and his duties and obligations.

Statutory duties triggered by appointment

- Get in the estate (s305). It will be the trustee's duty in due course to:
  - Realise for a proper price
  - Distribute
  - Account to the bankrupt for any surplus
- Maintain receipts and payments account.
- Take possession of books, papers and other records (s311).

2 B Reg 25 Insolvency Regulations 1994

3 C Regulations 27 Insolvency Regulations 1994

4 B Formerly an offence under s362, which has now been revoked, this is a matter to take into account when considering a BRO under paragraph 2(2)(j) Schedule 4A

5 B s305(3)

6 B

7 E s360

8 D R6.200(5)

9 B

20 Meetings of creditors – bankruptcy

1 Pursuant to rule 6.82 if the trustee is unable to act as chairman he will nominate a person to so act. That nomination will be made in writing. The person so nominated must be either: qualified to act as an IP in relation to the bankrupt, or an employee of the trustee (or his firm) who is experienced in insolvency matters.

2 C s302(2)

3 A R6.137

4 A s314 provides that creditors holding 10% by value of the total debt can force the Trustee to hold a meeting. 25% by value are required to force the OR to call an initial meeting of creditors (s294)

5 C R6.152 – The trustee should report in summary form where the committee has come into being more than 28 days after his appointment

6 D Rule 12A.21(2)(a)

7 D OR has 12 weeks to decide whether or not to call a meeting of creditors (see s136(5)(a)) and four months to actually hold it

8 B R6.84(1)

21 Bankruptcy estate and antecedent transactions

1 B s.341(1)(b)

2 (a) Note for the trustee setting out what assets could be claimed for the bankruptcy estate

File note

To: File

From: A Manager

Re: Bankruptcy Estate of Gail

Date: 1 July 20x6

Assets that can be claimed for the bankruptcy estate

Prior to the commencement of bankruptcy, the bankrupt has transferred all her assets away from her immediate ownership.

The principal assets available to the estate therefore consist of rights of action against the beneficiaries those transfers which fall fowl of the antecedent transaction provisions.

Types of claims that can be made

1. Transaction at an Undervalue – transferral of share in matrimonial home

   Gail transferred her share of the matrimonial home to her husband approximately 1 year ago. The transfer was undertaken for no consideration, at a time when the equity in the property stood at £120,000 (so, her share stood at £60,000).

   - It is likely that this transaction can be challenged under s339 as a transaction at an undervalue since:
   - The transaction provided for no consideration to received for the asset transferred;
   - The transaction took place in the relevant period, being within the five years before the bankruptcy petition was presented; and
   - As the transaction took place within the two years prior to the petition being presented, there is no need to prove that bankrupt was insolvent at the time or became insolvency as a result of the transaction.
   - If proven, the beneficiary of the transaction – Gail's husband – may be ordered to restore the estate to the position it would have been in had the transaction not taken place (by transfer of title to the property back to the estate or by making payments into the estate).

2. Preference transaction – transfer of horse to mother

   Gail transferred three horses to her mother a year ago in settlement of a personal loan that her mother had made to her previously. It is stated that she wanted to make sure they were not owed money if she were made bankrupt.

   This transaction could potentially be challenged under s340 as a preference since:

   - The transfer was undertaken with the desire to put a creditor in a better position than they would have been otherwise;
   - The transaction took place within the relevant period – in this case, as the beneficiary is the bankrupt's mother, the beneficiary is an associate of the bankrupt – the period is therefore any time up to 2 years before the date of the bankruptcy petition;
   - Insolvency is required to be demonstrated at the time of the transaction (or to have been caused by it) – either unable to pay their debts as they fall due or the value of their assets is less that their liabilities (including contingent and prospective liabilities).

- If proven, the beneficiary of the transaction – Gail's mother – can be ordered to restore the estate to the position it would have been in had the transaction not taken place (by transfer of title to the horses back to the estate or by making payments into the estate).

It would be unlikely that the Trustee could challenge the transfer of a further three horses to the saddler. This creditor had obtained a judgement from the courts; as the transfer was undertaken in order to satisfy the terms of the judgement, it would be difficult for the Trustee to prove a desire, on the part of Gail, to put that creditor in a better position.

3. <u>Post petition disposition – transferral of assets to the new limited company</u>

Gail's horse box and four horses were transferred to the new company after she was presented with a bankruptcy petition by HMRC. The transfer appears to have been undertaken to avoid the assets falling in to the hands of the Trustee as part of the bankruptcy estate.

The transaction may potentially be challenged under s284 as a post petition disposition, since:

- The disposition of assets was made after the presentation of the petition; and
- Any disposition in that period will be void except to the extent that it was made with the consent of the court or is subsequently ratified by the court.
- The new company will not have the defence that the transaction was in good faith, for value, and without notice of the petition.
- If proven, as the transfer will be void, the beneficiary of the transaction will be ordered to restore the estate to the position it would have been in had the transaction not taken place (by transfer of title to the business and assets back to the estate).

(b) In the absence of funds in the estate, the Trustee should:

- Consider instructing lawyers to pursue actions on a conditional fee arrangement basis;
- Consider approaching major creditors to provide funds to pursue actions;
- Consider approaching third parties to provide litigation funding; and
- Consider a negotiated settlement with the beneficiary of the transactions.

The Trustee should ensure that the estate's position is protected, and take out adverse costs insurance.

3 Section 283:

- – Such clothing, bedding, furniture, household equipment and provisions as are necessary for satisfying the basic domestic needs of the bankrupt and his family
- – Property held by the bankrupt on trust for any other person
- – A tenancy which is an assured tenancy, a protected tenancy, a secure tenancy, or tenancy of a dwelling house.
- Right of nomination to a vacant ecclesiastical benefice.
- Personal correspondence (Haig v Aitken).
- Titles of honour.
- Compensation claims for pain and suffering or injured feelings.
- Interest in an approved pension scheme.
- Items not vested in the bankrupt at commencement.

4 D S.283(1)(a)

5 C S.310(6)(b)

6 Under s307 written notice must be given to the bankrupt. Notice may not be served (except with leave of the court) after the end of the period of 42 days beginning with the day on which it first came to the knowledge of the trustee that the property had been acquired by or devolved on the bankrupt.

7 (a) **Payment to father**

Potential preference

- Transaction seeking to put creditor, surety, guarantor in better position in bankruptcy
- Taking place within 6 months of petition for non-associates, 2 years for associates
- Bankrupt must have had a desire to prefer the other party (presumed for associates)
- Bankrupt must have been insolvent or have become so because of transaction
- No presumption of insolvency

The repayment took place within the relevant period (as father is an associate) at a time when Bob appeared to be insolvent. His father has been put in a better position as he has been paid ahead of other creditors. There appears to be good reason to believe that the trustee will be able to overturn this transaction in court.

Payment to Paul

As above this is a potential preference.

Paul is not an associate and so the relevant time period is 6 months from presentation of the petition. The payment took place outside of this period and so is not a preference. The trustee may consider attacking this payment as a transaction defrauding creditors, as no time limit applies. However given that the trustee would have the onerous task of establishing that Bob intended to put assets beyond the reach of the creditors or otherwise prejudice their interests he is unlikely to do so.

Payment of tax bill

As above outside the time period of 6 months and so the trustee is not able to attack the payment. In any event given the scenario it is highly unlikely that there was any intent to prefer.

Surrender of life policy and payment into trust

Dispositions of property between presentation of the petition and appointment of the trustee are void save to the extent that the court has sanctioned/ratified the disposition.

On the face of the question it appears that the transfer took place after presentation and there is nothing to suggest that court consent was obtain (highly unlikely in the circumstance). Consequently the trustee should be able to restore this property to the estate.

Transfer of half share in matrimonial home to wife

Potential transaction at an undervalue

- Must be gift/sale at significantly less than m.v.
- Taking place within 5 years of presentation of the petition
- If within 2-5 years bankrupt must have been insolvent or have become so because of transaction
- Insolvency presumed if transaction with an associate

Here not clear whether or not the transfer was at significantly less than m.v. – will need to ascertain value of equity at time of transfer. Transfer however took place within the relevant time and there is a presumption of insolvency. On the facts as presented and subject to valuation of equity as at transfer it appears that trustee has good grounds to believe that court may set aside the transaction.

This transaction may also be a potential preference given that the transfer was to discharge a debt, however it took place outside the two year period and so the trustee will not be able to challenge it on this ground.

Transfer of second property to brother

As above potential transaction at an undervalue

The transfer was just within the 5 year period and appears to have been a sale at less than m.v. However, although Bob's insolvency will be presumed as the brother is an associate, it appears from the question that debts only started to accrue some time after the transfer and so Bob's brother may be able to defeat the trustee's claim on the ground that Bob was not insolvent at the date of the transaction and nor did he become so because of it.

(b) **Payment to Bob's father**

Matters for trustee to prove

- That payment took place within 2 years, whilst Bob was either insolvent or that he became so as a result of the transaction. Also that Bob intended to prefer his father and that Bob's father was placed into a better position because of the transaction. (All of which appear proven here.)

Presumptions that apply

- No need to establish 'desire to prefer' as Bob's father is an associate and so it is presumed that there is a desire to prefer unless Bob's father can convince the court otherwise, which will be difficult.

Payment to Paul

Matters for trustee to prove

- A discussed in part (a) there is no possibility of establishing a preference against Paul as the payment was more than 6 months from presentation and a friend is not an associate. As also mentioned in part (a) there is a possible argument that this was a transaction defrauding creditors in which case the trustee will have to establish that the payment was made with the intention to put assets beyond the reach of the creditors or otherwise prejudice their interests. (That would be very difficult to prove.)

Presumptions that apply

- Not applicable.

Transfer to trust

Matters for trustee to prove

- The trustee will have to establish that the transfer took place between petition and appointment of the trustee and that no sanction was obtained.

Presumptions that apply

- Not applicable.

Transfer to wife

Matters for trustee to prove

- As discussed in part (a) this may be a transaction at an undervalue and so the trustee will have to prove that the transfer took place within 5 years of presentation of the petition and that the consideration paid was significantly less than m.v. It will therefore be for the trustee to establish the value of the property at the time of the transfer.

Presumptions that apply

- As the wife is an associate insolvency will be presumed. It will be for the wife to establish that Bob was not, nor became insolvent as a result of the transaction.

Transfer to Brother

Matters for trustee to prove

- It will be for the trustee to establish that the transaction took place within the relevant 5 year period from presentation and that the sale was at a price significantly less than m.v.

Presumptions that apply

- The trustee does not have to establish insolvency as it is presumed for associates. However given that there is evidence to suggest that Bob's financial difficulties started after this transfer and there is no suggestion that this transfer caused those difficulties the trustee should be advised that the brother may be able to rebut the presumption.

8 **Associate of individual**

A person is an associate of an individual if that person is:

(a) The individual's husband or wife or civil partner

(b) A relative of:

(i) The individual, or
(ii) The individual's husband or wife or civil partner, or

(c) The husband or wife or civil partner of a relative of:

(i) The individual, or
(ii) The individual's husband or wife or civil partner

Associate of partner

A person is an associate of any person with whom he is in partnership and of the husband or wife or civil partner or a relative of any individual with whom he is in partnership

Associate of employee, employer

A person is an associate of any person whom he employs or by whom he is employed

Associate of trustee

A person in his capacity as trustee of a trust other than:

(a) A trust arising under any of the second Group of Parts, or
(b) A pension scheme or an employee's share scheme

Is an associate of another person if the beneficiaries of that trust include, or the terms of the trust confer a power that may be exercised for the benefit of, that other person or an associate of that other person.

Company associate of another company

A company is an associate of another company:

(a) If the same person has control of both, or a person has control of one and persons who are his associates, or he and persons who are his associates, have control of the other, or

(b) If a group of two or more persons has control of each company and the groups either consist of the same persons or could be regarded as consisting of the same persons by treating (in one or more cases) a member of either group as replaced by a person of whom he is an associate.

Company associate of another person

A company is an associate of another person if that person has control of it or if that person and persons who are his associates together have control of it.

9 C
10 D

11 (a) (i) A void disposition of property is one which takes place between the presentation of the bankruptcy petition and the vesting of the estate in the trustee.

S284 states that such dispositions (includes a payment in cash or otherwise) are void except to the extent that the court consents or subsequently ratifies the disposition.

Third parties having received payments from the bankrupt hold those payments as part of the bankrupt's estate.

Applications can be made by the debtor or any interested party.

(ii) Either Peter or the purchaser could apply to the court to have the transaction ratified.

(iii) Third parties receiving property for value, prior to commencement of bankruptcy, without notice, are protected by the legislation.

For this to apply here we would need to provide:

- Evidence that the transaction was for full value ie creditors interests were not harmed by the transaction, ie
  - Valuations of the property
  - Details of outstanding mortgage
  - Details of attempts to market the property
  - Advise from agent/ solicitors re accepting offer
  - Evidence of funds received from the sale
  - Details of any other prior offers made for the property
- Evidence that that the purchaser was unaware of the bankruptcy:
  - Confirmation that parties are not connected (or otherwise)
  - Confirmation that purchaser was not aware of the bankruptcy petition (or otherwise)
  - Information from purchaser's solicitor

(b) (i) Peter owes a number of duties to his trustee:

- Must deliver up to the trustee possession of any property, books, papers or other records of which he has possession or control and of which the trustee is required to take possession (s312)
- Duty to give trustee such assistance and attendance as the trustee may reasonably require for the purposes of s283 - 291 and s333
- Disclose any after acquired property to the trustee within 21 days (s333)
- Must notify trustee of any increases in income within 21 days (s 333)

(ii) The function of the trustee is to take possession of, realise and distribute the bankrupt's estate.

The trustee has a duty to take possession of the estate, including books, papers and records (s 311).

Under s303, if the bankrupt is dissatisfied with by any act, omission or decision of the trustee he may apply to court. The court may confirm, reverse or modify any act or decision of the trustee, may give him directions or may make such other order as it thinks fit.

The bankrupt has a right to complain to the relevant professional body of which the trustee is a member if he considers that the trustee is not complying with his ethical guidelines.

Under s304, the bankrupt can apply to court to seek a remedy against a trustee that has caused loss to the estate. The court must be satisfied that:

- The trustee has misapplied, or retained, or become accountable for, any money or other property comprised in the estate, or
- The estate has suffered loss in consequence of misfeasance or breach of fiduciary duty by the trustee in the carrying out of his functions.

The court may order the trustee to make such recompense as it thinks fit.

The bankrupt has a right to request that the trustee provide him with a statement of receipts and payments. The trustee must comply within 14 days of the receipt of the request.

(iii) Bankrupt's estate comprises all property belonging to or vested in the bankrupt at the commencement of the bankruptcy (s283(1))

Commencement is the date that the bankruptcy order is made.

The estate will therefore include the bank account.

On becoming aware of the bank account the trustee will have notified the bank of the bankruptcy order and required that the account be frozen so that the asset could be realised for the benefit of Peter's creditors.

The trustee will be concerned that the funds available to creditors have been reduced by Peter's actions and will look to see if any transactions can be overturned and funds recovered by the trustee.

S284 - dispositions of the bankrupt's property between the presentation of the petition and the vesting of the estate in the trustee are void unless sanctioned by the court. Third parties having received payments from the bankrupt hold those payments as part of the bankrupt's estate.

The trustee would look at what payments were made after the presentation of the petition and would seek to recover the funds. Third parties, receiving assets for value, without notice of the petition are protected however.

The trustee would look at the repayment of the loans to the bank and to his mother to see if either transaction could be challenged as a preference (s340).

To be a preference the trustee must show:

- The person was a creditor or surety or guarantor for any of the debtor's debts
- The debtor did anything which had the effect of putting that person into a better position, in the event of the debtor's bankruptcy, than would otherwise have been
- There was a desire to prefer (assumed where parties are connected)
- Must have taken place at a relevant time

Relevant time (s341(1)(a)) – at any time in the two year period ending with the day of the presentation of the bankruptcy petition.

Individual must also be insolvent.

Here, transaction with mother is likely to be a preference (no need to prove insolvency or desire to prefer).

(iv) Peter should be advised to bring his tax affairs up to date. He should produce accounting records showing the true tax position and should appeal against the estimated assessment providing full information to HM Revenue and Customs. The trustee should also be provided with all information so that the claim of HM Revenue and Customs can be rejected accordingly.

12 A S310A

13 An individual gives a preference to a person if:

(a) That person is one of the individuals creditors or a surety or guarantor for any of his debts or other liabilities, and

(b) The individual does anything or suffers anything to be done which (in either case) has the effect of putting that person into a position which, in the event of the individuals bankruptcy, will be better than the position he would have been in if that thing had not been done.

The individual must have been influenced by a desire to prefer (assumed in the case of an associate)

Transaction must have taken place at a relevant time:

(a) At any time in the period of six months ending with the day of the presentation of the bankruptcy petition on which the individual is adjudged bankrupt, or

(b) Within two years ending with that day if the person preferred is an associate

Individual must have been insolvent at the time of the transaction or became insolvent as a result of the transaction.

14 A S183

15 B S341

16 C R6.200(2)

17 D S316(1)

18 A S284(3)

19 (a) The OR may apply to the court for the public examination of the bankrupt (s290). The bankrupt will be examined as to his affairs, dealings and property and the causes of his failure. The trustee may attend and ask questions.

The trustee/OR may apply to court for the private examination of the following persons.

(i) Bankrupt

(ii) Bankrupt's spouse/former spouse or civil partner or former civil partner

(iii) Any person known or believed to have any property comprised in the bankrupt's estate in his possession

(iv) Bankrupt's debtors

(v) Any person appearing to the court to be able to give information concerning the bankrupt or the bankrupt's affairs, dealings or property.

Under s365 the trustee/OR may apply to the court to issue a warrant for the seizure of:

(i) Any property comprised in the bankrupt's estate
(ii) Any books, papers or records relating to the bankrupt's affairs or property

S369 – power to demand production of documents from HM Customs and Revenue

S371 – OR/trustee may apply to the court for an order redirecting the bankrupt's mail for a period of three months

Obtain Land Registry entries.

(b) It would appear that the property was transferred into the sole name of Mrs Depp for no consideration. At the time of the transfer there was equity in the property of £180,000, half of which was available to Mr Depp (assuming 50:50 split). This was in excess of the business loan of £50,000 which was taken on by Mrs Depp.

The trustee may be able to attack the transaction as a transaction at an undervalue s339(1). The court may make such order as it thinks fit for restoring the position to what it would have been if the individual had not entered into the transaction.

A transaction is at an undervalue if the debtor:

(i) Makes a gift or otherwise enters into a transaction on terms that provide for him to receive no consideration, or

(ii) Enters into a transaction in consideration of marriage, or

(iii) Enters into a transaction for a consideration the value of which, in money or money's worth, is significantly less than the value, in money or money's worth, of the consideration provided.

The transaction must have occurred at a relevant time:

(i) At a time in the period of five years ending with the day of the presentation of the bankruptcy petition.

(ii) If it occurs at a time less than two years before the end of the period, the debtor must have been insolvent or became insolvent as a result of the transaction.

In the case of a transaction with an associate, insolvency is presumed.

Here, the house was conveyed for no consideration and the transaction took place at a relevant time. The trustee has to therefore calculate what the bankrupt's interest in the house would be if the transaction had not taken place.

Need to calculate interest at today's date:

Estimated Outcome Statement
for Mr and Mrs Depp

		£	£	£
Value of house	1	350,000		
Less: Doubloon Building Society		(50,000)		
Black Pearl Bank		(30,000)		
Equity available		270,000		
			Mr Depp	*Mrs Depp*
			£	£
Split equity	2		135,000	135,000
Adjust re mortgage payments	3		(20,000)	20,000
Adjusted equity			115,000	155,000

WORKINGS/ NOTES

(1) Assume mortgage with Doubloon Building Society is in joint names since the property was purchased in joint names. Mrs Depp received independent legal advice re loan from Black Pearl Bank, therefore she is jointly liable for this debt also (cannot claim that she did not agree to her share of the property being charged in favour of the bank). Assume that debt was not legally transferred to her in 20X6 and that Mr Depp is still liable for the debt.

(2) In the absence of any further information assume that the equity is to be split 50:50.

(3) Need to take into account the fact that Mrs Depp has been paying the mortgage and loan repayments by herself since 20X6. This needs to be reflected in the equity split. Adjust for 50% share of repayments made by her.

	Doubloon Building Society	*Black Pearl Bank*
	£	£
Debt outstanding as at 20X6	70,000	50,000
Debt outstanding today	50,000	30,000
Reduction in debt by Mrs Depp	20,000	20,000

(4) Occupational rent is not applicable here since both Mr and Mrs Depp have continued to reside at the property.

Depending upon the time of the transaction it would appear that the trustee could claim the sum of £115,000 from Mrs Depp for the benefit of the estate.

(c) Need to calculate the benefits which might accrue from pursuing the action.

Approach the creditors' committee (or if none, the main body of creditors). Outline the benefits of taking action, advise them that no funds in the estate to pursue such a claim and invite them to form a fighting fund to pursue the claim.

20 D S316(1)

21 D S342 A – F

22 C Associate is defined in s435 and includes relatives – but a cousin is not a relative according to sub-section (8).

23 **Part one**

(a)

			£
Property Value			150,000
Agents Fees (2%)			(3,000)
1st Mortgage			(50,000)
2nd Mortgage			(20,000)
Equity			77,000

		Estate	*Denise*
		£	£
Equity Split	1	38,500	38,500
Improvements	2	(4,000)	4,000
Mortgage Capital	3	(5,000)	5,000
Possession Fees	4	(1,250)	(1,250)
Final Equity Split		28,250	46,250

(b) **Notes to Equity Split**

(1) **Equity Spilt**: In the absence of any information to the contrary it is assumed that the equity should be split between the estate and Denise in the ratio of 50:50.

(2) **Improvements**: Need to credit Denise with the estate's portion of the cost of the improvements. Credit her split of the equity with 50% of the cost or the increase in the equity whichever is the lowest.

Cost of Improvements = £15,000
Increase in Equity = £8,000
Therefore the relevant figure is £8,000

(3) **Mortgage Capital**: Need to credit Denise with the estate's portion of the capital element of any mortgage payments. There is no credit for mortgage interest as mortgage interest can only be offset against occupation rent.

(4) **Possession Fees**: Possession fees to be split equally between the estate and Denise.

(c) By s336(4) – the court will make such order as it thinks just and reasonable having regard to:

(i) Interests of the bankrupt's creditors

(ii) Conduct of spouse/ former spouse as contributing to the bankruptcy and needs and resources of spouse/ former spouse

(iii) Needs of any children

(iv) All circumstances of the case (but not the bankrupt's interests)

There may exist rights of occupation which may delay the trustee in obtaining the order for possession:

- Under s1 FLA the non-bankrupt spouse has a right of occupation,
- Under s337 IA 86, the bankrupt has a right of occupation where:
  - He has a beneficial interest in the property and
  - Any person under 18 has their home (at the time of the presentation of the petition) with the bankrupt

S337(6): Where such an application is made after the end of the period of one year beginning with the vesting of the bankrupt's estate in a trustee, the court shall assume, unless the circumstances of the case are exceptional, that the interests of the bankrupt's creditors outweigh all other considerations.

Part two

Memo format

Re: Bryan Adams in bankruptcy – Matrimonial home

Problem: The trustee is unable to obtain his release where assets (ie the bankrupt's share in the matrimonial home) remains unrealised. In this case, there is not expected to be any benefit to creditors in securing possession and sale of the property at this time.

Solution:

(a) Apply for a s313 charge (whether or not the court makes a charging order)

(b) The Secretary of State certifies on the trustee's application that it is inappropriate or inexpedient to apply for a charge

The trustee can then seek his release.

The effect of a s313 charge:

(a) The benefit of the charge is comprised in the bankrupt's estate,

(b) The property ceases to be comprised in the estate and re-vests in the bankrupt.

(c) The practical effect is that the trustee has now lost control of how and when the property will be sold.

24 D S283 Necessary for use personally by him in employment, business or vocation

25 D

26 D S341

27 (a) (i) **Steps to obtain an Income Payments Order**:

1 Obtain full details of the bankrupts' income and expenditure

2 Negotiate with the bankrupt to determine an acceptable level of voluntary contributions

3 If no agreement can be reached apply to court for an Income Payments Order under s310.

Trustee applies and court fixes venue

Trustee must give 28 days notice of the venue to the bankrupt and a copy of the application and a short statement of grounds of the application

The notice must tell the bankrupt that he must either:

– Attend the hearing and show cause why the order should be other than that applied for, or

– At least 5 business days before the hearing notify the trustee and the court that the bankrupt accepts the trustee's proposals.

The level determined by the court will be so much of the bankrupt's income which exceeds the amount necessary to meet the reasonable needs of the bankrupt and his family.

Here, the court might be unwilling to allow James Cannon to pay all of the school fees out of his income. Motor expenses may also be deemed to be unnecessary given that he has use of a company car. The level of pension contributions would also be looked at and the possibility of reducing mortgage payments by refinancing the loan or realising the equity in the property. Allowances would have to be made for any rental costs should the family home be sold. The level of Mrs Cannon's income would be taken into account and any contributions made by her towards the family's costs.

(ii) Trustee can apply to court for an order that the Post Office redirects the bankrupt's mail to the trustee

Trustee seek information re the bankrupt's affairs from HMRC

Trustee can apply to court under s365 for the issue of a warrant for seizures of:

- Any property comprised in the bankrupt's estate
- Any books, papers or records relating to the bankrupt's affairs or property

Trustee can apply to court under s366 for an order that any of the following be summoned before it:

- Bankrupt
- Bankrupt's spouse or former spouse
- Any person known or believed to have any property comprised in the bankrupt's estate in his possession
- Bankrupt's debtors
- Any person appearing to the court to be able to give information concerning the bankrupt or the bankrupt's dealings, affairs or property

(b) (i) Give notice of intention to declare a dividend to all creditors who have not yet proved their debts – r11.2

Request further information from creditors whose claims have been queried

Discuss these claims with the bankrupt

Trustee may require a claim to be verified by statement of truth

Trustee must adjudicate all claims. Where the trustee has rejected all or part of a claim, he must, in writing, inform the creditor of his reason for doing so – r6.104

Any creditor who is dissatisfied with the trustee's decision to reject his proof may apply to the court within 21 days of receiving the notice from the trustee for the decision to be reversed or varied

Any creditor who has not submitted his claim by the date stated in the notice given under r11.2 will not be entitled to participate in the dividend

(ii)

- Confirm that all sums due to the OR have been paid
- Confirm all proofs dealt with
- Ensure all assets realised or disclaimed
- Ensure matrimonial home dealt with
- Confirm all fees and expenses paid
- Confirm remuneration agreed and drawn
- Obtain certificate of balance from Insolvency Services Account
- Issue s330(1) notice of intention to declare dividend
- Declare dividend within two months of notice
- Adjudicate claims (within five business days of expiry of notice)
- Calculate dividend
- Request cheques from ISA
- Give notice of dividend to all creditors together with Receipts and Payments Account and distribution statement and cheque
- Obtain OR's authority to destroy records

- Update IP record
- Call final meeting s331
- Notice to Court and OR

28 (a) The estate comprises all property belonging to or vested in the bankrupt at the commencement of the bankruptcy – s283(1)

Commencement of bankruptcy is the date of the bankruptcy order.

S283 – Certain property is excluded from the bankrupt's estate:

(i) Tools, books, vehicles, items of equipment necessary to the bankrupt for his personal use in employment, business or vocation, and

(ii) Such clothing, bedding, furniture, household equipment and provisions as are necessary for satisfying the basic domestic needs of the bankrupt and his family.

The following assets will comprise his estate:

(i) **Pension fund**: petition is post 29 May 2000 so pension will NOT vest in trustee.
(ii) **Box van**: possibly excluded by virtue of above if necessary for income or employment
(iii) **Cash at bank**: this will vest in the trustee
(iv) **Matrimonial home**: Mr Powell's interest in the property will vest in the trustee

(b) Bankruptcy automatically terminates a joint tenancy.

It is only the bankrupt's beneficial interest in the property which vests in the trustee.

In order to calculate the interest, we have to consider ownership of the property.

Is there equity in the property? Obtain an up to date valuation and redemption statement.

The property is held jointly, so we must establish in what shares the equity is held. In the absence of any express declaration, assume that the equity is held 50:50.

May be challenged if evidence to the contrary - who paid initial deposit?

Who has paid ongoing mortgage and interest payments?

Was the business loan in joint names which is secured on the property, or was it only secured against Mr Powell's share of the equity?

Mrs Powell may be able to claim equitable exoneration if she can show that she received no benefit from the business loan and was not party to it.

Need to investigate the circumstances of the loan.

(c) (i) Payment of £50,000 to the pension scheme:

Two matters to consider:

1 **Disposal of the lorries**

Was the disposal of the lorries for fair value, at arms length, were specialist agents used to advise on the sale.

Possible transaction at an undervalue.

2 **Payment of monies into pension scheme**

Payments may be deemed to be excessive and recoverable by the trustee.

Investigations required:

- Obtain sales documentation re sale of lorries
- When did sale take place
- Compare monies received with valuation of vehicles
- To whom was sale made
- Obtain pension documents

  - Record of payments made into the pension fund
  - Seek legal advice

(ii) Purchase of diamond ring:

- Possible transaction at an undervalue.
- Where an individual subsequently becomes bankrupt and at a relevant time has made a gift to a person.
- Relevant time is within five years of the presentation of a petition.
- Court can order restoration of the position.
- Investigations required:
  - Look at history of gifts made to the wife – Could this be deemed excessive/ unusual
  - Obtain valuation of the ring

(iii) Payment of £20,000 re daughter's wedding:

- Possible transaction at an undervalue, however persons who enter into such transactions in good faith, for value and without notice are protected.
- Investigations required:
  - Investigate to whom payments made and what for.
  - Unreasonable extravagance contributing to bankruptcy?

(iv) Payment of £15,000 to Mr Elliot:

- Possibly a preference.
- Where a person is one of the individual's creditors and the individual does anything which has the effect of putting that person into a better position in the event of his bankruptcy than would otherwise have been the case.
- Mr Elliot was a creditor (note NOT an associate per the definition under s435 IA 86).
- The transaction must have taken place at a relevant time – within two years/six months of the presentation of the petition (to an associate/non-associate)
- Individual must have been insolvent at the time of the transaction, or as a result of it
- There must have been a desire to prefer (assumed in the case of an associate)
- The court shall make such order as it thinks fit for restoring the position to what it would have been if the preference had not been given.
- Investigations:
  - Check relationship status of Mr Elliot
  - Ascertain insolvency of Mr Powell at the date of the transaction
  - Look at circumstances of how the debt arose
  - Was it repaid under ordinary terms of business
  - Were demands for repayment made
  - Were other creditors paid at the same time.

29 C R6.200(1) – Within 21 days of his becoming aware of the relevant facts

30 C Para 44(7)(c)

31 A S343(2)

22 Bankrupt's home

1 (a)

The matrimonial home

To: Trustee
From: Insolvency administrator
Subject: Mike's interest in the matrimonial home
Date: dd/mm/yy

- The property is currently valued at £260,000, with a mortgage of £110,000, resulting in a total equity of £150,000.
- The property appears to be in Mike's sole name, so prima facie, it would appear that 100% of the equity therefore vests in the trustee.
- However, Mike's spouse, Tracey, may be entitled to a share of the property based on any contributions she has made towards the cost of the house.
- Tracey contributed £30,000 towards the initial deposit for the purchase of the property and will be entitled to a share of the equity based on this contribution.
- The couple also set up a joint account shortly after the purchase and all mortgage and other costs were paid from this account which shows that Tracey has also contributed to the mortgage payments.
- Both parties earned similar incomes so it appears that the contributions towards the mortgage would have been equal.
- Based on these facts, it would appear that since both Mike and Tracey have contributed equally to the property, Mike's share in the property would be 50% ...
- ... and as such valued at £75,000

(b) The holiday home

- The property is currently valued at £150,000 and is free from any mortgage or charges, which means the equity is £150,000.
- The property was purchased as joint tenants, which means that the couple owned the property jointly at 100%.
- However, joint tenancy is severed on bankruptcy, and the couple will become tenants in common, each with a specific share of the house.
- Since the property was purchased as joint tenants, the couple would not have signed a deed of trust.
- The trustee can therefore assume 50:50 per Stack v Dowden 2007.
- It would therefore appear that Mike's interest would be £75,000.
- However, if one party appears to be entitled to more than 50%, the onus is on that party to show that this is the case.
- Since Mike is bankrupt, the onus to show that he should be entitled to a higher share would be on the trustee.
- This could be achieved by the trustee showing that Mike paid the whole £150,000 from his inheritance money, and has hence contributed more to the property than Tracey …
- ... and as such it would appear that he is entitled to a higher share than 50%.

(c) The joint bank account

- The bank account is in joint names, and it would appear that both parties are entitled to 50% of this money.
- Further, their incomes, which are paid into this account appear to be similar which would support the case that they are entitled to an equal share of the monies.
- However, the trustee may be entitled to claim more than half of funds in the account, for the benefit of the estate, if he can show that Mike has paid more money into the account in total – unlikely however as they are operating a joint account.
- The income from the holiday home has been paid into the joint account, and as it appears that Mike is entitled to more than 50% of the property, it would appear that he would be entitled to more than 50% of the rental income paid into the account.
- It would therefore appear that the trustee can claim more than 50% of the £6,000.

2 [Note that the reference to 'partner' in this question should be interpreted as meaning civil partner in accordance with s.283A of IA86.]

Under rule 6.237 the notice in Form 6.83 should contain:

- The name of the bankrupt;
- The address of the dwelling house;
- If the dwelling house is registered the title number.

3 C S313(3)

4 B S283A(1)

5 (a) (i) It is possible that the trustee could challenge the transfer of the property as a transaction at an undervalue. In order to do this here the trustee must show that:

- There was a gift (or other zero consideration transaction)
- The transaction must have taken place at a relevant time (in the five years prior to presentation of the bankruptcy petition)
- If the transaction took place within two – five years prior to the petition the debtor must have been insolvent at the time of the transfer. If the transfer took place within two years of the petition it is assumed that the debtor was insolvent at that time.

If proved, the wife will be asked to transfer back to the trustee Fred's share of the equity.

(ii) The value of the trustee's interest will be as follows:

	£
Value of property	150,000
Less outstanding mortgage	(50,000)
Equity	100,000

	Notes	*Fred Smith* £	*Mrs Smith* £
Equity	1	50,000	50,000
	2	(1,000)	1,000
		49,000	51,000

Notes

(1) Assume held 50:50 (in absence of a formal agreement)

(2) *Re Pavlou 1993* – Where a couple have separated, the spouse in occupancy should be credited with 50% of any capital payments made under the mortgage.

(3) As Mrs Smith has sole enjoyment of the property she should also be debited with an occupational rent being 50% of the rental value of the property. This

should be payable from when Fred Smith was no longer welcome in the home. There is insufficient information available to calculate an occupational rent in this case.

(iii) The trustee could protect his interest in the property in the following ways:

- Register a restriction at the Land Registry
- Insure the property
- Notify mortgage provider of his interest in the property
- Apply for a s313 charging order

(iv) (1) The trustee could approach Mrs Smith with a view to her purchasing Fred's interest in the property. A lower sum could be negotiated to reflect the avoidance of sale costs and possession proceedings.

(2) Fred's wife could voluntarily place the property up for sale on the open market. Fred's share of the equity following any sale would be passed to his trustee.

(3) If Fred's wife is unco-operative, then the trustee may apply for an order for possession and sale under s14 Trust of Land and Appointment of Trustee's Act 1996. It is likely that due to the wife's rights of occupation, any sale would be delayed by 12 months after which period the rights of the unsecured creditors would be paramount.

(4) The trustee must deal with the interest in the property within three years of the date of the bankruptcy or the property will re-vest in the bankrupt and will no longer form part of the bankrupt's estate.

(v) In order to defeat a transaction at an undervalue claim the wife would have to show that the criteria did not apply ie Mr Smith was not insolvent at the time of the transfer, that the transfer did not take place at a relevant time and that the transfer was for consideration.

Alternatively she could claim that she is entitled to a greater than 50% share in the property (assumed 50% in the absence of other information). In order to do this she would have to show that she contributed to the deposit and to the ongoing mortgage repayments in such a way that entitled her to a larger share of the equity in the property, or that it was their intention that the property be held in unequal shares.

Alternatively, to frustrate an order for possession she would have to show that there were exceptional circumstances. This would not include hardship to herself or the children but a sudden, grave illness would be exceptional.

(b) (i) It is unlikely that the trustee would be able to pursue a claim to an interest in 1 New Road. The house was purchased by Fred's partner in her own name using moneys provided solely by her. She makes all mortgage payments.

The trustee has no claim therefore to any equity in the property and there appears to be no evidence of intention that Fred should share in the equity in the property *Lloyds Bank v Rossett 1991*.

(ii) In *Stack v Dowden 2007* in order for a claim for beneficial ownership to be established the court would need to look at:

- The purpose for which the property was acquired
- Whether any parties have any children for whom they have responsibility to provide a home
- How the purchase was originally funded and subsequently
- How the parties arrange their finances, separately or together

In *Gissing and Gissing* a beneficial interest could be established where detriment has occurred to the non owning spouse. This is shown by:

- Payment of the deposit/ purchase price
- Payment of mortgage instalments
- Some other substantial contributions referable to the acquisition of the property

Here, whilst no financial contributions have been made it may be possible to argue that Fred's labour could be deemed to be an 'other substantial contribution' (*Cook v Head 1972*). This would give him an interest in the property.

(iii) If Fred had contributed to the initial deposit this would give rise to an equitable interest in the property and could be evidence that the property was to be held in shares based on the amount of the deposit provided by each party *(Stack v Bowden)*. At the very least Fred would be entitled to recover the deposit provided by him. (Note that shares are established at the date of acquisition but valued at the date of sale.)

6 C S283A

7 C

8 (a) Any four of the following:

- Office copies showing title to the property.
- Declaration of trust to show ownership shares.
- Evidence that equity is more than £1,000.
- Bankruptcy order and certificate of appointment to show that more than one year has lapsed.
- Evidence the papers have been served on occupiers.

(b) Apply to court under s313 for imposition of a charge.

Realise the property – either sell bankrupt's share to spouse or sell on the open market with bankrupt's permission.

Apply for an order for sale or possession.

Enter into an agreement with the bankrupt whereby the bankrupt gets the property back in return for a promise to pay money into the estate in the future.

9 D R6.237

10 A S313

11 **Part One**

To: Trustee
From: Assistant
Re: Bankrupt's matrimonial home

(a) Establishing the extent and value of the trustee's interest:

The bankrupt's share of the equity in the property will vest in the trustee.

(i) Establish the value of any equity in the property:

- Obtain up to date valuation
- Contact mortgagee and obtain mortgage redemption statement

(ii) Establish bankrupt's share of the equity:

- House is owned in joint names
- Need to establish in what shares the house is owned

- Check title deeds - may identify an express trust
- In the absence of an express declaration, assume held 50:50
- This may be rebutted depending on who made the mortgage payments, provision of original deposit etc

(b) Options available to Trustee when dealing with the property:

(i) Approach debtor's wife and enquire whether she wishes to purchase her husband's share of the equity. Trustee is likely to accept a reduced sum to reflect the fact that costs of selling the property on the open market have been avoided.

(ii) Agree with bankrupt and his wife that the property may be placed for sale on the open market (unlikely here given non co-operation of bankrupt so far). Trustee will receive the debtor's share of the equity when the property is sold.

(iii) If an agreed sale cannot be made, the trustee can apply to court for an order of sale or possession.

The court will make such an order as it thinks just and reasonable having regard to:

- Interests of the bankrupt's creditors
- Conduct of spouse/former spouse as contributing to the bankruptcy and needs and resources of spouse/former spouse
- Needs of any children
- All circumstances of the case (but not the bankrupt's interests)
- After a period of one year the creditors interests are taken to outweigh all other considerations

(iv) Where the trustee is unable to realise the equity in a property occupied by the bankrupt, he may apply to court for a charging order under s313

- This has the effect that the benefit of the charge is comprised in the bankrupt's estate and the property ceases to form part of the estate and re-vests in the bankrupt
- Trustee loses control of how and when the property is sold

(v) Trustee can reach an agreement with the debtor, whereby the debtor incurs a specified liability to the estate in consideration for which the interest will cease to be part of the estate

Note: If the equity in the property is less than £1000, the trustee is unlikely to take any steps to realise the property

Part Two

The trustee cannot obtain his release unless he has dealt with his interest in the property. This may have to be by s.313 charge unless the Secretary of State certifies that it is inexpedient to apply.

It may be in the equity (at the time of application) is less than £1,000 that an application to the Secretary of State may be the most appropriate action to take.

Early re-vesting of the estate's interest in the property (back to the bankrupt) is also possible provided that the trustee serves notice under rule 6.237 A.

Disclaimer is also an option where property is not readily saleable but unlikely here.

12 D Article 3 Schedule Part II Insolvency Proceedings (Monetary Limits) Order 1986

13 A Mortgage interest can only be netted off against occupation rent

14 MEMORANDUM

To: Principal
From: Administrator
Subject: Property interest
Date: XX.XX.XX

(a) **Protecting the interest in the property**

(i) Notify mortgagee of trustee's interest in the property

(ii) Carry out Land Registry Search – Register restriction if considered necessary

(iii) Confirm property is covered by insurance. If in doubt, arrange cover

(iv) Ensure that mortgage repayments continue to be made by debtor and his wife to prevent repossession proceedings by Building Society

(b) **Establishing trustee's interest in the property**

(i) Obtain up to date valuation by professional valuers

(ii) Request redemption statement from Building Society

(iii) House was purchased as joint tenants, in equal shares, so 50% of the equity in the property will vest in the trustee 150,000 – 80,000 = 70,000 @ 50% = £35,000 equity

(iv) Since couple have not separated, equitable accounting will not be necessary

(c) **Realising equity**

As Trustee you have three years from the date of the bankruptcy order to deal with the equity in the property. After this time the property will re-vest in the bankrupt.

Can 'deal with' the property in the following ways.

(i) Realise equity
(ii) Obtain s313 charging order
(iii) Reach an agreement with the debtor

(d) **Realising equity**

(i) Initially the trustee will approach the non bankrupt spouse with a view to her purchasing the bankrupt's equity in the property

(ii) Alternatively the house could be put up for sale on the open market. This would require the co-operation of the non-bankrupt spouse. Upon a sale being completed, the sale proceeds would be split between the bankruptcy estate and the non-bankrupt spouse

(iii) If the non-bankrupt spouse will not co-operate, the trustee may apply to court for an order of sale and possession.

The court will make such order as it thinks just and reasonable, having regard to:

- Interests of the bankrupt's creditors
- Conduct of spouse as contributing to the bankruptcy and needs and resources of spouse
- Needs of any children
- All circumstances of the case (but not the bankrupt's interests)

After a period of one year the creditors interests are taken to outweigh all other considerations.

The non-bankrupt spouse has a right of occupation since she has a beneficial interest in the property additionally the bankrupt will have a right of occupation also as a child (under 18 at the time of presentation of the petition) lives in the property.

After a period of one year from the date of appointment of the trustee, the court shall assume that the interests of the creditors outweigh all other considerations, unless the circumstances of the case are exceptional.

(There do not appear to be any exceptional circumstances here.)

(iv) If the equity cannot be realised for any reason, the trustee can apply to court for a s313 charging order.

This has the effect that the benefit of the charge is comprised in the bankrupt's estate and the property ceases to form part of the estate and re-vests in the bankrupt. The trustee loses control of how and when the property is sold

(v) The trustee may also come to an arrangement with the debtor whereby the debtor incurs a specified liability to the estate in consideration for which the interest will cease to be part of the estate.

15 D

23 Powers of the trustee

1 The bankrupt or bankrupt's spouse or former spouse [or civil partner, former civil partner]

Any person known or believed to have any property comprised in the bankrupt's estate in his possession, or believed to be indebted to the bankrupt.

Any person appearing to the court to be able to give information concerning the bankrupt or the bankrupt's dealings affairs or property.

2 (a) Obtain permission of the creditors' committee or the court s314(2).

Permission must relate to a particular proposed exercise.

(b) Trustee cannot disclaim property which has been:

(i) Claimed for the estate as after acquired property under s307
(ii) Claimed for the estate as an item of excess value under s308

3 B s315

4 B s315 – Disclaimer (general powers)

5 Any four of the following:

- Power to sell any part of the property being comprised in bankrupt's estate
- Power to refer to arbitration, or compromise on such terms as may be agreed, any debts, claims or liabilities
- Power to make such compromise or other arrangement as may be thought expedient with respect to any claim arising out of or incidental to the bankrupt's estate
- Power to give receipts for any money received by him
- Power to prove, rank, claim and draw a dividend in respect of debts due to the debtor
- Power to exercise the powers vested in him under the Act in relation to property comprised in the bankrupt's estate
- Power to deal with any property comprised in the estate to which the bankrupt is beneficially entitled as tenant in tail

24 Proofs of debt – bankruptcy

1 D r.6.101

2 D All others are non-provable rule 12.3

3 (a) Generally, an IVA proposal will incorporate the bankruptcy rules re proofs of debt. Claims in foreign currency must be converted into sterling at the official rate as at the date of the bankruptcy order r6.111.

Claims in the voluntary arrangement are calculated as at the date of the creditors' meeting. The exchange rate at the date of the meeting is 300 yen/£.

Claim is for 60,000 yen @ 300 yen/£ = £200.

(b) Secured creditors can only vote in respect of any unsecured balance of their claim. However, where the claim is unascertained (as here, the actual claim will not be known until the property is sold) the chairman of the meeting can agree an estimated minimum value for the debt and allow the creditor to vote.

The creditor will then be bound by the terms of the arrangement.
The claim should be admitted to vote for £1.

4 B s324

5 B R11.2

6 B s175 Insolvent Partnerships Order 1994

7 C Debt payable at a future time

8 s325 – The creditor can prove for the balance of his debt, however, he cannot disturb the dividend already paid before he proved his debt.

He will be entitled to receive payment of the first dividend on his debt before any further dividends are paid by the trustee.

If the trustee refuses to pay a dividend, the court may, if it thinks fit, order him to pay it and also to pay out of his own money:

(a) Interest on the dividend from the time it was withheld, and
(b) The costs of the proceedings in which the order to pay is made

9 **Part One**

(a) Debt is over six years old – therefore if no acknowledgement of the debt has been made during last six years, the debt will be statute barred and unenforceable.

However if the debt has been acknowledged the creditor may be able to claim, however more detail is required ie:

(i) How the debt arose
(ii) Details of the dispute

The claim should be discussed with the bankrupt and legal advice taken as necessary.

(b) Interest will only be payable if the creditor (prior to the date of presentation of the petition) serves written demand for payment of interest, stating that interest would be payable from the date of service of demand to the date of the bankruptcy order.

The rate of interest charged is that in the Judgments Act unless the demanded rate of interest is lower in which case that will apply.

Providing the letter claiming interest pre dates the petition - the claim for interest will be allowable in full.

(c) Commencement of bankruptcy is the date of the bankruptcy order ie 26 May 20X9.

A bankruptcy debt is defined as any debt or liability to which the bankrupt is subject at the commencement of bankruptcy.

Since this debt was incurred after commencement it will not be allowable as a bankruptcy debt and the claim should be rejected.

(d) Debts in respect of credit supplied by a person who is the spouse of the bankrupt at the date of the bankruptcy order are claimable. However, for dividend purposes, payment of such debts are deferred for payment until after payment of preferential and unsecured creditors in full including interest on such debts payable for the period after the bankruptcy order to the date of payment.

Accept claim in full.

(e) Where, before the commencement of the bankruptcy, there have been mutual credits, mutual debts or other mutual dealings between the bankrupt and any creditor of the bankrupt proving or claiming for a bankruptcy debt:

(i) An account shall be taken of what is due from each party to the other in respect of the mutual dealings and the sums due from one party shall be set off against the sums due from the other

(ii) Sums due from the bankrupt to another party shall not be included in the account taken if that other party had notice at the time they became due that a bankruptcy petition relating to the bankrupt was pending

(iii) Only the balance of the account taken is provable as a bankruptcy debt.

Need to obtain a full account of dealings with the creditor and offset the book debt against the monies claimed by the creditor.

Part Two

(a) In convening the meeting the trustee should have regard to the following;

(i) The place and time of the meeting should be convenient to creditors
(ii) Meeting shouldn't be held immediately before or after a known holiday period
(iii) Meeting should commence between 10.00 and 16.00 on a business day
(iv) 21 days notice to be given to all known creditors
(v) Proxy forms should be sent out with the notice
(vi) Guidance should be given about the requirements of SIP 9.

The following matters should be stated in the notice of the meeting:

(i) Purpose of the meeting ie that a resolution for remuneration of the trustee will be passed

(ii) Date and time by which proxies and outstanding proofs must be lodged (by 12 pm on the business day before the meeting).

(b) (i) Creditors are unable to vote in respect of claims which are unascertained unless the chairman agrees to put an estimated minimum value on the debt and admits the proof for the purposes of voting.

Chairman should accept the estimated value, but should mark it that this is not in agreement of the proof for dividend purposes, but for voting purposes only.

Use to vote in favour of resolution.

(ii) Secured creditors can only vote in respect of any unsecured element of their debt.

Chairman should be advised to ask creditor to deduct the value of its security for voting purposes.

Vote against the resolution in respect of the unsecured element of the claim.

(iii) R8.6 – a proxy holder shall not vote in favour of any resolution which would directly or indirectly place him in a position to receive any remuneration unless the proxy specifically directs him to vote in that way.

Should not therefore use this proxy to vote for the resolution.

(iv) The creditor has lodged a valid proof of debt and is therefore entitled to vote at the meeting. A proxy is not required because the creditor is an individual who is attending the meeting in person.

Accept vote against the resolution.

(v) Company can be represented at the meeting - he must however have a signed authority to act on behalf of the company, which the chairman may request sight of. In order to vote at the meeting, the company must have lodged a valid proof of debt form and a proxy, by the deadline, giving the office holder power to vote on behalf of the company.

No proxy has been lodged therefore the company officer is not entitled to vote.

(vi) Faxed proxies are acceptable, providing they are backed up by a hard copy. Should allow the creditor to vote subject to the original being received.

(c) If the chairman is in any doubt whether a proof should be admitted or not, he must mark it as objected to, to allow the creditor to vote subject to that vote subsequently being declared invalid if the objection to the proof is sustained. R6.94

(d) R12.4A(2)(a) - a quorum is at least one creditor entitled to vote, present in person or by proxy.

10 D R6.101

11 B (R12.3(2))

12 By r6.98

- The creditor's name and address, and company registration number (if a company)
- Total amount of claim including any VAT as at date of bankruptcy order
- Whether amount includes uncapitalised interest
- Details of how and when debt was incurred
- Details of any security held, date it was given and value which creditor puts on it
- Details of any ROT in respect of goods
- Name, address and authority of person authenticating proof

25 Discharge and annulment

1 The court has the power to annul a bankruptcy order under s.282 where:

On any grounds existing at the time the order was made, the order ought not to have been made (s.282(1)(a)), or

That, to the extent required by the rules, the bankruptcy debts and the expenses of the bankruptcy have all, since the making of the order, been either paid in full or secured to the satisfaction of the court (s.282(1)(b)).

[Note that a bankruptcy can also be annulled where an IVA is approved in regard to an undischarged bankrupt however that is under (s.261(2))/(s.263D) *not s.282.*]

2 D Section 261

3 A Paragraph 1(2) Schedule 4A

4 D R6A.2A – R6A.58

5 B S281(1)

6 A S282(3)

7 A Sch 4A s4

8 D S281

9 B The Secretary of State rule 6A.1 under which the Secretary of State maintains an individual insolvency register which includes bankruptcies and IVAs as well as BROs.

10 C S261 – This is because the creditors can appeal during the period of 28 days beginning with the day of filing of the chair's report in court

11 (a) S282 That on any grounds existing at the time the order was made, the order ought not to have been made, or

(b) That, to the extent required by the rules, the bankruptcy debts and the expenses of the bankruptcy have all, since the making of the order, been either paid or secured for to the satisfaction of the court.

12 1 Any balance due to the Official Receiver on account of expenses properly incurred by him and payable under the insolvency legislation and any advances made by him in respect of the estate.

2 Any disbursements made by the nominee prior to the approval of the arrangement ie costs of interim order application

3 Any fees, costs, charges or expenses which would be payable, or corresponds to those which would be payable, in the debtor's bankruptcy ie trustee's remuneration and disbursements etc.

13 D The trustee is only required to report on a s282(1)(b) application (debts and expenses of bankruptcy all paid or secured). For the content of that report see R6.207.

26 Vacation of office – trustee

1 D R6.137(6)

2 B R6.137(5)

- If there is no quorum present at the final meeting, the trustee shall report to the court that a final meeting was summoned in accordance with the Rules, but there was no quorum present
- The final meeting is then deemed to have been held and the creditors are deemed not to have resolved against the trustee having his release
- The trustee is released when the above notice is filed in court

27 Individual voluntary arrangements

1 The standard conditions state the following:

'The supervisor has the discretion to admit claims of £1,000 or less, or claims submitted that do not exceed 110% of the amount stated by the debtor in the proposal, without the need for additional verification.'

2 B Rule 5.11(1)

3 D S262A and Schedule 10

4 C Changed from £10 to £15 by Insolvency Proceedings (Fees) (Amendment) Order 2009

5

MEMORANDUM

To: Principal
From: Administrator
Subject: IVA proposal
Date: XX.XX.XX

IVA proposals should include the following matters

(a) Nature of the arrangement - whether it is a composition in full and final settlement of debts or a scheme of arrangement.

(b) Short explanation of the desirability of the VA and reasons why the creditors may be expected to concur with it.

(c) Background and explanation of present insolvency.

(d) Extracts from previous years trading accounts.

(e) Details of debtor's assets and estimates of values:

(i) Details of charged assets

(ii) Proposals re dwelling house

(iii) Details of excluded assets

(iv) Funds contributed by third parties (and confirmation that they have sought independent legal advice)

(f) Details of debtor's liabilities and estimates of amounts:

(i) Include excluded liabilities
(ii) Secured, preferential and associate creditors and how they are to be dealt with
(iii) Contingent liabilities
(iv) Overseas creditors.

(g) How debtor's business is proposed to be dealt with:

(i) Cash flow forecasts
(ii) Provision of working capital
(iii) Credit requirements
(iv) Function of the supervisor is not to manage the business
(v) Provision of timely trading information to the supervisor
(vi) All tax and VAT returns to be completed on time.

(h) Details of claims which may be pursued by a trustee under s339, s340 and s343.

(i) Proposed duration.

(j) Comparison of the estimated outcomes for creditors under bankruptcy and VA.

(k) Whether any guarantees are to be provided.

(l) Manner in which Supervisor is to be remunerated and his expenses defrayed.

(m) Name, address and qualification of the Supervisor.

(n) Supervisor's powers, duties and responsibilities:

(i) To call meetings of creditors
(ii) Agree creditors claims
(iii) Retain funds to petition for bankruptcy of the debtor in event of failure/ default
(iv) Basis of reports to creditors

(o) Estimate of dividends and proposed dates of distributions.

(p) Manner in which funds are to be held:

(i) Open bank accounts
(ii) How to deal with unclaimed dividends

(q) What constitutes failure/ default and what should happen in such circumstances?

(r) What will happen to unclaimed dividends or unpresented cheques when the VA is concluded?

(s) Express trust

(t) Requisite majorities required to pass resolutions of meetings of creditors.

(u) How to deal with after acquired assets and windfall gains.

(v) Procedure for varying the terms of the arrangement.

(w) Whether a creditors committee will be appointed.

(x) What happens to surplus funds?

(y) How to deal with creditors who have not submitted claims.

(z) Confirmation of when the terms of the VA have been successfully completed and confirmation that creditors will no longer be entitled to pursue the debtor for any balance of their claim.

(aa) How to deal with claims of non notified creditors.

(bb) Whether EC Regulations apply.

(cc) Whether within 24 months preceding date proposal delivered to nominee whether or not a proposal for an IVA submitted for approval of debtor's creditors or for purpose of obtaining an interim order.

6 D

7 MEMORANDUM

To: Principal
From: Administrator
Subject: Voluntary arrangement for Mr Bodgit
Date: XX.XX.XX

(a) IVA is more flexible than bankruptcy. Bob Bodgitt can choose which assets form part of the arrangement ie may wish to exclude the family home. Creditors would seek compensation for any assets excluded.

In bankruptcy, all assets belonging to the bankrupt at the commencement of bankruptcy will vest in the trustee. This will include the available equity in the family home.

In bankruptcy the trustee has power to claim the Porsche as an item of excess value and replace it with a cheaper alternative. A supervisor of an IVA has no such powers.

(b) **Trading**

Under IVA scenario, Bob would be able to set up and trade the new company. Creditors would wish to see cash flow/ trading forecasts to support Bob's estimates of future trading. The IVA proposal would also include obligations to produce to the Supervisor regular trading figures, controls re obtaining new credit and what would happen in the event that the new venture failed.

If Bob were declared bankrupt he would be unable to act as a director, or directly or indirectly take part in the promotion, formation or management of any company except with leave of the court.

This would directly impact on Bob's plans to set up a new company.

If a sole trader, cannot trade other than by the name in which he was adjudged bankrupt.

Restrictions on obtaining credit without disclosing bankruptcy status.

(c) **Stigma**

More stigma attached to being declared bankrupt than entering into a IVA

(d) **Returns to creditors**

Creditors will seek a better return in an IVA than compared to bankruptcy

Reduced costs in a IVA ie no Secretary of State fees, will improve returns to creditors

(e) **Duration**

Creditors would seek a longer duration in a IVA, say up to five years, in order to maximise the period of time during which voluntary contributions would be made

In bankruptcy, automatic discharge after 12 months

(f) **Costs**

In IVA Bob would have to pay the proposed nominee's fees and the costs involved in gaining the creditors approval

If a creditor presented a bankruptcy petition, there would be no cost to Bob personally

(g) **Bankruptcy offences**

In bankruptcy the trustee has wide powers to investigate the actions of Bob and take action re any bankruptcy offences which may have been committed. The trustee also has powers to augment the estate by taking action re preferences, transactions at undervalue etc

A supervisor in a IVA has no such powers, however such transactions have to be disclosed in the proposal

Trustee may seek a bankruptcy restrictions order for a period of two to 15 years; a supervisor has no such powers.

Creditors may prefer Bob to be investigated by a trustee.

(h) **Other**

IVA avoids obligations imposed by bankruptcy ie to co-operate and provide information to the trustee

Bankruptcy may give debtor a clean break. All creditors are dealt with by the trustee. Bankruptcy debts will not survive the bankruptcy.

In IVA, debtor has continued interaction with creditors over a long period of time

If IVA fails, bankruptcy will result

Any other relevant points

Style

8 (a) **Initial contact with the debtor**

Consider code of ethics

Money laundering checks

Explain IP's role as nominee in relation to the debtor's proposal

Emphasise that it is the debtor's proposal

Explain IVA procedure

Ensure IVA is the most appropriate insolvency procedure

Ensure no ethical problem with accepting role as nominee/supervisor

Explain IP's requirement to maintain independence

Explain IP's duty to perform an independent objective review and assessment of the proposal

The IP has to prepare a report to the court giving his opinions on the proposal

IP has to balance the interests of the debtor and the creditors

Explain costs associated with an IVA and ensure funds are available to cover costs and fees

Send a letter of engagement to the debtor setting out in writing their respective duties and responsibilities in relation to the proposal

Form an opinion as to the credibility of the debtor

(b) **The position of any third parties who may be affected by the proposal**

The nominee should consider the need for separate representation of any 3rd parties who intend to inject funds into the IVA or who are otherwise affected by the VA eg spouse in relation to the matrimonial home.

(c) **Consideration of the need for an interim order**

Need to be satisfied that the four conditions for the court to make an interim order are satisfied:

(i) IP willing to act as nominee
(ii) Debtor could petition for own bankruptcy
(iii) Debtor has not applied for an interim order in the last 12 months
(iv) Debtor intends to propose an IVA

An interim order has the effect of preventing creditors taking action against the debtor. Creditors who are likely to take enforcement action should be identified.

It may be necessary to make an early application for an interim order based on an embryonic proposal.

(d) **The Statement of Affairs**

The debtor must submit a statement of affairs to the nominee to assist the nominee in preparing his report s256(2)

Should detail the nature and amount of all of the debtor's assets and liabilities

The debtor commits an offence if he makes any false representations or commits any other fraud for the purpose of obtaining the approval of the creditors to the proposed arrangement.

A Statement of Affairs is not required if the debtor is an undischarged bankrupt and one has been prepared or delivered to the OR/trustee.

Nominee must ensure that all known liabilities are included

The nominee should take steps to satisfy himself that the value of assets is appropriately reflected in the statement of affairs, obtaining independent valuations where appropriate

Details of any business assets should also be included if relevant

9 C Transactions at undervalue must be disclosed in the proposal (see rule 5.3)

28 Individual voluntary arrangement procedures

1 B s.252(2)

2 C Section 255

3 Rule 5.19:

The nominee shall be chairman of the meeting.

If for any reason the nominee is unable to attend, he may nominate another person to act as chairman in his place. The person so nominated must be:

(a) A person qualified to act as an insolvency practitioner in relation to the debtor;
(b) An authorised person in relation to the debtor; or
(c) An employee of the nominee or his firm who is experienced in insolvency matters.

4 The nominee's report states:

Whether in his opinion the voluntary arrangement which the debtor is proposing has a reasonable chance of being approved and implemented

Whether in his opinion a meeting of the debtor's creditors should be summoned to consider the debtor's proposal

If in his opinion such a meeting should be summoned the date and time and place at which he proposes the meeting should be held.

5 A R5.23

6 A

7 R5.10 provides:

Nominee
Bankrupt
Official receiver
Trustee

8 Any two of the following:

- That the debtor's true position as to assets and liabilities is not materially different from that which it is represented to the creditors to be
- That the debtor's proposal has a real prospect of being implemented in the way it is represented it will be
- That there is no already manifest yet unavoidable prospective unfairness

9 B S252(2)

10 A

11 D (Change introduced 6.4.2010 – R5.14A)

12 C S256 IA 2000

13 D S262

14 B S261(1)(b)

15 D R5.27

16 C S253

17 C S262

18 (a) No bankruptcy petition relating to the debtor may be presented or proceeded with

(b) No landlord or other person to whom rent is payable may exercise any right of forfeiture by peaceable re-entry in relation to premises let to the debtor in respect of a failure by the debtor to comply with any terms or conditions of his tenancy of such premises, except with the leave of the court

(c) No other proceedings and no execution or other legal process may be commenced or continued (and no distress may be levied) against the debtor or his property except with leave of the court

19 C SIP 3 Voluntary Arrangements

20 Willing nominee who is authorised to act

Debtor has not applied for an interim order in the last twelve months

Debtor could petition for own bankruptcy

Debtor intends to propose an IVA

21 C R5.21(2)(c)

22 C s4(3)

23 D R5.6

24 E s256(2)(b) and r5.5(3)

25 C R5.24 – Meeting may be adjourned for not more than 14 days

26 D s253

27 C s255(1)(c)

28 B This provision is now in s262A. The maximum sentence is set out in Schedule 10 of the Act.

29 C s256(1) and r5.11(1)

30 D

31 A R5.12 – The debtor shall give to the nominee at least five business days' notice of his application

32 B, C, F, G R5.29

33 C (R5.5(4))

29 Post approval matters

1 ▸ s.263 IA86: an application may be made by:

- The debtor, or
- Any of his creditors, or
- Any other person who is dissatisfied by any act, omission or decision of the supervisor.

▸ On such an application, the court may –

- Confirm, reverse of modify any act or decision of the supervisor, or
- Give him directions, or
- Make such other order as it thinks fit.
- The court may also appoint another person qualified to act as supervisor either in substitution for the existing supervisor or to fill a vacancy.

2 A S.424(1)(b)

3 Rule 5.29 provides that the report should state:

- ▸ Name and address of debtor, gender and date of birth
- ▸ Date of creditor's approval
- ▸ Name and address of supervisor
- ▸ The court in which the chairman's report to court has been filed

From 6.4.2010 Report must also have details of any name by which the debtor was or is known, not being the name in which the debtor has entered into the VA.

4 B S263

5 (a) Report the default to creditors.

Convene meeting of creditors to obtain views on the situation given that VA had been successful to date and debtor is taking steps to rectify the situation.

Seek to vary the arrangement to allow for current situation.

If creditors are not happy for arrangement to continue,

Issue notice of default.

Take steps to fail the arrangement and petition for bankruptcy of the debtor.

Could apply to court for directions under S263.

(b) The supervisor has the discretion to waive the default and give the debtor the benefit of the doubt and allow the arrangement to continue.

This can be done in circumstances where the default is not due to the debtor, for example, due to failure of internal reporting systems and error in cancelling direct debit.

6 B S262B

7 Under s262B(2), the nominee/supervisor should forthwith:

(a) Report the matter to the Secretary of State, and

(b) Provide the Secretary of State with such information and give the Secretary of State such access to and facilities for inspecting and taking copies of documents as the Secretary of State requires.

s262B(3) – where a prosecuting authority institutes criminal proceedings following any report under subsection (2), the nominee/supervisor shall give the authority all assistance connection with the prosecution which he is reasonably able to give.

8 B, D (Requirement to send to court removed 6.4.2010)

9 (a) The debtor has failed to comply with obligations under the voluntary arrangement

Contributions are three months in arrears and it would appear that there is no prospect of further contributions being received.

Other obligations under the arrangement are not due until the end of the arrangement and are therefore not yet applicable.

The proposal states that the Supervisor must fail the arrangement if contributions are two months in arrears.

The supervisor could call a meeting of creditors to seek their views, however since the creditors modified the original arrangement to include the failure clause, it is unlikely that they would now wish to see the arrangement continue.

S264(1)(c) – Where the debtor has failed to comply with obligations under the arrangement

The supervisor, or any creditor bound by the arrangement can present a petition for the bankruptcy of the debtor

The effect of presenting a bankruptcy petition is:

S284 is triggered, dispositions by the debtor of his assets will be void unless court sanction is obtained.

If the bankruptcy order is made, the arrangement is terminated.

A well drafted proposal should create an express trust of the assets in the IVA in favour of the IVA creditors.

If it does not then case law provides that such a trust will arise by implication.

The proposal should be checked to see if it makes any provision as to whether or not the express or implied trust will survive the bankruptcy.

If the proposal is silent the *N.T. Gallagher* case says that the trust will survive.

The effect of this is that as trust assets are excluded property in bankruptcy, the IVA trust assets will not vest in the Trustee in bankruptcy but will remain available for the purposes of the IVA (eg to pay costs and a final dividend to creditors).

If the IVA creditors do not receive 100p in the £ they can prove in the bankruptcy for the unpaid balance and will rank pari passu with the bankruptcy creditors.

Preferential creditors position will be weaker in a subsequent bankruptcy. This is because the relevant date for the purposes of calculating preferential debts is the date of the bankruptcy order rather than the (much earlier) date of the Interim Order here.

So, the supervisor should:

(i) Establish that the debtor has failed to comply with obligations under the arrangement

(ii) Agree preferential creditors and pay a dividend out of funds held

(iii) Issue a default petition

(iv) Report to creditors, debtor, the Secretary of State and the court within 28 days of the termination of the arrangement (R5.34)

The report must include an explanation of why the arrangement has not been implemented in accordance with the proposal as approved by the creditors meeting

(v) Vacate office

(b) IVA trust assets will not vest in the Trustee.

Only those assets which were excluded from the IVA will be available to the Trustee. These assets here are:

(i) Motor vehicles

(ii) Shares
(iii) Tools of the trade

However both the tools and the motor vehicles will be excluded in the bankruptcy if they are necessary to the trade. In practice the Trustee is likely to require trading to cease given that Mr Pownell does not believe that he can trade profitably. The tools & vehicles would then be available to the Trustee.

(c) Since the *N.T. Gallagher* case the situation is the same as that outlined in the solutions to part (a) and (b) above, whether a petition is presented by a Supervisor or creditor bound by the IVA or by a new creditor, as here.

10

- Full details of inability to pay must be shown to the supervisor's satisfaction
- No more than the equivalent of 3 months payments can be agreed to be missed in this way
- The duration of the IVA will be extended by the same number of months for which payments have been suspended to recover the sums due, unless the debtor has made good the shortfall

11

- Inform the supervisor within 14 days of notice of redundancy
- Inform supervisor of the amount of any redundancy payment within 14 days
- Pay to supervisor within 14 days of receipt any redundancy payment in excess of 6 months net take home pay
- Where possible continue to make monthly contributions
- Keep supervisor informed of any changes in employment status